Ballad O' Stone...

The Trail of a Lonesome Fugitive

To John & Sandy

By
Robert B Cronkhite
and
Sarah Henry Cronkhite

from Sarah

Other Books by Robert B Cronkhite:

Non-fiction
Hypersphere: A Journey at the Speed of Geometry

Non-fiction
Architecture for a Third American Republic

Dedication

I would like to dedicate this book, <u>Ballad O' Stone</u> to my mother, Ruth Paton Cronkhite, who bought me my first typewriter and encouraged me to be a writer. She persisted in this vocation for me when I was a teenager. I remember the first word that she taught me to read, and that word was 'book'. I was not even in kindergarten yet when she had me learning to read, as she read to me. When I was so sickly with bronchitis and pneumonia in first grade, that all I could do was read, she got me books for children about archaeology, the classics, history and even science.

As time would pass by, the works of H.G Wells, Mark Twain and so many other authors would be my friends as I had to outgrow many illnesses of my lungs. It was when I was so weak that she helped me to grow so intellectually strong.

This book was originally written when I was in my early twenties; but it had laid quietly in dormancy as I had travelled on in life with its trials, tribulations and maturing. And finally it has been finished and refined in 2014, and has been born. She had such a passion for the higher things for me that God in His time has answered her prayers.

Thank you, Mom
Your son, Robert

Acknowledgements

This book has been a real journey for me. Inspired by reading Mark Twain's books, forty years ago I wrote the original manuscript for this Civil War adventure. Now my lovely wife, Sarah has helped me rewrite several parts and has with her special touch added characters, dialogue, and embellished what I had already written. The final project has become a Civil War novella, co-authored by my forever friend; an experience we will both cherish.

We would like to thank our friends David and Susan Morrison for their assistance in developing this text. David's illustrations helped give a visual aspect that significantly added to this work, while Susan tirelessly assisted in editing the language of the text.

Chapters

Title	Page
I Stone Joins Capt. McDonald's Unit	1
II The Running Begins	18
III Young's Prison	42
IV Stone Meets Ellen	65
V A Way Out	85
VI The Southern Line's Queen	103
VII Why Are We Fighting	126
VIII Stone and Ellen Part	148
IX The Betrayal	171
X The Old Abandoned Church	194
XI Harrisburg Federal Prison	210
XII The Escape	220
XIII Unionville	245
XIV Amos	265
XV The Wedding	286
XVI The CSS Alliance	308

Chapter I

It was one forty-five that afternoon, as a partial company of Confederate regulars was waiting at the railroad station in Memphis for their complement. The men were just milling around, as were the sergeants and officers.

It was a warm day on this fourteenth of June, 1863. The sun was shining down quite strongly, the heat only making the wait longer and Captain Orrey McDonald's patience shorter. He was in charge of a small detachment of soldiers who was on the train in course. He was a stocky man and not very handsome, rough looking inside as well as out. And the type of men he was in charge of was as bad as he, or worse. The captain was waiting for twelve men on the train, and on the list before him were the names of those expected.

As he pulled out a few cigars from his stained and dusty coat, some of which fell apart in his hand, he dropped the list. Immediately McDonald put one of his travel beaten boots on the paper and then commenced to clean out his pocket of a couple of broken cigars and loose tobacco. Picking up the list, he lit one of his old stogies and again looked over the names on the paper. As he was reading, one of the more mannered and far more egotistical officers, Lieutenant Wilson Gray, with all the spit and shine of a younger man, put on one of his disgusted looks. Gray could not stand sloppiness and as Capt. McDonald was his commanding officer, the embarrassment the lieutenant had to suffer was just unbearable. With the heat and the long waiting, the lieutenant's properness had not failed; with boots well shined and clothes well cleaned and pressed, he stuck out in the fairly crowded railroad station like a sore thumb. He was standing like a great Victorian patriarch as his captain wandered around aimlessly and clumsily.

It was two o'clock when the train, an engine with four cars and no caboose, finally arrived. It was an hour late and the officers on board seemed to move slowly as they got off the train. They re-organized near the station. Everyone appeared tired except the lieutenant who immediately went to inquire why the train was so late. As the officers and men were assembling in rank, an insulted Lt. Gray was returning from an angry, festering engineer.

In the station Colonel William Parker was welcoming the men. He was a polished man and understood well the mood of the men under him.

"Welcome to Memphis, men. My name is Colonel Parker and I will be the commanding officer of this small company. I know it is quite hot this afternoon and I realize you are tired from your two hour train ride, but after some rest we will have to get on with the business of war. By the way, I would like to meet with the division leaders at about eight tonight. So let us begin making our way to camp."

As he was about finished, one of his staff whispered in his ear. The colonel then made an announcement. "Will the men in Capt. McDonald's unit stay here? I understand that you men are to be transferred to Richmond." With a smile, the colonel curtly left the railroad station with the other troops.

The captain and the lieutenant looked at each other, "What's he talkin about?" asked McDonald. The lieutenant looked just as bewildered. The captain ran after the superior officer. "**Colonel Parker**, *Colonel Parker*!" The colonel quickly turned around.

"Captain McDonald, what seems to be your problem?" asked the colonel brusquely.

"Suh, I was ordered to be stationed in Memphis."

"Captain, do you have your orders with you?"

"Suh, they weren't written. I-- I --."

"Well, Captain McDonald, your orders have been changed. Check the schedule. You and your men are to take the next train to Richmond. And I don't care if it's a cattle car train or what. You *do* know how to read a train schedule, do you not, Captain?" The colonel seemed to be preoccupied trying to degrade the captain in front of his own staff and soldiers, as well as McDonald's, for the captain's men were in ear distance.

"*Yes suh*," said the captain with a sudden firmness, controlling a note of disrespect.

As the colonel and one of his staff mounted their horses, with the enlisted men in formation and ready to march, the staff officer said privately,"Suh, I didn't know about such a transfer myself."

The colonel now a little peeved replied, "Mr. Purvis, I am not going to have a shiftless lot like that ruin my military career. Let's get going!" As the company moved on from the railroad station the captain and his men, a group of fourteen including the lieutenant and McDonald, waited for the next train for Richmond.

It was late afternoon when the train, known as the Dixie Zephyr, departed the Memphis Station; the trip to Richmond would be at night, one of the most dangerous times to travel. There were many railroad incidents caused by both Union and Rebel forces. Trains were frequently ambushed and the passengers were advised to wait and take the first train out in the morning. Only the soldiers were on board. Slowly the train picked up speed and glided away from the Memphis railroad yard. On board a tired group of soldiers and their officers were making their way to Richmond by way of the Tennessee hills. A sleeping, dirty Captain McDonald and his aide Lieutenant Gray, felt slighted and took the whole incident personally.

As the train was crossing a small bridge, an explosion suddenly shook the ground and the sleeping occupants were abruptly thrown to the floor. First there was a flash of light, then a loud thunder, a column of smoke and a shower of falling debris. The Dixie Zephyr had no engine. As a matter of fact there was no longer a bridge and all four cars were off the tracks, one was laying on its side. There were no fatal injuries and the captain was relieved he and the soldiers were the only ones on the train. As soon as McDonald pulled himself together, he and a still dazed Lt. Gray gathered the men together. Slowly and grudgingly the soldiers fell into a somewhat decent formation.

The captain, satisfied with the results of a near tragic situation, began to instruct the men on how and where they were going to sleep the rest of the night ... in a wooded area nearby; and also about what had happened to their train. Most of the men were hard to discipline and were just out of boot camp, so they were confused. Then McDonald explained about a new type of pressure mine used on train tracks. After he was finished and the men were beginning to break formation, the lieutenant interjected with a small and unneeded speech on 'not panicking'. Lieutenant Gray, as though he had nerves of steel, held the unit up for five more minutes, until the captain interrupted him and had the men start moving on.

Eventually the small unit of Confederates made it to the top of a small, but well sheltered hill and set up camp for the night. The captain was very watchful for Federals, as Union soldiers were called. Among this small detached group of 'rebels' of society and nation, were two men ... Richard Harold Stone, age twenty-one of Parkinson, Tennessee and Donald Michael O'Reilly, age thirty-one of Creekville, Tennessee. The two men had met in boot camp and had been buddies ever since. Both were high spirited; Stone was many times reflective and O'Reilly over-reliant on liquor, either happily drunk or dangerously mad at the world. Just two men in a group of soldiers that a society and now a nation had no room for, or didn't know how to accommodate. As everyone was worn-out, it was soon quiet with everyone asleep except the single guard, who was awake on and off.

Though seemingly awkward and reckless, Captain McDonald's ability in military strategy and survival were not surpassed by any officer on either side. His lack of respect for authority, and most people in general was because of his poor upbringing. Treated as a misfit himself, McDonald knew his men and how to control them. Sometimes, it seemed he was almost a father to them. His greatest respect came from the men for his manner of discipline. The captain would never degrade a trouble maker or the hard to control type in front of the troops, but would take them aside for discipline. He would use enough muscle or understanding, whichever the situation called for, in handling each man. Captain McDonald would make the soldier feel that he was worth something, even though throughout all his life, that man had probably been told how worthless he was.

The captain was perhaps the first man in the form of authority that Richard Stone would have any deep respect for. And Stone wasn't the only one. O'Reilly and the others after having had some meeting of fists and hot words with the captain, were just as respectful. Captain McDonald always tried to build confidence in his men. He knew you couldn't win a fight if the men were feeling confused and worthless.

The following day came swiftly. Captain McDonald arose at about ten in the morning, clumsily stood up in front of his tent and yawned. After checking on his guard as though he expected to find him asleep, he had the cook start some coffee and a light breakfast. An intermittent breeze blew across the tree sheltered hilltop on a very sunny morning. The captain had soon awakened the men and placed several two men guard details around the camp, which would work in four hour shifts. With each of the two guards flanking the camp and on the hill, the approach of any Federal forces would be immediately noticed.

There were seven wall type tents set up. Each housed two men, un-cramped even with all their personal belongings and gear. Inside the captain's tent was a small foldable desk, where he was sitting this warm afternoon. Much of their gear on the train had been recovered by the soldiers, who were making their way back to the woods and finally the hill.

Inside the tent Capt. McDonald, still at his desk and Lt. Gray were trying to decide what to do. To continue on to Richmond would be expected, but looking at the map in front of him, he decided to send two of his men to a small town four miles away and telegraph word to Richmond. Maybe they would allow his unit to stay where it was or possibly another transfer was waiting. It was about four thirty when the two men finally left camp. They didn't return until nine o'clock that night.

The camp was quiet and a small crackling fire made the only noticeable sound. Coffee was being brewed for the two returning men. They were tired after hiking the distance and the coffee was refreshing. The two were met by an anxious Captain who hurried them to his tent. One left just after entering, while George Sherman, the other man, relayed the reply from Richmond.

"George, what's the story?" asked the captain as the two sat down, the soldier on the captain's cot and the officer on a small fabric and wood folding chair.

"Well, here's the telegram," George replied handing the letter to his captain. McDonald read it slowly and seemed finished, but then read it all over again.

"They want us to move north into Kentucky. How tha hell are we gonna do anythin there? They want us to be close to Louisville, but not too close as to cause any concern for the town there. *'Be alert to all Federal movements of any kind and report anything significant to Richmond immediately. Good luck, Thomas Hanly Cole, Col., Army of Virginia, C.S.A.',"* was the reply the captain read aloud.

"Ya know, George, I wonder if we were supposed to be in Richmond, after all?" commented Capt. McDonald skeptically.

"Don't know Captain. If ya don't mind my personal opinion, Suh, I don't think they know what to do with us," replied George with a grin.

McDonald grinned back and said, "Well I guess

we'll move on up to Louisville tomorrow."

Soon George left the officer's tent and made his way to his own. A sudden shot rang out and the captain immediately grabbed his rifle. He looked out his tent to see George lying dead on the ground. Fear gripped his throat. His eyes nervously twitched as he stared into the darkness in the trees. McDonald could see his men in the tents awake, some looking out. He could sense their fear too. The woods that once seemed to give them protection now was infested with a large regiment of Union soldiers, leaving them with no cover and nowhere to run. A Colonel Maxwell Ames commanded them. His only dilemma was whether he wanted these Confederates dead or alive.

Within the opened tent fly, the still and fearful captain stood. The small fire lit his figure and he knew his place at this moment of time. He knew of no other place to go, and neither for his men. The best thing to do would be to surrender. How he now wished he wasn't so casual at times. He knew better. The mining of the train was by no one that he knew of, for Federal forces were obviously around.

The Union colonel was slowly loading his revolver in the now deathly still night. He expertly checked it one last time, then slowly taking aim through a part in the tree limbs and leaves, he squeezed the trigger. The bullet made its mark into the captain's brain, throwing him to the ground unconscious. Colonel Ames, with almost stoic handsomeness, straightened in his saddle; he had made his strike, his proud duty had been served once again. From the woods, the colonel's firm triumphant voice called out to the Rebels. And slowly from their tents, the soldiers in gray, and others in colors they themselves, or their poorly financed army had provided, lined up in a much straighter and stronger line than they had known.

The Union soldiers except for a few, were still hidden in the surrounding woods, as officers were inside the small Rebel camp. As if he had been waiting to go on stage, the colonel resolutely and arrogantly walked his horse along the line of soldiers, now numbering thirteen. The once talkative lieutenant, silent in line, interested the colonel. The camp and woods, still very quiet, only increased the fear of the Confederates. Each was hoping that this was just the colonel's way of scaring the enemy and so no serious harm would come to them; but Colonel Ames' game was a long one.

"**Sergeant!**" suddenly shouted the colonel, "Question the lieutenant in the officer's tent back at camp." Almost as swiftly, a sergeant and two other soldiers, all three quite burly, dutifully and soberly appeared. The lieutenant, almost crying and slightly hysterical, was swiftly swept from the eyes of the Rebel soldiers.

After Lt. Gray and the three Union soldiers disappeared in the surrounding woods, the colonel walked his horse over to George. He slowly leaned over the dead man, smiled and then 'thanked' him with a mock salute.

The small camp still quiet, but not the deathly

silence as before, was suddenly interrupted by the wounded Confederate Captain McDonald rising awkwardly and asking for 'Lillian'. His head was covered with blood. The soldiers in his troop were sickened by the scene, as were most of the Union soldiers. Many of them never really wanted to be in a war with its real tragedies, but their powers were matchless against the authoritative controls on either side.

The delirious captain aimlessly crawled and half-walked away from the camp. The colonel's pistol now raised again shattered the uneasy, quiet night releasing the remainder of its load into the captain's body, leaving just the slightly twitching and blood soaked remains of a man.

In the minds of the Rebels, memories of the past were quickly revived. The fear that had harbored within the soldiers was now gut and throat filling anger toward the Union colonel ... not only for Ames, but those like him in authority, that these men had learned to hate. Without any sign of compassion or remorse, Colonel Ames led his prisoners, without their boots, to a Union camp four miles away.

It was starting to sprinkle just as the prisoners arrived in camp. Many of them were looking for some kind of sign of the lieutenant's presence, but so far no one could see or hear anything. Already, the colonel was in his tent talking to some of his staff, while the prisoners were left out in the mild rain still at attention. Stone and O'Reilly both moved slightly enough to look at each other. The summer shower, now coming down just a little bit harder, warranted the officer's attention and the prisoners were soon escorted into a small tent. Stone noticed only two guards by the tent. He looked at O'Reilly and slightly grinned, to which his friend raised his eyebrows. Inside the tent, the two men could talk without being overheard for the rain was drowning out other sounds.

"Look, without too much trouble you an me could make a run fer it," offered Stone.

"I don't know. That's quite a risk," said O'Reilly, who then paused and asked, "What about these other guys? What about the lieutenant?"

But Stone's answer would wait. For suddenly, six of the Rebel soldiers were moved to another tent leaving Stone and O'Reilly still together. Except for the colonel's arrogance, the Union army seemed just like the Confederate army to two rag-tag soldiers. The officers were the big men and the enlisted men and non-commissioned officers seemed to either tolerate the whole thing as a boring, but necessary job, or they were really excited by the fighting, the uniforms and all that goes with armies and war.

For Stone as well as O'Reilly, the beginning had been a grand adventure. They could fight, shoot guns and kill guys and never get in trouble. But as the dream faded away, they found you couldn't really do just what you wanted to; the novelty was gone, grimly replaced with the reality of war. When he first joined up, Stone figured he'd be in about eighty battles and easily be famous for something and probably go down in history. O'Reilly, just a little less ambitious figured he'd make colonel before the war was over. That was probably the only major motivation for the two unlikely soldiers to join the army, except for the posted bills and propaganda on either side telling of everyone's duty to God and country, to stop the merciless and deranged mob of cut-throats on the 'other side'. So the two men, never having gotten along with some of the finer parts of society, joined the army in Tennessee. Of course, they didn't know that the 'other side' had been telling their young men the same things ... about *their* side.

So in a leaking tent on a rainy night somewhere in Tennessee, the two men decided the whole thing to be less than the adventure they were expecting and not promising to be very historic to them personally. Richard Harold Stone and Donald Michael O'Reilly made plans to leave the brutality of war behind; and if they survived, make their way to the gaiety of New Orleans.

At about one o'clock the following morning, Stone and O'Reilly each jumped one of the two guards, then ran for the woods. The escape was seen by the two guards at another tent. Though the escape was not very well executed, Donald falling down twice and Richard following him down the second time, they miraculously made their way into the woods. As soon as they were spotted, the fire rang out and bullets streaked past them. Maybe their uncoordinated, unconventional manner had a lot of influence on the aim of the Union rifles; but whatever, the two men had succeeded in escaping not only a Federal prison camp, but as far as they could see, they had just escaped the war as well.

After running through the wet woods and rain for about half an hour, they came upon a small flat-board cabin, and finding it unoccupied, entered; also finding that the abandoned cabin, having broken windows and a leaking roof, still had some decent dry spots and would do for the night. After a cautious night of sieving and watching, the two escapees moved on just after dawn. If the Union soldiers hadn't gotten this far yet in their search for them, then on this sunny morning they wouldn't be far behind.

Having already left the cabin a couple of hours ago, the two Rebels being in good moods but tired, were walking through an alfalfa field. It was up to their waists and could be cover if spotted by the Federals, who were probably closing in on them. As they briskly walked through the ripening grain, Stone stopped and looked at something way out in the field. O'Reilly stopped, looked back at him and followed his gaze; both could see a small farm out across the field. As O'Reilly looked at the farm, then back at Stone, he noticed that his friend wasn't looking at the farm.

"Alright, now I see the farm, but what's over there?" asked O'Riley pointing to where Stone was looking.

"Look, did ya see?" answered his buddy.

O'Reilly, a little impatient and obviously worried about the Federals said, "Yea. I don't see nothin. But I know somebody isn't far behind us."

Stone looked at his friend and suggested, "Let's see if we kin stay at that farm."

So the two men made their way toward the farm; one walking briskly with eyes straight ahead, while the other was trying to keep up while attempting to see whatever it was out in the field that Stone had seen. Eventually, they made it to the farm. Richard had a smile on his face which O'Reilly saw, but didn't understand. They made their way up on the porch to the door which was on the front of the house and where they were met by a middle-aged, but attractive woman.

"Well, how are ya? What can I help ya with?" asked the surprisingly friendly woman.

O'Reilly was feeling somewhat unsure, but Stone seemingly calm and happy answered, "Well, we don't wanna trouble nobody, but we wuz lookin fer some honest work an a place ta stay. We wuz wonderin if you er yer husband could put us up?"

"Well, I ... I haint married an ...," as she quickly pulled herself together and continued, "I might have some work fer ya, but you'll have ta stay in the barn. I don't allow strange, young men in my home at night."

She suddenly withdrew into the house, leaving them standing on the porch not knowing how to take her.

"She seems like she's quite friendly," O'Reilly

said softly.

Stone smiled again and added, "Let's see somethin," and led O'Reilly out toward the barn at the edge of the field.

There they could see a young woman just out a small way in the field. O'Reilly looked at Stone and grabbed him playfully and started to laugh. For now coming back from the field, they saw she was a young woman maybe in her twenties. The closer she got, the prettier she got. Immediately the two disheveled men started tidying themselves up. As she came toward them, she seemed to notice them. But she walked right past them without saying a word. The two men just grinned, looked at each other and followed her into the barn.

Standing in the doorway a moment, Stone watched her get a drink of water while O'Reilly smiling, stared out across the field on the side of the doorway.

"How're ya today, miss?" greeted Stone, remaining in the doorway. She looked up and smiled; Stone smiled back and then went over to O'Reilly. "She hardly says a word; the other one's more talkative," he whispered.

"How come there aren't any Federals following us?" asked O'Reilly, now with a serious look on his face.

Stone replied, "B'cuz they wuzn't never really

far behind us."

O'Reilly came back with, "Now that is, if they were following us, right?"

Stone looking slightly bemused, just made a face and turned back toward the barn. O'Reilly couldn't understand how he took it so casually.

Chapter II

The evening came silently as Stone and O'Reilly ate supper with the two women. The meal had been almost completely without conversation, except during the passing of the food. No one had been introduced to anyone else, no names; but it didn't seem to bother anybody. As they ate, the two women, each without noticing the other, were taking turns looking at Stone. He had a unique handsomeness; it was an earthy, yet almost noble type of look. And as the women each looked at him, in turn he looked at each of them, maintaining the looking game. O'Reilly on the other hand was too busy eating to notice anything. Just as the meal ended, the older woman offered the young men separate bedrooms inside the house for the night, explaining how 'cold it'd bin gettin lately' and also how she 'wouldn't want new help gettin sick on ther first day a work'.

Soon Stone and O'Reilly were asleep soundly in their bedrooms, as were the two women in their separate rooms. As the night slowly progressed, each of the women would get up separately and on their own, look in on Stone. At one point in the night when the older woman went into the room where Stone slept, she stood silently by the side of his bed watching him sleep. In her mind, she thought of how young he was and how not so old she was. As she continued to stand by the side of the bed, she remembered how her husband used to love her, how he used to be with her and her with him; but the war took that away. Now it was just her and her daughter.

From within her, a sense of shame and passion grew for the young men who had courted her daughter. The shame was of herself for her rightful, lonely feelings that had found relief in her passions for her daughter's courters. She loved her daughter dearly, but she herself was still a woman with desires and needs. Slowly and earnestly she eased herself to the side of the bed and sat softly on the edge. Stone was still sleeping soundly and seemed so boyish, while at the same time manly enough to satisfy her ... if he wanted ... or if she could make him want her.

Purposefully she removed her robe and let it fall gently to the floor. Now, completely and fully she would give herself to him. Carefully she placed her hand under his sleeping head and even more cautiously, she kissed him. Stone was starting to awaken, so she quickly drew back. As she remained sitting on the side of the bed, her still youthful body catching the faint light of the night, she waited for Stone's sleep to deepen again. She was a very frustrated woman as her eyes filled with anticipation for the young man lying before her. Her increasing passions had overcome the shame she had felt. With determination to have what she needed ... to have what she deserved ... she slowly slipped under the covers, then losing her restraint, began to satisfy her desire for him. As she quietly and yet forcibly seduced him in his now awakening state, Stone and his need for a woman immediately responded. For the young man and the woman of more mature years were now in this almost perfect moment, without shame or any state of remorse; feeling alive during the hardest and loneliest times in their lives.

Soon the morning came and the daughter was preparing breakfast while the rest of the house was still asleep. As she placed the dishes on the table, one could sense an almost extreme peacefulness about her. The younger woman seemed so innocent and delicate. Just as her breakfast was almost ready, she noticed Stone in the inside doorway of the kitchen. He appeared irritated, but not extremely so. As she looked at him, but not ever saying anything, she noticed that his mood seemed to be more of concern and somber bewilderment. The daughter quickly turned away and said, "It'll be ready in jes a few minutes. Why don't ya sit down?"

Stone, after a short pause, firmly sat himself down at the large hardwood table. "Have ya got a boyfriend miss? Aint that odd, we don't even know each other's name?"

"Listen you jes work here an ya mean nothin ta me. An my personal concerns, are *my* personal concerns," retorted the daughter.

"Aw don't take me so hard, young lady, I don't hafta be nice. I kin git away with murdering you, among a lot o other things if I wanted ta be that way. But I'm not. Why're you two so quiet?" asked Stone. To which she gave no reply. Disgusted, but still concerned, he left the table and walked onto the porch to cool off and wait for breakfast.

Outside, as the smell of pancakes filled the air, Stone sat down on the wooden chair next to him. As he waited, he could see the quiet and brilliant morning sun over the fields. The morning air was also filled with the sounds of song and flight of birds. Leaning the chair back against the side of the house, he placed his dusty boots on the porch's weathered railing, supporting the chair back with his legs.

A feeling of peace came over him this morning that he hadn't felt in a long time. Though he was disturbed about the older woman and his affair with her during the night, and confused about the relationship between the two women, Stone could sense their common loneliness and needs stirring within them. He was beginning to consciously figure them as mother and daughter, though he always felt they were. From the kitchen, he could hear the others sitting down at the table. Somehow he felt he could help the women beyond staying here with them and working. He and O'Reilly could take them along; 'they couldn't be that great a burden', he thought. The two men were headed for New Orleans where they could get away from the grimness that they all had been feeling and living. Stone stood up, stretched and then went inside.

Across the field on this beautiful morning sat a burly Union captain and four other soldiers on their horses. They seemed to have a sense of urgency, but their manners were well disciplined and experienced. The captain using field glasses was surveying the farm buildings. Silently he put his glasses in his saddle bag and motioned his men to proceed toward the farm.

At the table everyone ate quietly. While Stone was tense and seemingly over-contemplative, the older woman was very preoccupied, never raising her eyes. O'Reilly, having had a good night's rest seemed quite cheerful, and the younger woman stole quick glances at Stone.

"How long're you two gonna stay?" asked the younger woman.

Stone looked at the older woman who didn't seem to notice and O'Reilly cleared his throat saying, "Well, we're not planning on staying long, young lady. Rich an I are headed for New Orleans."

"Do you ladies realize that no one has introduced themselves?" O'Reilly stated bluntly in a rather cheerful voice to a silent and uncaring audience.

"Well, my name is Donald O'Reilly and this is my partner and friend, Richard Harold Stone. We're from western Tennessee."

The younger woman seeming to open up more introduced herself and the other woman. "Well, this is my mother, Madeline Harrow an my name's Cynthia. Mother, don't ya have anythin ta say?"

Her mother sat up straight and looked coldly into her daughter's eyes, then rose from the table, set her plate, cup and utensils into the sink and went out on the porch. Immediately, she spotted the Union soldiers coming through the field. She remained on the porch and called her daughter. "*Cynthia*, hide the men! Them damn Yankees're comin!"

Cynthia and the two friends were soon in the hallway, as she pointed, "Go down in the cellar." Stone and O'Reilly immediately went for the door and into the dark, cool cellar. The Union soldiers moving cautiously and still on horseback, arrived at the front of the house. The captain and his men, all carrying rifles, came around to the side of the house by the porch. Madeline nervously standing there was quite frightened by the Federal soldiers.

"Good morning, ma'am, I'm Captain Tryon. I'm looking for two Rebels that escaped from our camp a couple of nights ago. I was wondering if they have come by here at all?" greeted the captain coldly, but politely.

"N ... no sir. Not that I seen. Have ya seen anyone like the captain says, Cynthia?" asked her mother.

"No, mother, 'cept fer a couple a hobos over by the creek last night," her daughter answered from inside the house.

"Did you see which way they were headed, miss?" asked the captain without emotion. The young woman came to the back door and just shook her head 'no'.

Captain Tryon looked down at the ground angrily with his jaw muscles noticeably tensing. Then quickly raising his head, he surveyed the house and barn with an apparently well-trained eye. The morning was quiet and the captain's silent surveillance made it feel even more still. Slowly the captain dismounted and the men followed.

"I have a job to do. I am not calling you liars, but we're going to check around. Out of the way!" ordered the captain.

"But there's nobody inside," pleaded the mother.

The captain now more determined than ever to find the Rebels, gently shoved the women out of the way, and with two of his men entered the kitchen. Tryon spotted the table with three places hastily left. Grinding his teeth quietly, he opened the cellar door. The women, holding on to one another, were terrified. He had one of his soldiers find a lantern and light it.

"Alright, we're not here to hurt you," the captain called down into the cellar with a steely cold voice. "We're coming down, if you don't come up."

The captain waited, but there was no reply. Stone and O'Reilly were just under the stairway in the crowded cellar. Determinedly the captain stepped down the stairs with his rifle ready. The two still under the stairs remained silent in the darkness. Tryon now on the cellar floor and his men at the top of the stairs looking down, left no hopeful escape for them. Carefully, the captain checked every nook and cranny where one or two men could hide. As Stone's eyes nervously searched the crack in the stairway to see where the captain had gone, a rifle barrel slipped in front of his face.

"Come on, let's go," said Captain Tryon, his voice now tense and even sharper than before. Slowly, and with much apprehension, Stone and O'Reilly removed themselves from their unsuccessful hideaway.

The two men were brought up and the captain had them seated. The women upstairs were already bound and seated at the kitchen table. Chains were placed on Stone and O'Reilly and they were searched. The captain was a rough man and so were his men. There was no polite attention given to the women either, for as the captain searched the two Rebels, one of his soldiers was stroking Cynthia's cheek, which she unsuccessfully tried to avoid. Then the captain saw the man.

"Alright Douglas," said the captain disgustedly to the offending man. Tryon, after finding nothing of importance, instructed his men to place the prisoners each on a horse from the barn. Madeline said nothing as she and her daughter sat bound in their chairs. She just seemed accepting of the whole incident. After the prisoners were removed from the house and placed on their horses, the two women were untied.

"Ma'am, I realize your loyalties are not the same as mine. You are not a soldier, neither is your daughter. So I have no need to keep you. I've gotten what I wanted and have done my job. Sorry to have troubled you," said the captain, as he touched the brim of his hat.

The two women said nothing. Madeline just stared after the Union captain angrily. Cynthia looked sorrowfully out the kitchen window at Stone and he was looking back at her. She had felt something for him and now wished she had been friendlier toward him. She wanted very much to help him, but alone she felt so helpless.

As Stone and O'Reilly rode back across the field with the Union soldiers, Cynthia purposefully wandered out of the house and hurried toward the barn. There were many times she had passed the Union camp out in the hills and she figured that's where Stone would be kept. After preparing a horse, she returned to the house and went to her room. Her mother was cleaning up after their interrupted breakfast and noticed her daughter's behavior. She knew very well what Cynthia was going to do, but she also understood her and acted reservedly. As she was easily passing back through the kitchen, Cynthia came to an abrupt stop at the door and watched her mother.

"Mother, don't feel too bad; they were prob'bly no good fer anything anyway," ventured Cynthia, waiting for her mother to answer her. Madeline paused, then slowly turning toward her daughter, just looked at her with a slight grin.

"Um, I'm goin fer a ride," stated the unnerved younger woman. Her mother's eyes revealed that she knew exactly what her daughter was doing. Cynthia turned away, then looking back at her mother, noticed she was about to cry. Then, wanting to comfort her, she ran into her mother's arms.

"I love you mother. I love you very much," cried Cynthia. As the two women embraced very lovingly, her mother was now crying too.

"Cynthia, I know how ya feel, but he's gone now. There's no way ya can help 'im," her mother said. Thinking back on last night, she was filled with shame and remorse. Her daughter needed someone more than she. "Darlin, yer a grown woman now," her mother paused, "I can't really stop ya if yer in ... if yer in love with 'im." Cynthia slowly pulled back and wiped her eyes. Her mother just looked at her, keeping one arm around her.

"I don't know if I love him," Cynthia cried. Then hesitating, "But I need a man; an I need *him*. I want desperately ta help him." The two women looked at each other, then Cynthia kissed her and said firmly, "I'll be back mother. I promise, I will be back." She walked out the door and went to her waiting horse, still in the barn.

In a couple of hours, it would be noon. Her mother quickly put together a basket of food and met her in the barnyard. "Here's somethin ta eat later on. Ya know what yer doin haint gonna be easy," her mother simply stated. Cynthia smiled and touched her hand; then as her mother stood in the barnyard, she started on her way across the field and to Richard Harold Stone.

Captain Tryon, his men and his two prisoners were only a two-day ride from the camp where Stone and O'Reilly had escaped. The noon sun was beginning to warm the day, so the captain and the men spent a little time under a grove of trees near the road that they were to travel. Here they had lunch. Stone and O'Reilly still bound and chained were under the trees with them.

"You know boys, I don't hate Southerners and I don't hate you two either. It's just that I've got a job to do. Can you understand that?" asked the surprisingly pleasant captain. The two somewhat frightened prisoners just nodded their heads in agreement.

"Now to show you that I'm not so bad, how about a game of poker, huh?" asked the captain with a grin. Stone and O'Reilly just looked at each other skeptically and didn't say a word.

"Aw, c'mon boys! Look you're not going to some horrible place. Union prisons aren't as bad as you think." The two Rebels were beginning to lose some of their apprehension as the captain continued, "I've got some cards. Wait a minute ... yea they're all here. Okay now, what was I saying?"

"Oh, yeah. Now you two will wind up ... now I'm guaranteeing this ... you two boys will probably wind up in a Federal work camp like the one near Hickman, Kentucky. Now," as he dealt both of them a hand, his men stood around watching, "that's right on the bank of the Ol' Mississippi. So you see it's not going to be that bad. You two will probably dig holes and trenches and things like that. Now take a look at your cards." The two men looked over their hands and Stone said 'Two' and O'Reilly 'One'. Captain Tryon dealt the respected amount of cards and grinned.

"Ah, sounds interesting. Hm-m-m," the captain mused. They all looked at each other and O'Reilly folded. Stone looked at the captain and laid down a pair of aces. Tryon at first looked surprised, then he leaned back and grinned sinisterly. He laid a royal flush on the grass.

"*I always win!*" The captain continued with a mocking laugh, "Well, that was a lot of fun; but you see the war must go on. So now we're going right up to Hickman." The Union soldiers helped their prisoners back up on their horses, then remounted their own.

'I almost fell fer his friendly gestures,' Stone said to himself, 'I knew he wuzn't a nice guy. He's jest like all the rest of 'em. I gotta be on my guard"

From a fair distance, Cynthia had just caught sight of the Union soldiers and their prisoners. She was too far away to hear and didn't realize they were going up into Kentucky. The brave, young woman squinted and stared hard, trying to make out Stone. When she found him, she noticed the chains on his ankles and wrists. Rushing to her horse she mounted. Still watching, Cynthia felt some remorse in having left her mother alone, but soon shook the thought out of her head when she noticed the men had disappeared. Hurrying down to the road, she could spot them going northward. She began to ride close enough to always be able to keep them in sight.

It was almost evening and the Union soldiers,

along with their prisoners were only a few miles from the Tennessee-Kentucky border. Cynthia Harrow was not far behind and was still able to see Stone and the other men. Soon the captain had his men set up camp for the night. The soldiers removed their chains under the order of Capt. Tryon. While still under the watchful eyes of Cynthia, he also had his men tie Stone and O'Reilly to the trunk of a tree. It was a clear night and the air was warm, so the threat of rain was remote. A small camp fire was started and the soldiers, with only one placed guard, called it a day. The weary Rebel prisoners were soon asleep. As an hour passed and then another Cynthia waited lying on the ground watching the stars. The camp was silent except for the snoring and rustling of the sleeping men.

It was about two o'clock in the early morning and Cynthia was cautiously walking toward the night guard, who had laid his rifle against the tree he was leaning on. As she crept up near the soldier, she had her hand under the shawl she was wearing. The guard became alert when he heard a small stick break. Suddenly, he grabbed for his gun and just as quickly Cynthia shoved a sharp, long bladed kitchen knife into the man's throat. She pulled back in terror at what she had just done to another human being. She muffled her cry as she watched and heard him gag on his own blood and die. The distraught young woman was sitting on her knees, rocking back and forth, but soon quieted as she saw Stone still asleep. Getting herself together, she straightened her dress and hair and went over to him.

The two prisoners still sleeping, startled when the rope that held them to the tree fell heavily to the ground, and one awoke. Upon seeing Cynthia standing with a knife dripping with blood, O'Reilly realized what had happened; they were no longer bound to the tree. She had cut the rope.

"Hey, what's goin ...?" O'Reilly started, but was quickly gestured to be quiet by Cynthia, seemingly pleased, despite how she looked. He quickly and quietly awakened Stone, who was also surprised at what was happening and who was doing it.

"What're ya doin here, Cynthia?" gasped Stone. She was now sitting on the ground by him and smiling yet still in shock.

"We better get outta here b'fore somebody else wakes up," whispered Cynthia. The three quickly left the area.

"What happened ta the guard?" Rich whispered to their rescuer with widened eyes.

"Well, I stabbed him, um, right here," pointing to her throat.

"Right'n the throat? How could ya ... er any woman do a thing like that?" he responded with another muffled gasp.

"I don't know; but it was the only way I could think of. I really didn't want ta kill 'im; I jest didn't know what ta do. What would you have done?" Cynthia questioned with tension in her voice. Stone looked at her and she could see that he understood.

They continued to walk quickly, but in a more westerly direction.

Meanwhile Captain Tryon, having just discovered the body of his guard, was walking around the camp looking for signs of his escaped prisoners. Turning the corpse over with his boot, the captain quickly turned his head in disgust.

'Those dirty rotten …! They haven't got a decent bone in their bodies,' he said to himself. He looked around and could see three, barely recognizable figures walking briskly up a hill in the near distance. Immediately he picked up the dead guard's gun and checked to see if it was loaded; then aiming, he fired the magazine at the fleeing figures.

Suddenly they could hear bullets whizzing over their heads, and Stone motioned toward a nearby clump of trees. The rifle shots began to make their marks; first Stone was hit in the right thigh, then in his left upper arm. He fell in pain as Cynthia and O'Reilly went over to his aid; they were only about fifteen yards from cover. All of a sudden, there was silence.

"They're probably changing magazines or something. Let's get into those trees fast," O'Reilly gestured with his head. As they were half-carrying Stone, the rifle fire resumed and the bullets were whizzing by again.

"C'mon, c'mon! Move, move, move! C'mon, get him over here," ordered O'Reilly as he and Cynthia carried their injured friend. Just as they got to the safety of the trees, the rifle fire ceased again.

"Just when we find cover, they don't shoot anymore," said O'Reilly.

"Oh-h-h, look at his arm; look at all the blood!" Cynthia cried. She seemed to be falling apart. "I've got you two in real trouble now. Oh-h-h- no-o-o; no-o!" she continued, nearly hysterical.

"Shut your mouth and pull yourself together. Do you hear me? *Pull yourself together!*" O'Reilly firmly ordered. "Now the only way we got to move him, is to keep our heads … alright?" he said firmly, but more calmly.

Cynthia now just sniffling, nodded her head. "Tear off part of your dress and here's part of my shirt; now we can slow down the bleeding. Are there any doctors close by?" O'Reilly asked, as he peered down the hill at the still visible camp.

"There's a doctor about a mile down the road, but he's older than these hills. I don't think he kin even see too good. I guess he's quit doctorin," answered Cynthia a bit more composed. Stone was moaning.

"Well, he's better than nothing. Alright, let's get started," ordered O'Reilly. Stone was on his feet again, supported on each side by his friends.

The captain and his men had just packed their guns and were on their horses coming up the hill. The three fugitives were too far into the woods to be caught now. It was too dark and Tryon was too smart to search the wooded area. Through the closely grown trees and bushes continued the two men and the young woman. Soon, the three were coming down the other side of the hill and Cynthia thought she could spot the old doctor's farm house. They paused and tried to get their bearings.

"There it is!" Cynthia said, pointing to the house. "See, he used ta run a farm there, but after a while he couldn't handle the work an tried to sell it."

"But where's the barn? All I can see is the house," wondered O'Reilly.

"Well, I had heard nobody would buy it, so he burnt the barn down. I guess he's a little odd sometimes," she said with a slight smile. O'Reilly looked at her with an expression of surprise.

"Well like I said before, Miss Cynthia, he's better than nothing," said O'Reilly with a grin. They immediately began to make their way toward the house down by the road.

"Wait a minute. If we go in now, then these Federals will probably come by and check the house. Maybe we'd better wait in the woods for a little while yet," offered O'Reilly.

"Yea, but *he* needs help *now*. Look at 'im; he's even breathin slow. We better let the doc do what he kin," responded Cynthia.

O'Reilly looked at the young woman and was surprised at her already collected manner. He agreed and they proceeded to carry Stone to the house of the old doctor.

In the woods, Captain Tryon and his men were heading down the hillside back to their small camp.

"You know, I think we'll continue on this way and see if we can catch up with them. I figure they'll avoid the road, but will be close enough to use it for their own sense of bearing," said the now confident captain. In his hand he was stroking a whip. Tryon's men seemed more confident themselves as they looked at the whip. This Union unit had not figured a loss yet; their pride made them arrogant.

As the captain and his soldiers made their way down the hill, he remembered how he had tried to be a fair man with his prisoners; but when they crossed him, then he changed; and now, he had definitely changed his thoughts about Stone and O'Reilly.

The night continued and the hours passed as O'Reilly and Cynthia were sitting at the kitchen table in Dr. Grant's house while the doctor was treating Stone's wounds in the bedroom nearby. An old clock was ticking. That and the old doctor's intermittent use of his tools and the slight moans of a half- conscious Stone, were the only sounds in the house.

O'Reilly looked at a drained Cynthia and really began to notice how much of a woman she was. Her soft, dark, brown hair had a slight wave to it; he could see that her blue eyes and her light complexion framed by her long, wavy hair, adorned quite a strong- willed young lady.

"Doesn't he have a wife?" whispered O'Reilly to an almost sleeping Cynthia.

She opened her eyes and looked across the table and answered, "She's been dead fer a couple years er so." He just leaned back, and the two tried to get as much rest as they could in the kitchen chairs.

The next morning found the two exhausted friends, Cynthia and O'Reilly in one bed, with the doctor between them. Stone was in the next room. Cynthia began to awaken first. As she laid there in the bed opening her eyes, she noticed surprisingly her fellow occupants ... the old doctor sleeping and snoring flat on his back and a sleeping, snoring O'Reilly facing away from her on the other side of him, with almost all the covers. A little chilled, she began to pull the covers back, when she noticed her night gown. Now sitting up in bed, she couldn't decide if the doctor, yes good old respectable Dr. Grant, was a dirty old man or if O'Reilly wasn't as innocent as he appeared. As she looked around the room, she noticed her petticoat, dress and some other undergarments laying across the chair. She stood up out of bed and the long nightgown met the floor.

"Oh, all ya men want an think about is one thing!" she hissed softly. She was quite upset about the whole matter. And what angered her even more was the sight of the two guiltless looking men, asleep as though neither of them had anything to do with her present situation and state of undress. As she made her way to her clothes, she began tripping and suddenly fell, her foot catching in the hem of the long gown. She landed on the floor on her stomach waiting for someone to awaken, but all that could be heard was the repetitive snoring of the two men.

Slowly she got up and removed her nightgown, exposing a very attractive form. As she stood naked in the bedroom, she purposely waited for one of the men to awaken and look at her. "Well, you two have seen enough already?" she whispered a little loudly; then proceeded to redress in her original attire.

With a good night's rest, Captain Tryon sat drinking a cup of coffee with his sergeant. The morning was crisp, but the day would soon be warm. The captain was silent as he threw the cup's dredges on the ground. On his face was a look of strong determination while he rubbed his hands together, demonstrating the impatience of the man for the capture of the two Rebels.

"C'mon we haven't got all day," ordered the captain, as slowly the Federal bounty soldiers gathered themselves and their belongings, then continued their way down the road, unknowingly approaching the old doctor's farm house.

It was two o'clock in the afternoon when the Federals arrived at the old doctor's place. They were taking their time, though the distance was shorter through the hills than by the road. It was easier the longer way around, because the horses would have had a difficult time making their way through the heavy, well grown, underbrush in the hills of this area.

Inside the farmhouse, the injured Rebel still laid in bed sleeping. Cynthia was sitting on the back porch with Dr. Grant and O'Reilly was in the kitchen drinking coffee and reading a week old newspaper. As the soldiers approached, Captain Tryon had his sergeant lead a few men around the back of the house. There was sufficient cover of bush and trees to hide them. All the while, the young miss and the old doctor sat lazily chatting, the young man drinking his coffee, reading and the injured soldier unable to do much of anything else but rest. At the front of the house, the Union captain and another soldier flanked the front door. There, directly in line of the front door was the archway to the kitchen where O'Reilly sat calmly at the table; and without any design, he was an inescapable target of the captain's now cocked, long-barreled pistol.

In the rear of the house, Federal rifles were aimed at Cynthia and Doc Grant. The sergeant wasn't sure of the young woman's part in the conspiracy, because he was actually too far away to recognize her. But at the same time, she appeared to be the same woman from the farm where the two Rebels were first caught, and he felt sure she was the same one he had seen running up the hill with the two men the night before. It was a certainty in his bones, rather than in his mind, that he felt she was a conspirator more than not.

Swiftly, the captain kicked open the front door and aimed his pistol right at the head of O'Reilly who was sitting, holding the coffee cup in his hand and about to take a sip. A look of shock and sheer terror covered his face.

"Stay right where you are and don't make a sound," ordered the captain in a tensed, but hushed voice. He motioned his soldier to proceed out the back door and O'Reilly to move to the side. As the soldier passed between the Rebel and the Union officer, O'Reilly suddenly grabbed the soldier and used him as a shield. He swiftly ran into the kitchen and out onto the back porch to warn Cynthia and the old doctor. Here the Federal sergeant opened fire ... and O'Reilly, Cynthia and old Doc Grant met their end.

Inside the house, Capt. Tryon had shielded himself behind the archway; his other soldier laid on the floor as the spray of bullets marked the kitchen walls and door and shattered the windows within their trajectory. An odd silence hung in the air after the sound of the shots died down. The captain and the soldier quietly made their way upstairs. Here they cautiously kicked open the door to each of the rooms, three in all, until they got to Stone's room. The top of the captain's boots suddenly appeared in front of the wide eyes of the weak Rebel soldier, who had been making his way toward the door by crawling on his stomach after hearing all of the ruckus.

"Mr. Stone, you are coming with me and you have nobody left to help you now," said the captain in a cold and determined voice. Stone's macabre facial expression revealed to the captain that the injured man already knew that his friends had been killed. Their deaths seemed to be a fact of the matter, from what he could make from Tryon's words and attitude.

Stone's health was poor at this time and his weakness extended to his mind. He was exhausted and his ambition to escape had faded. As the captain and his soldier half-carried him down to the back porch, Tryon turned Stone's head so he could see the bodies of Cynthia, O'Reilly and old Doc Grant. After seeing them lying there so still, Stone closed his eyes and choked up silently. He was now a very beaten man and within himself felt a numbing grief unlike any before. The captain and his men fashioned a suitable stretcher, then made their way down the road to another farm Tryon knew about. Here they put Stone on a buckboard and under their watchful eyes, took him straight to Norwalk, Tennessee.

Norwalk was a small town, but there was a doctor who could look over the prisoner and Federal military officials would process him for his incarceration. In this part of Tennessee, the Union Army had made some ground and it was also where Captain Tryon was paid a 'commission', better called a bounty for the escaped Rebel. Richard Harold Stone was now a prisoner and within three days he would be in Young's Prison, a small swiftly set up make-shift rural prison for Confederate soldiers. It was located about ten miles into southern Illinois and not more than six miles from the Mississippi River. It was about two and a half days north of the Illinois city of Cairo.

Stone was in a physical and emotional daze. He was trying to explain away what had been happening to him, as a dream, but the reality of it was raw and too overwhelming. 'How horr'ble', he thought, 'three dead an the only wrong they did was to try ta help me. Where is the justice in all o this? I should be the one dead … and here I am alive and alone.

Chapter III

In a hotel room in Norwalk, Richard Stone was lying in bed. There was a guard outside the door, while in the room another guard and a doctor were looking over the new prisoner.

"Mmm ... all I can tell is that he was hit twice. Here in the shoulder and in his thigh. All he's suffering from is shock and some lost blood," said the doctor to the observing guard. "He can be moved the day after tomorrow."

The soldier just nodded his head agreeably as the doctor, an older man from the area began to pack up for the next prisoner in a nearby room.

The day arrived soon for Stone's departure for Young's Prison. It was a sunny and warm Thursday morning without a cloud in the sky. It was about ten o'clock when Stone was brought down on a stretcher to the Federal prison wagon. He was slowly eased in, then the door was closed and locked behind him. Inside there were other wounded prisoners; one young man had his hands bandaged, another with crutches and one eye bandaged, and the last one appeared to have nothing wrong with him except that he just stared and never said a word. There were four in all in the back of a wagon that could easily hold eight. So they had enough room and the ride would be of a decent, while still rough, kind of comfort.

The black sheet metal wagon with chicken wire windows wobbled away from the hotel with its cargo drawn by two horses. The driver and a guard sat up front; two more guards rode on horseback a short distance behind, where each could see the back and one side of the wagon. Painted on both sides in faded letters was 'FEDERAL PRISONERS'. The wagon was well-used as one could tell by looking at it and the men moving the prisoners were just as used to their job as the wagon was to its. The prisoners inside were raggedy, though sufficiently clothed. As a matter of fact, most of the soldiers on both sides and even the civilians were getting used to wearing well-worn and mended clothing. The exceptions to the case were the higher ranking officers.

Stone was somewhat better physically, though his morale was very poor. Inside the wagon, he was silent and just watched the other wounded prisoners. Occasionally he would sit up, though still feeling sore and trying to figure out where he was. Then with a disgusted and uncaring look, he would lie back down and close his eyes. If one could know, they would find that the loss of O'Reilly and Cynthia tore at Stone far more than it appeared. But he continued to keep silent and just rode along with the others.

With night stops in small, uncomfortable yet tolerable hotels along the way, Stone and the other prisoners finally arrived at the gate of Young's Prison. It was a hot Saturday afternoon, but a breeze made it comfortable on this day in southern Illinois. As the wagon slowed to a stop, Stone sat up and looked at his point of destination.

The once dirty, rocky and dusty road gave way to a heavily rutted entrance to the prison. The prison itself was nothing more than a collection of fairly constructed barrack-type buildings, except one; the only two story structure looked to be the best built. The prison was completely encompassed by an eight foot high fence made of chicken wire, heavily supported by eight foot long stakes nearly a half foot thick. At each corner was the unmistakable form of the guard tower, which loomed about twelve feet above the ground. Each was well-manned and well-armed.

An archway of black painted sheet metal mounted on plank board over the prison gate read, 'YOUNG'S PRISON'. Stone laid back down onto his stretcher and from the window of the wagon watched the prison gate open. The rig took the well-rutted roadway, making its way in roughly toward the two story building. Stone could smell a stench from what must have been an open sewer. As they continued on, the smell became less noticeable until it all but disappeared when the wagon stopped in front of the larger building.

Almost immediately the door was unlocked and opened; Stone was eased down to the ground on his stretcher. The other prisoners were also given aid out of the wagon depending on the severity of their injuries until they formed a recognizable row. Here they waited in front of what was labeled on another black sheet metal sign mounted on a post, 'THE OFFICE OF

ADMINISTRATION'. On the porch stood two well-dressed officers ... a colonel and a captain. Three guards came to help with the newly arrived prisoners.

As the prison wagon pulled away and headed back out the gate, the colonel walked sternly down the steps and stood in front of the four injured Confederate prisoners of war.

"I'm Colonel Masson and up there is Captain Hardy. We try to run an efficient and somewhat bearable institution here. Of course your cooperation is needed for this level of operation to be maintained. If you do not know how to cooperate, we will certainly show you how. Now for your own information, this is where the captain and I, and our respective staffs live and work. This is where the prison hospital is also located," said the colonel, as he pointed at the two-story building behind him.

"Over there will be your home until the end of the war," Colonel Masson said, pointing toward the barracks. "You will live and work here without too much grief from Captain Hardy or me. Just do as you are told, and everything and everyone will be fine."

"Sergeant, take the one on the stretcher and the one on crutches straight to the hospital and get them checked over. The other two may as well get checked, but they look good enough to me to be placed in a barracks. Yes, have those two checked also," the colonel ordered. Two guards eased Stone off the ground and took him behind the building where the entrance to the prison hospital was located.

Opening a small door, the guards entered the hospital with the two prisoners. Inside were many beds, almost all of them filled; moaning and the smell of sickness filled the air. The guards stopped at a desk and the doctor pulled off Stone's single blanket.

"Got hit a couple of times, hey? A couple of days here and you'll be fine. The last bed down," said the young doctor with a smile, as he pointed at the row of beds. Stone wasn't in a light mood, but just wanted to rest.

As the guards carried him to his bed, he looked from side to side on the stretcher and found the patients pitiful. After placing Stone on his bed, the guards rolled up the stretcher and left. Lying in his bed, Stone could look out the window to his right and see a woods. He looked into the distance and noticed how the hills seemed to form around a valley; an unconscious, but noticeable suspicion filled him with hope. As he continued to look, the idea came into his mind that the Mississippi River was just a matter of a few miles away.

He turned his head and could see the other patients and also some prisoners. As he looked, he counted about thirty beds with only two empty. An uneasiness rose within him as he thought about the causes of so much sickness and suffering in one place. Stone, while an idealist who was always being surprised if not shocked by the realities of war, was realistic enough to harbor the thought of brutality as one cause. As he lay thinking, a nurse entered the room. She stopped and checked some of the prisoners' moanings. She noticed Stone and with a compassionate look on her face came over toward him.

"Ah now, I haven't seen ya around here before. Just come in today?" she asked with a smile. Stone smiled back and then nodded.

"I wuz captured a few days ago in Tennessee," he answered. "I wuz hit a couple o times. The doc said I'll be out in a couple o days."

The nurse was still smiling and then looked out the window. "Well, ya got a beautiful view of the Mississippi Valley." Stone looked out the window too as she added, "I wouldn't get any ideas though, if I were you. You'd just get yourself killed."

She looked at him and began to leave. Stone just stared at her and asked himself, "How kin a woman work in a place like this?"

She lost her smile, taken aback as she quietly answered, "That's a good question. I was an orphan and the government had a nursing program. See I'm from a home in Chicago, well near there; they had a need in the army for nurses and some of us girls at the home took advantage. And that's why I'm here." Her smile returned and she left Stone's bedside.

After she left the room, Stone looked up at the ceiling and felt lonely for Cynthia. The nurse must be in her early twenties he thought. In his mind he tried to picture her without her cap and imagined what she would look like with her long auburn hair loose down around her shoulders. His loneliness for Cynthia and a sense of responsibility for her death crept upon him again, as it had been. The young nurse was a relief to him. She was a woman he could at least dream about. As he looked back out the window, he tried to figure which way south was. Now with a little bit of hope and a sense of the future back again, Stone closed his eyes and went to sleep.

He slept through from late that afternoon until ten o'clock the next morning. With a soft moan, Stone was awakened by the doctor checking his wounds.

"Now take it easy, will you?" said the doctor, as he finished checking his arm and went to the leg wound. Stone winced as the doctor touched the wound and then began replacing the bandages.

"You'll be out of the hospital by tomorrow afternoon, Richard." Stone showed surprise that he knew his first name. "I read the prisoners' admissions' list last night," the doctor smiled knowingly. The patient winced again as the doctor finished replacing the bandage on his leg.

"You're kind of quiet. Well, you might as well relax, because you'll probably be here at Young's for quite a time," the doctor said. Stone laid there, feeling well rested as the doctor went to another bed down the row. He looked out toward the Mississippi Valley, determined not to stay in this place long.

Down by the side of the bed he had seen some newspapers on the little stand that was there. He picked one up and looked at the date. It must have been the latest issue, for it was only a week old. Most of the news was about the war. As he turned the pages of the Cairo Weekly, he came across an advertisement for *'men needed for a St. Louis River Transportation Company'*. It had an illustration of a riverboat, which only furthered the desire in Stone to escape down the river.

As he looked out the window, Richard noticed the fence around the prison formed a very troubling obstacle for his plans. He laughed to himself about the nurse's mention of not getting 'any ideas'. 'What the hell am I supposed to do here?' he whispered to himself as his eyes returned to the newspaper.

Deep inside Stone could feel his desire for freedom become more intense, while in his mind the images of the young nurse, the Mississippi River and New Orleans raced by. As he looked back up from the paper the reality of his present situation came back, along with the question of how this freedom was to be obtained. He began wondering about where this nurse stayed. 'Would a young woman like this live in the prison er would there be someplace nearby?'

As Stone put down the newspaper he could hear bells in the distance. He listened and then remembered that it was Sunday morning. A quieter sounding bell began ringing. In his mind he pictured a smaller handheld type bell that seemed to originate from within the prison grounds. In the bed next to Stone laid an older man, who looked about thirty-nine or forty. He watched Stone's preoccupation with the sights and sounds from outside the hospital.

"Well, it's another church mornin, friend," the other man said in a voice that was not loud enough to break Stone's train of thought immediately.

"Huh? Oh, yea, that's what I thought wuz goin on. My name's Richard Stone," he replied as he extended his hand.

"I'm Tom Silts," the other man said as he shook his hand. "I'm from Atlanta, an been here fer 'bout a year. The only thing that bothers me is what happened ta my brother in Jackson, Mississippi. Ya know, Grant took the city in the first week a May."

"I'm from Parkinson, Tennessee," said Stone. "They caught me last Thursday er ma'be it wuz Friday. It was jest a few days ago near Memphis."

Silts let a pause linger after Stone spoke, then very quietly interjected, "Seems ta me far too easy fer someone ta escape frum here. I been wonderin 'bout our very dear, considerate nurse ... even the staff here er some of the Union officers that come 'round." He had Stone's undivided attention now. "Why're they so kind an eager ta make us all git better? Why don't they jus shoot us? After all, we're the enemy."

Tom was glad to share his suspicions, even if Richard might consider him to be delving into fantasy. So he continued, "Ya know there's a way of makin a lot of cash fer anyone on either side playin this 'bounty game' of findin escaped prisoners; lots a money that'd make bein on only one side er the other, a fool's game. If such is goin on, then maybe it'd be easy ta escape; an fer those gettin money at all this … ta capture 'em agin an make quite the rich man's life," Silts now being so extra cautious in his whispering to Stone.

While Stone was digesting all this, he reflected on all the opportunities seemingly presenting themselves, even though suspicions arose about Silts. 'Wuz this prisoner part o this schemin too? The nurse? Some o the Federals? Yeah, what a racket ta take advantage of? Filthy lucre in this war seemed ta be part o the human game o survivin; an what side *did* really matter after all?'

There had to be quite the danger in all this; some of those who 'escaped' must have been of lesser value than others. Could they be expendable enough to be killed, while others are more valuable with their bounty? Slavery was not the only peculiar institution. Everyone even the free could be bought or sold, or worse.

Stone and Silts regarded each other, then Tom picked up the same Cairo Weekly and began to read it. Richard turned his attentions outside again. The day would be warm and the sun's heat could already be felt. He was eager to get out of bed and now, impatient to escape. The thought of escape scared him, but the thought of staying here for maybe years was worse. His desire for freedom was now strong and the obstacles hindering his escape were not as deterring as would be expected.

Everyone seemed so contented on being trapped or bound by things and circumstances that they really didn't want. Stone felt alone with his desire for freedom. 'Maybe Tom was wrong in his speculations; maybe he's a coward and afraid to try to escape'. Stone's own spirit and determination didn't seem to stir the same desire in the others around him. This frustrateded him, but he had learned earlier that people do things only if they really want to. He would like to take that nurse with him to New Orleans, but only if she sincerely wanted to leave her present situation. Stone didn't believe Silt's ideas about her and he couldn't believe she would want to stay here in this depressing place. If she wanted to change her life, she would have to tell him so.

As noon arrived at Young's Prison the young nurse who so preoccupied Stone, was serving meals to the hospital patients. A soldier was assisting her. He was a young man apparently in his twenties and seemed overly anxious to help the young lady. Stone's face showed irritation as the nurse's helper was doing a fair job of keeping her smiling and laughing with his charming manner. As they approached, he sat up a little straighter in his bed and tried to look as sure of himself as was possible under the circumstances of his painful wounds.

"There he is on such a lovely day. How are ya today?" asked the young, pretty nurse. The soldier looked at Stone as though he didn't have a chance for her fancy; and if he had any chance at all, then this fella would stop him fast and sure. At least that was the impression that the young man was trying to give. To this, Stone looked with a carefree grin right into the tender eyes of the young woman. She appeared even more pleased with serving Stone and seemed to linger, detaining herself at his bedside over the others.

"I'm feelin a lot better today Miss ... Why, what's yer name?" he asked. The young soldier's face looked more serious as Stone seemed to be able to please the young woman without much else to show than his pleasant personality.

"I'm Ellen Marshell. Didn't I mention that yesterday?" she responded.

"No, ya didn't."

She paused over his bedside for a moment and briefly looked into Stone's eyes. In that brief and still moment, she sensed a difference between him and the other prisoners she had met so far. As a matter of fact, he had some indefinable quality that she had never seen in any man in her life. It was a warm feeling, a genuine wholesomeness that stirred within her.

With a hand on her elbow the young soldier suddenly, but gently directed the young nurse away from Stone's bedside and on to the next patient. His annoyance toward Richard wasn't more than irritation at the moment. 'For what could a pretty, young woman want with a sickly, scrawny Rebel prisoner? All he probably knows is farming and what kind of life would that be for Miss Marshell,' the young man thought to himself. Stone was unaware that this soldier was dating her and considering asking for her hand in marriage.

Stone's wounds were healing and the pain had

lessened since the day before. Tomorrow afternoon he thought he would be out and on the grounds where he could get a better view of his confinement. Looking down the row of beds, he thought about what he saw in Ellen's eyes. 'An unhappy young woman', he whispered to himself. His face had a determined look as he watched her, still with that soldier as they continued to serve food to the patients.

Monday morning arrived with rain and Stone awakened as the doctor was probing his wounds and replacing bandages. He looked at the clock; it was half past nine.

"Well, you ought to be able to have mess with the other prisoners, but maybe you'd rather have dinner with Captain Hardy?" asked the doctor as he watched Stone's face.

"Yeah, I might like that," replied the patient.

The doctor pausing a moment, added, "I think it would be wise." He continued with a suddenly brighter nature, "It might do you some good to get out and around."

Alone again, Stone was confused. Being a prisoner-of-war for him wasn't so bad so far. He had heard stories, but this place and the people here made it seem almost like home ... almost. In his heart he was becoming suspicious of some of the people working here. 'Was Silts right?' He began thinking about the newspaper, the friendly nurse who just happened to be young and very pretty, and that almost cheerful doctor.

Stone, putting his hand to his head began to feel that while his suspicions loomed, he should remind himself not to jump to any conclusions.

At about noon Captain Hardy came to meet Stone who was sitting on the edge of his bed getting dressed. "Good morning, Richard. I'm Captain Hardy. I think you remember me. Well, at least I hope you do," he greeted cheerfully as he stretched out his right hand.

Stone smiled back and shook his hand, but sensed the captain's opinion of him ... a poor, dumb, southern boy who should consider this a special honor for the great captain to want to have dinner with him ... Richard Stone, some plowboy from the sticks of Tennessee. "Cap'in, why'd ya wanna have dinner with me?" asked Stone, as he played it a little slow.

"Well, Richard, I'm a fair man," the captain began. Because of Stone's condition, the two of them walked slowly from the room. He offered Stone a cigar and he accepted. "I can't see carrying the war right into the prison camp. Do you know what I mean?" the captain continued, as he lit Stone's cigar and then his own.

"Well, I guess so. We're all friends here. Is that what ya mean?"

The captain caught the touch of sarcasm in his reply, but still figured Stone too dumb for even that at the moment. "Well, Richard, now I wouldn't say that either," smiled Hardy as he placed a hand on Stone's shoulder and led him into his office.

"Have a seat there Richard. Some brandy or scotch?" offered the gracious captain. Stone could see an almost amateurish manner to the officer, so he figured to play along. Maybe he could throw something advantageous in. The captain didn't seem all that smart, thought Stone.

Captain Hardy sat down, poured himself a glass of scotch then motioned for Stone to join him. The captain, in order to form some kind of psychological advantage, sat there with such a sincere look on his face. He was trying too hard; Stone felt quite relaxed as the captain became a less formidable and almost ridiculous opponent.

"Ya don't mind if I jest have one, do ya, Suh? I kinda talk a lot when I'm drinkin," Stone revealed.

"Oh, don't worry about that. You can have more. I didn't pay for it and besides, you are my guest," the captain's eyes revealed the hope that he might succeed at whatever it was that he was planning to accomplish. This Stone could see clearly.

Dinner was brought in and placed before them by an old black man who seemed to be some kind of military servant, but without the finer clothes. This Stone noticed and thought to himself about all the abolitionists who would come down to preach about the evils of slavery and how the North had a better view of things. Now right here in a Federal prison camp was a black man who didn't look any better off than his Southern brethren.

"Richard, what did you do in the Confederate Army? Anything special?" asked the now more serious captain.

Stone didn't know what to say. "Well a lot o things, sir," he answered. "I done a lot o work. Ya know, like diggin holes an cleanin 'round the camp where I was stationed. Um, but mostly I joined to be a soldier. Ya know carryin a gun an fightin the enemy wherever he was." Captain Hardy nodding, was taking in every word that Stone said.

"Now Richard, you can tell me the truth without any fear. Did you do any kind of espionage work? In other words, did you do any type of spying?" asked the captain, still showing a friendly attitude.

Stone's face showed surprise. While he wasn't taking Hardy very seriously, Richard started feeling a little wary about the whole interrogation procedure. "No, Suh. I didn't do no spyin."

"Any sabotage?" asked a more serious Hardy, offering the soldier another drink.

"No, Suh," he answered, shaking his head and refusing the drink.

"Now Richard, do not get the impression that you will be punished for what you have done in the past. Just as long as you cooperate with us, then everything will be fine," the captain said as he returned the scotch and the glasses to his desktop.

Captain Hardy's attitude had grown a little cooler, but he still remained friendly toward Stone. He slowly turned the pages of his notebook and would occasionally look up at the man and slightly smile. The bottle of scotch and the two empty glasses were on a metal tray on his desk, separating Stone from total view. Slowly the captain stood up, easily moved to his right and then sat on his desk directly in front of him.

"Now Richard, what was the name of your outfit?" questioned the captain.

"Well, we didn't really have a name, Suh."

"Well you mean to say that your outfit, your group of men had no name or identification?"

"No Suh, not the type ya mean."

"What do you mean?"

"Well, we wuz only called Captain McDonald's unit; any other kind o name is completely unknown ta me," answered Stone firmly.

At this Captain Hardy became irritated. He went over to his office window and looked out across the camp. He felt sure about this prisoner and he was going to get the truth out of him. "Stone, you are lying to me and I don't care for liars."

"Cap'in ya bin here too long. I aint lyin to ya, b'cuz I aint got nothin ta lie 'bout. Maybe ya got me mixed up with somebody else," retorted the Rebel, his temper slightly flaring. He thought he knew the captain's intent, but really didn't know how to handle being accused of something he didn't do, without losing his temper.

"Cap'in Hardy, we wuz a group o men that wuz considered ta be a problem. What I mean, we wuz a bunch of ex-cons an petty criminals. Um, some o the men jest didn't control themselves very well. They were jest sick o people lookin down on 'em an never gittin any respect from nobody, b'cuz most of us wuz from out in the sticks an poor! It's as simple as that. We didn't do nothin special. No spyin er anythin like that." Stone's answer had a slight apologetic tone. Hardy, somewhat nervous, sat down. Stone could see he was shaking and could sense the captain was feeling sick.

"Richard, I got to have a drink," he said then continued, "I'm going to tell you something. Now, I'm supposed to interrogate you, but all I do six days a week and nine hours a day is interrogate. We get prisoners here every day. I don't mind the military, but I can't say that I like everything that I do for my part of it. You see Stone, I had a suspicion about you ever since I saw your admission. It's just a hunch on my part, but I feel I should pursue it," said the captain, calming himself with the drink that he had just made. Stone was getting nervous, and felt that he was in more trouble than he deserved and for reasons he couldn't understand.

"Now Stone," Hardy continued in a more open but authoritative tone. "I'm going to ask you something and I want you to answer me truthfully."

"Suh, I don't know what ya suspect me of, but all I am is...," Stone tried to say.

"Stone, do you or anyone with you, remember killing a young woman and child about three months ago? It happened near Memphis and ... and it was my wife and boy. Answer me truthfully. I've got to find out who did it," said the captain now almost with a hysterical look on his face.

"*No Suh*," said Stone emphatically.

"I've almost ... never mind. As you can see I'm becoming a very sick man. Richard, I'm sorry," the captain was almost in tears as he trembled.

"Cap'in, I aint a educated man," said Stone as he stood up in front of the breaking man. " I honestly don't know who the animals are, that's what I think they wuz. But I kin understand yer hardship. I aint got no real family; ya see I wuz a orphan. But I lost somebody I ... I really cared fer ... jest a few days ago. An those wuz Federal animals! I lost my best friend too, an then there wuz Captain McDonald; he wuz the only man I ever respected an some other Federal animals got him."

Stone caught himself quickly and then, almost apologetically sat back down. The two men were both quiet now. Both seemed to be taking each other's roles as a man in prison quite differently. The captain's sudden loss of face was recovered by the strange, but interesting exchange between the two men about their stories of personal tragedy.

"Stone, you know, for not knowing one another and being enemies, supposedly enemies, and for your confidence ... well, I wish I had met you sooner. Colonel Masson was right and I mean what I say. We don't torture anyone here or kill anybody with work. Every one of you men is just a simple soldier so far as we know. I've been carrying this personal revenge for the killers into too many lives ... maybe. But it doesn't lessen what's been done. Some day and some where I will find them and well ...," the captain's voice faded. Stone stood up and put out his right hand.

"Stone, I don't know you and I shouldn't have confided in you. I always keep my distance with the prisoners and I don't know why I left my guard down. You are a prisoner, and that's about it. We are not friends, beyond two men who have met in a prison. I may have my weaknesses, but I am not an easy man. From now on you go your way and I will go mine; and what was said here can be forgotten. Or, I can guarantee you an unpleasant stay," instructed Hardy, still a little shaky and with a tone that was clearly understood. Sitting back, the captain just looked at Stone's once extended hand, dismissing him. Stone left the room.

Once outside he began to wonder about the way people seemingly get caught up in circumstances that in the long run aren't worth the trouble. He slowly made his way away from the administration building and walked toward the barracks. The rain had stopped and the afternoon sun had begun to dry up the muddy campgrounds. As he walked, lost in thoughts about himself and those around him, a guard near the front of the administration building came up behind him. Stone was slowly and tiredly dragging along when the guard's left hand pulled on his sore shoulder, painfully stopping him. He stooped over to relieve the pain and as he gritted his teeth, held back a vocal attack at the guard who he found to be as cold and rough as he looked.

"What're ya doin'?" asked the guard, as he pulled Stone up straight by his sore arm.

"I jest got out o the hospital," angrily answered Stone through gritted teeth.

"Where's your paper?" the man asked as he held onto Stone's arm firmly.

"I don't have one."

"You don't have one, huh?"

"Look, ya kin ask Captain Hardy. I wuz jest in his office."

"Now *I* know you were coming from the fence and *you* know you were coming from the fence, right?" questioned the guard as he pointed to the camp fence near the building. This soldier seemed more concerned with having Stone admit to something that they both should be able to tell he couldn't do in his condition. Richard's manner was slow, almost like an old man, though his spirit and determination were at the same time very high. This the guard may have misinterpreted.

"Look, ya little bas ...," the guard began to say.

Suddenly Captain Hardy's voice interrupted from the porch of the building, *"What's the trouble over there?"*

"He claims he jus got out of the hospital, but I figure he was comin from the fence," the guard responded as he proudly held Stone firmly.

"You ass, he just did leave my office. Does he look like he could climb an eight foot high fence? *Use your head!*" the captain shouted as he came down the porch steps, murmuring to himself about the stupidity of the guard.

The guard removed his hand from the prisoner. Stone, massaging his arm after the guard's tight grip, watched as the silent, but authoritative stare of the captain ordered the guard to more constructive things without saying a word.

"We'll be done by this afternoon, sir," replied the guard in a low voice. He looked at Stone and his eyes showed a dislike, almost hatred toward him. Stone returned the stare, confused at the guard's accusations and the look in his eyes.

"Here, you'll need this Richard. You'll be excluded from work for the next three days," the captain said, as he gave Stone the paper that he should have shown the guard. The captain, still cool toward Stone, was not trying to hide some slight warmth, even while maintaining his reputation of a hard, but fair man. Hardy went on his way immediately toward the other side of the camp.

Stone stood in the huge prison yard, looking all around at the prisoners doing senseless work ... some digging holes, others filling holes, some marching in the hot sun, while others relaxed under trees. 'My Lord. What's goin on here?' Then his thoughts wandered back to the prisoners in the hospital suspicious of how they had really gotten their wounds. Coming back to his present surroundings he muttered, 'What's that smell?' From here he could see the outdoor sewer running from the barracks to the side of the gate. He knew for sure now where the stench was coming from. He turned and could see past the building out to a greater view of the Mississippi Valley. 'If I could git over er under that fence ...', he thought as he pondered his confinement and attempt at freedom.

He looked around and could not understand how they could have allowed themselves to become the miserable rogues they were, and live in conditions like this. To be free is worth dying for. He would rather be dead than stay here and get as messed up as those he had observed.

Chapter IV

The remainder of the day, Stone wandered around the camp occasionally having to show his paper to the guards. Other than that, he found life at Young's Prison or 'Youngs' as it was familiarly called, very boring. The only change of pace came at mess time around five thirty, the supper hour and surprisingly to Stone the food wasn't too bad. Well, this particular meal wasn't too bad.

At mess the men formed a line of two abreast half-way across the camp. The food was served at the administration building where the kitchen was located. From there the prisoners ate in a barracks nearby that was converted into a mess hall or they could eat somewhere on the grounds. Many of them would take advantage of the warm weather and eat outside where it was shaded by large weeping willow trees. Here a steady breeze blew fresh air into their lungs, contrasting the almost constant, though sometimes slight stench of the open sewer and latrine.

The stream served the camp in a dual function … the board running alongside the ditch was the outdoor toilet and the contents of these makeshift toilets were carried away by the stream that flowed on outside the camp. It was also in this stream above the sewer outlet, that the Young's men took their baths. Sometimes a new prisoner would be anxious to wash off the grime of the war and the men would get a big laugh out of watching him do it unknowingly downstream of the latrine.

Soon evening came and Stone went to one of the guards to find out where he would sleep for the night. The guard took him to a sergeant who in turn took him to barracks number four. There were about thirty barracks each holding about twenty men, some thirty. Since every couple of days there would be new arrivals or a death every once in a while, even a suicide about once a week or so, the total number remained around six hundred.

Stone entered barracks number four with a small box he had picked up that afternoon from the administration building. In it were some personal belongings and a few things he originally didn't have, like a comb and a razor. As a matter of fact for a twenty-one year old, he didn't have much of a growing beard; it had been cause for his sometimes feeling less than a man, therefore trying to be tougher than he was. He appeared at times to be about eighteen. 'So what?' he would muse to himself as he looked in some handy mirror. 'When I'm thirty, I'll look twenty-seven. An when I'm forty, I'll look like thirty-seven.' But that type of reasoning still couldn't replace those parts of a beard that needed to be filled in. So he would usually try to find something more interesting to do with his thoughts.

The sergeant showed Stone his bunk in a corner, the lower tier of the double-decker type that was in all of the barracks. A small table was in the middle of the building and a now dormant pot-belly stove. The table had four old wooden chairs, each of a different type. It looked as though they picked up the chairs from just about anywhere. Inside it was well lit from the sun shining through windows. They were rather large allowing air and sunlight in most of the day. There were two windows to each wall of the uniform rectangular structures.

"If you have anything to put away, use one of these trunks under your bunk," offered a seemingly tired sergeant.

A little weary himself, Stone laid down in the unfamiliar barracks. It was almost seven o'clock. The sergeant picked up a paper off the floor and saw it was somebody's excuse from work.

"Is your name Richard H. Stone, boy?" asked the sergeant.

"Yeah, that's me," said Stone wearily.

"Well, don't lose this or I'll have you working. And when you work for me, you work! I'm Sergeant Doale and I run this barracks," he said, extending his right hand. Stone sat up, shook it and smiled. He looked weak and the sergeant saw this clearly.

"You know Stone, I'll be leavin next Monday. I'm goin back home to Albany, New York. I'm forty-five. I've got one daughter left at home, though I did have five," the sergeant said with a relieved look on his face.

"Yep," he continued in an easy tone, "my wife and daughter. I haven't seen them for six months. Huh, I haven't even met my one daughter's husband. They're all going to be married though. Yep, every one of them," the sergeant shared, then noticing that Stone was almost asleep, he quietly left the barracks and went outside, easily shutting the door behind him. Doale went for a walk toward the fence and looked out at the light of a twilight sun gleaming red across the Mississippi River Valley; for he also seemed to find an escape there, as many others must have silently and privately done.

Tuesday morning arrived and Stone found himself alone. As he looked around he could tell the bunks had been used during the night, even though they had been made up. Stone slowly sat up and tried to look for a clock. Unable to find one, he headed for the door. He looked himself over, just to double check to see if he was dressed ... he found that he was. So he opened the door and stepped outside.

"Wow, o-o-h!" he said as he happened to pick up the scent of the latrine. He stepped back inside to the warm, close smelling air of the barracks. Stone was quite awake now and found another reason to escape. The fear of getting killed trying was at times well present; but when compared with staying inside a place like this for maybe even years, he would surely rather die trying to escape.

Richard collected himself and his thoughts, then proceeded again out the door of the barracks. Outside wincing at the smell again, he pulled out his paper to see what day he would have to start work. This was actually the first time he had read it. He was so exhausted before, that he just wanted to sleep.

'Now today's Tuesdey, tomorra's We'nesdey, then Thursdey', Stone thought as he counted the days on his fingers. 'Fridey, I'll have ta start work. Pro'bly the stinkin sewer ditch', he told himself. He folded the paper back up and put it in his pocket. He walked along and tried to decide what to do with himself.

'I wonder where Nurse Ellen comes from. I bet she's already here. Well she's gotta be, she wuz there ev'ry mornin with me', he said aloud to himself. He quickly looked around. He was hoping nobody had heard him talking to himself. He stood taller with a straighter posture and started walking briskly toward the administration building. Stone was so bored yesterday and was wondering what he would do with himself for the rest of today, tomorrow and Thursday if he didn't have Ellen to think about.

Richard was pondering about how much a woman affects a man; how much even women who are far away ... even dead. Stone's affections for the late Cynthia had never died. They had faded as the permanence of her death finally was accepted by his mind and heart. But a man must have some particular woman to think about, even make plans with, who could even in the remotest sense include her. Stone was sure about these feelings. He did know of men who claimed that they don't need a woman; and women in general, they said they could do without. But Stone was different and he knew himself well enough to know his need for female companionship. He had to have a woman in all his plans.

Now with Cynthia gone, Ellen fit that need. Stone was more interested in her than actually in love. But especially under these conditions, it wouldn't take much to stir his passions. The nurse was an attractive young woman and he wondered why she preferred this kind of life. He couldn't understand why she hadn't tried to catch some rich man and be pampered by him and society for the rest of her life. He was nearing the hospital entrance.

Ellen was in the hospital supply room which wasn't too far from the entrance where Stone was standing. He could easily take a peek in, trying to catch a glimpse of her. The young nurse wiped her hands on her apron and headed for the entrance to get some fresh air. As she stepped outside, she immediately noticed Richard. He was looking the other way trying to make sure no one could see what he was up to. Actually, most everyone else had enough of their own private thoughts to keep them busy. The only ones to worry about were the guards, and most of them knew already that this prisoner was supposed to be convalescing.

Stone now confidently leaned against one side of the door frame, as Ellen stood on the other side just quietly refreshing herself. This was their situation; and Richard, if only he'd turn, could not have asked for a better coincidence. Luckily, he did and immediately noticed her with pleasant surprise.

"Hi there. Aint too bad out here," Stone said

nervously as he straightened up, a little embarrassed, while knowing there really wasn't anything to be embarrassed about.

"Yes it is nice as long as the wind blows the right way," she responded, seemingly a little shy.

"Um, my wounds're practic'lly healed. A great job o medicine, Miss —," he muttered as he forgot her last name.

Slightly irritated, but seeing how nervous he was, "Miss Marshell, Mr. Stone," she replied.

"Miss Marshell, I'm sorry," he apologized then putting his hand to his head said, "I'm still tryin to a'jest."

She relaxed more to Stone's innocent, but refreshing humor. "I didn't think you've had it that rough," she said with a smile and eyes that could see right through him. He playfully appeared outsmarted, but as he looked down at the ground, the soldier who had been accompanying her in the hospital appeared in the doorway.

"Everything alright, Ellen?" asked the soldier who Stone remembered well. The man was coldly looking him down, while standing as Miss Marshell's great protector.

"We were just talking John."

"Aren't you supposed to be doing something

young fella?" asked the soldier who wasn't much older than Stone.

"I bin excused. I gotta paper ... right here."

"Oh, you've been excused. Did you hear that Ellen?" exclaimed the soldier condescendingly. "He has an excuse. Well Stone, no, I don't want to see it. I hope you wind up working under me, because I would really find something constructive for you to do."

'Yeah, like fillin holes?' he smirked to himself. Stone put back the paper that he had only gotten half way out of his pocket. The other two then turned to go back inside the hospital, leaving a disgusted Stone standing by himself outside. He looked down at the ground groping for the answer to his dilemma of escape with Ellen.

'I bet they git married', Stone angrily thought to himself. He started walking back toward the barracks, but stopped as he looked way down the perimeter line at what appeared to be a bundle of some kind at the base of the fence. After being unable to focus his eyes on it, he started walking toward it; but something inside made him move cautiously. As he got nearer, it appeared to be a bundle of clothes. Then a little closer, it was clothing, but almost at the same time, it looked like a man; but his position was peculiar. When Stone finally got to it, he quickly turned his head, first at the smell and then at what he thought he saw. Slowly he looked back; it was what he thought ... a stiff body. The skin on the remains looked brown ... a color and texture only a dead body would have. Stone figured he had been dead for days. The flies had taken their toll and so had the ants and worms. He looked so thin, maybe tortured, Stone feared, or at least starved.

Richard slowly walked back toward the barracks, hoping that no one had seen him. He was surprised at his find and wondered why they would leave the body by the fence. Suddenly Stone had an awful thought and an awful chill in his bones. The dead man had probably been trying to escape. He didn't remember seeing any bullet hole, but he really didn't think to look for any. He assumed it was an escape attempt. But he must have been starved, tortured or severely punished too, Stone imagined. This verified his suspicions of the guards' brutality and what could happen if you tried to escape. 'That's why them Federals didn't bury him'.

Once inside the barracks, he stayed there with his thoughts and questions for about an hour. It wouldn't be long till mess. Stone felt nervous and was even more suspicious about the people in this place. Even his thoughts about Ellen were not as clear and pleasant as before. 'What kinda woman her age would wanna work in a place like this?' he asked himself again. He could think of no reasonable answer. 'Ma'be she's sincere, er then ma'be she's not trustworthy ... er ma'be Silts could be right.' Stone was so bewildered.

He diverted his thoughts to those of escape ... if she comes or not, at least he was still determined to try. He would just keep thinking about the illustration of the riverboat in that ad he had read in the newspaper. 'Man, I gotta git out o' here,' he said aloud. He looked around hoping nobody was in ear range. He found himself to be still alone.

All he had been doing for this past hour was walking around inside the barracks, talking to himself. He turned a corner and saw a couple of inmates. They were just standing around, doing nothing. Stone looked at them and they stared at him; they didn't appear too friendly. Stone kept walking toward them, still feeling completely alone even with his many thoughts.

At first glance, Stone, not yet in the best of health, appeared meek. This was the sense these two got of him. As he approached, the men stood apart yet remained close enough to make him feel physically uncomfortable. Richard looked up and stopped right in front of them. His eyes didn't show the meekness that they wanted to see. But they didn't acknowledge anything as Stone began his walk again.

Suddenly, one of them shoved Stone against the other man, who caught him and hissed into his ear, "Hey, boy. Hain't ya got no manners?" He held Stone by the neck of his shirt, then almost immediately threw him to the floor.

The two inmates then stood apart and allowed Stone to get back up. Slowly, he regained an upright stance, but tightened his legs in a slightly bent manner. One of the men began coming up from behind Stone and this Richard caught out of the corner of his eye. Suddenly, the once meek form had become a skilled opponent as he sprung and kicked the inmate to the floor, knocking the wind out of him. Stone spun around, silent all the while and readied himself for the other one. The second inmate was surprised, but Stone began to feel dizzy as his remaining strength was being taxed. He involuntarily closed his eyes for just a second when the man's fist hit him right in the chin, knocking him out, right onto the floor.

His partner had just caught his wind. "Man, that little guy kin kick!" said the first opponent. They both were standing over Stone now, deciding what to do with him. "Wanna kill 'em?"

"No, it'll be too much bother with hidin'im an all that kinda stuff," answered the other as he went through Stone's pockets. "Nuthin, nuthin at all."

"Let'em be. C'mon," suggested his first attacker. At that, they both disappeared as Stone gradually regained consciousness.

"Oh-h-h, my head," groaning, as he slowly got up. He put the lining back in his pockets and then slapped the dust off his clothes.

It was noon now, mess was being served, and Stone found himself starved. He was in line, watching the other men as they left the line and found a place to relax and eat. It was soon Stone's turn. Mashed potatoes and a slice of ham were placed on his grey metal plate. He dipped his metal cup, which came from his personal mess kit, into a large bucket of water. All prisoners received a mess kit upon entering the prison. He moved away from the line and scanned the camp for a place to settle and eat.

As he was looking, a young man came up behind and startled him. "Nice day we're havin, hey?" he said in a friendly voice. Stone turned around, smiled and nodded. "Ma name's William Boice," he said as he extended his right hand. Richard adjusted his tray and shook his hand.

"Stone, Richard H. Stone." William smiled in response and took a bite of food from his plate. "Let's find us a place ta sit down," Stone suggested and then pointed to some trees near the fence. Boice agreed and they walked over and settled down.

"Ah'm from Baton Rouge," Boice started with an accent. "Y'know, Baton Rouge?"

"*Oh yeah!*" exclaimed Stone. "I'm from Parkinson, Tennessee."

"What's so excitin about Baton Rouge, Richard?" he asked, puzzled by Stone's enthusiasm about his hometown.

"Well, it's in Lou'siana aint it?" Richard came back, "An it aint far from New Orlins, right?" William nodded, but was still puzzled.

"So, what about Lous'ana an New O'leans? Are ya leavin soon Stone?" Boice asked with a chuckle.

"Yeah, sometime next week. I can't stand it here," replied Stone seriously.

"Ya musta lost yo mind. What yo gonna do ... escape?" kidded a surprised Boice.

"Ya bet yer ass. Ya wanna go?" teased Richard.

"Yea sure ... I wanna get killed climbin over the fence sometime next week," mocked William.

"How long ya bin here, Boice?" asked Stone as he continued to eat.

"Four months. Why?"

"Ya mean ta tell me ya bin in this rat hole place fer four months, an ya can't un'erstand somebody wantin ta 'scape?"

"Well, Ah guess Ah ken."

"Boice, ya gotta be crazy, that's all. Jest plain crazy!"

"Now hold on Stone," Boice was becoming irritated at his smartness. "Ah jus don't wanna get killed coz some jack ass wants ta escape ta New O'leans coz he can't stand a work camp."

Stone was stunned at Boice's devil-may-care attitude. "Work camp! Ya think this sew'r hole is a work camp? Well Buddy, ya *are* nuts!" Richard looked around to see if anyone overheard him.

"Wait a minute, smart guy. This place hain't so bad as the others. I been in Union prison camps for a year an a-half. An this place has got food that haint so bad cumpared ta other places. An better places ta sleep. Hey, yo really are new, haint ya? Wow, have yo got a lot ta learn. Have yo got a *real* lot ta learn," lectured Boice.

"Oh, hey, I didn't know ya were in other places," said Stone apologetically, a bit softer, "but I can't see why er even how anyone kin stay fer years in a place like this."

Boice shook his head and replied, "Ya jus gotta learn ta stomach some things, Stone."

"How old are ya, Boice? Twenty five, six … ma'be twenty-nine?"

"Twenty-nine. Yep, twenty-nine years old an ya know what?" asked an almost tearful Boice.

"What?" surprised at the man's interesting character.

"I got a wife an two kids that I haint seen in two years. Ya know that. Two years, wow. I betcha, them kids won't reco'nize me right off. That's a course, *if* I escape with ya, an if we, well … make it."

Stone was surprised … this was the first person who wasn't in some authority position, just another regular guy, who seemed to have more brains than him. As a boy, Richard was always the leader, but only because he could beat most any of those his own age.

Now he was feeling that this man had made such a quick change of heart in agreeing to escape, when moments before he thought it an insane idea. Stone thought that it could not have suddenly been Boice's memories of his family that would have caused him to think of escape. Though Stone reasoned Boice must think of his family quite a bit every day; he was puzzled, but not for long. Richard's face brightened and Boice, now quiet, noticed it. Stone felt he must have been the first prisoner to convince this man that he could have enough faith and spirit to escape. Stone had now figured William to be a very smart, but an overly practical man. He seemed almost afraid to dream.

"What yo thinkin about now?" asked Boice, returning Richard's staring gaze. His face was reflecting great enthusiasm over another one of his strange and possibly impractical ideas. Stone may not have been one of the smartest men of his day, but as to having insight into another person's character, well, he'd be a hard one to beat.

The rest of the day found Stone alone. Boice had gone back to a work detail which was outside of the camp. This would have sent Richard soaring, if he had known of the 'out-of camp' work details. William could have said something, and even should have, but his inhibition to dream would never have allowed that information to surface. Understandably, most of his thoughts were about his family. Stone, doing a lot of thinking himself, would use this as the fire that might inflame Boice's subconscious to want to change his circumstances.

At about seven that night, Stone was in his barracks. Two other prisoners were there too, but they kept to themselves. Stone was lying on his bunk and looking up at the planks on the bottom of the bunk over his head. The door opened and Sergeant Doale entered.

"Stone, there's a man who'd like to see ya," the sergeant said as he pointed outside. Stone slowly got himself out of his bunk, stood up and stretched. He put his boots on and then went outside shutting the door behind him. He looked around and didn't see anybody at first. The moonless night was very dark to Stone's unadjusted eyes.

"Hey, Stone. It's me, Boice," came a loud whisper.

Stone could just barely see him. "What's the problem?"

"Ah been thinkin 'bout our discussion this afternoon an Ah … Ah decided ta try it with ya," Boice nervously replied.

"Well, I really aint come up with any kinda plan yet. I bin tryin ta figger somethin fer the fence. Do they let prisoners work with the horses?" wondered Stone aloud, as the two men walked away from the barracks. An unseen guard was watching them, but he couldn't hear them.   Richard's original misgivings were true though, as all the guards were suspicious of any close discussion between two or more prisoners.

"Look, Ah'll talk ta ya at mess tomorrow noon.

Ma'be, I ken think a somethin," offered Boice.

Stone motioned him not to leave yet, as his eyes searched the area. "Why aint nobody troubled 'bout ya talkin ta me outside the barracks … an at night yet?"

"Nah, don't worry 'bout it Stone. Ah wouldn't," he smiled nervously.

Richard immediately sensed William's deceptive attitude. He smiled back as he shook Boice's hand. Stone's plan to escape was known to no one else. Boice was the only one. And Ellen had only suggested that he not try it, so he didn't feel he would have to worry about her. His old thought returning, 'kin anyone here be trusted'?

Stone was disappointed in Boice and figured he would be telling someone about his plan of escape. 'Now, what could I do?' he thought to himself. 'I gotta accept the chance that William is informin someone 'bout me.' He had forgotten how long he had been outside his barracks. Boice had disappeared immediately after shaking hands. Richard turned and went back inside his barracks.

Sergeant Doale was at the table looking over some papers and the other two prisoners were at their bunks, one reading a book and the other writing a letter. Stone entered and everyone acted as though nothing was unusual. They were all preoccupied with their own private thoughts and business. He closed the door easily and went over to his bunk. Stone laid there in silence.

"Ya seem to be makin friends here, Stone. Everything fine?" asked the sergeant. He seemed interested, but not suspicious.

"Yeah, that was Boice. I met 'im at noon mess today. Seems like an alright fella." He wondered again about the lack of greater concern for his activity outside the barracks

"I don't think I've met him," said the sergeant seeming to want to make conversation. Stone looked at him and nodded dismissively.

A reflective mood had come over him as he laid there. He remembered about his younger days back in Parkinson and his zest for fun that was so easy to find. He was remembering his depressive moments too, especially his failings with love and sometimes his friends. He was thinking of Cynthia and O'Reilly and that poor old doctor who had helped him. He had been raised in an orphanage that was more like a large house and school. There was room to play outside and the children worked in the garden, growing many vegetables. It was run by a middle-aged widow who took very good care of the children, making the place very homey. Her name was Miss Hale. She made the children feel like a family.

It was in his adolescence that Stone lost his innocence and became a problem. Around thirteen he started stealing and got involved in small scale vandalism. When he became too much for Miss Hale to handle, a judge in Parkinson had Richard sent to a reformatory near Memphis. After a year there, his attitude toward people, life and especially authority radically changed. An ever present zeal for freedom, and a distrust and lack of respect for authority and anyone in it, became his major motivation. He later returned to Parkinson to live with an uncle, which didn't help at all. Richard had a problem with self-control and he knew it.

Stone had considered the army a good place to develop some kind of personal discipline for his life. It had been working fairly well. He even began to respect a man in authority, Capt. Orrey McDonald and his best friend, someone who thought like he did, Donald Michael O'Reilly. 'Why did they have ta die?' he'd asked himself many times. '*Why?*'

And then there was Cynthia. He really loved her he had now concluded. Her mother wasn't too bad either, he thought to himself with a grin. Cynthia was his real first love. Oh, he had met and liked other girls through the years, but none had the style or whatever it was that had attracted him to Cynthia. She radiated from inside. She was such a brave young woman, and a real lady too. He realized this some time ago. Why did she have to die? Everyone who meant so much to him met tragic ends. How unfair life could be? They were all very special to Stone. He was a man who needed something in his life. What was it? He couldn't figure it out. Maybe he felt the lack of belonging ... he needed a purpose.

Stone looked down at his feet, then at the prisoner who was writing. His eyes darted to the sergeant. Everyone needs something to stay alive for.

'But what is it that I need?' he asked himself.

He turned onto his side and faced the barracks' door. He started to stroke his sore arm. It was then that he came to a conclusion. Ellen! Stone needed a woman; he needed freedom. He had known this all along, but didn't realize it until now.

'That's what's wrong with everybody', he thought to himself. 'That's what generals, soldiers, men an women need ... an everybody kills, works an dies fer. Yeah! They need love an freedom.'

Stone's mind flashed images ... the captain of the prison camp, the prisoners, Ellen, Cynthia, her mother ... and everyone he had met in his life. He turned over on his back. Even Boice with all his brains needs it. His only trouble, Stone concluded, is that he doesn't know it. Well, maybe the love part, but he is ignorant about his need for freedom. Yep, that's what it was, Stone figured. Everyone needs love and freedom ... yep, and some kind of discipline.

Stone stretched his arms above his head, yawned and rubbed his eyes. 'Whew', he thought, 'I aint done that much thinkin in years.' He turned back on his side and fell right to sleep.

Chapter V

Stone awoke Wednesday morning at about eight o'clock. The rest of the men had gone two hours earlier to their work details. The work schedule ran from six in the morning until six in the early evening. There were the noon and five-thirty mess times, and a fifteen minute break in the morning with another one in the afternoon. Then from six to eight at night the prisoners could visit or do whatever on their two hours of free time. Many lingered and stretched it to nine, which was the time every inmate had to be in his bunk. Many of the guards and staff didn't mind the extra hour stretch, because it gave them a ploy to use on the prisoners in some disciplinary procedures.

Again Stone was alone in the barracks and slowly dragged himself outside. The air was already warm from the bright summer sun, which felt good to the man now stretching, for the night had been a bit chilly.

In his office, Captain Hardy and a very stoic and important looking man were sharing coffee and discussing one of the prisoners.

"Captain, I am very grateful for your coffee, but I would like to get this job finished as soon as possible. The fourth of July is next week, you know," said the visitor.

"Oh, of course. Washington wouldn't want a delay in such matters, aye, Mr. Palmer?" jokingly asked Capt. Hardy. The visitor just ignored the captain and sipped his coffee delicately.

Hardy feeling a little uneasy and embarrassed, offered Mr. Palmer a cigar, but he refused. The captain accidentally spilled the box of cigars while trying to replace it on his desk. "Well, now ... now, I'm sorry Mr. Palmer," mumbleded the captain.

"Captain, do you have the man I'm looking for or not?" Palmer immediately wanted to get back to business. Hardy quickly threw the cigars back into the box to the raised eyebrows of his visitor, then threw the box in one of his desk drawers.

"Well, I don't believe we have any spies here, sir. I can assure you, and those in Washington, on that," boasted the captain with a smile. Palmer looked at him with no humor or feeling. He appeared cold and egotistical. It was obvious that Hardy did not like the man and Mr. Palmer did not like the captain.

"Captain, do you drink?" asked Mr. Palmer, with staring eyes.

"Well, just socially. You know at parties and toasts. Do you drink, Mr. Palmer?" He was a bit surprised at Palmer's interest.

"Now level with me Captain. You're shaking like a leaf," he stated, leaning forward in his chair.

"Sir, just socially. Why are you interested?" responded the captain, now leaning forward in his chair with hands folded on his desk.

"Get away from your desk, Captain," ordered Mr. Palmer.

"Sir?" angrily retaliated the captain.

"Get away from that desk or I'll have you locked up. Get away from there now!" Palmer demanded with clenched teeth. He stood facing the captain. Hardy reluctantly moved himself to the side of his office, as he watched the man from Washington meticulously search each drawer and compartment of his desk.

"What right do you have to search my personal belongings, Mr. Palmer?" questioned the steaming captain.

"The right that I see fit, Captain! I can't stand drunkards running our facilities," responded an indifferent and efficient Palmer. He continued his search until he found the bottle of scotch Captain Hardy and Stone had shared just two days before.

"Well, now ... I'm a drunkard, right?" he came back, as Palmer with the look of wrath, held the bottle at arm's length toward the captain.

"You're a drunk! That's why you shake, isn't it Captain?" T he captain looked to the floor and dropped his defensive attitude.

"Yes, sir maybe I am," he responded.

Palmer set the bottle on the desk easily, then went over to him and seemed to be a bit more sympathetic.

"Captain, I used to be a drunkard. And I could tell you were almost as soon as we started our meeting. Now I am not the ogre that many think I am. But if you're having problems, I think you would be better off solving them or just forgetting about them; and begin making a responsible life for yourself," advised Palmer.

"I wouldn't tell anyone Captain, but try to get some kind of help," continued Mr. Palmer. As he looked at Hardy, he proceeded to straighten the desk as the captain, embarrassed, didn't know what to do.

"Do you want some time off?" Palmer seemed to be suggesting, but more with an air of an order.

"When sir?"

"Oh, how would you like the month of July. I could have you transferred to Washington for the month or longer. How's that?" offered Palmer. The captain did like the idea, but seemed hesitant as he sensed the man's concern might be a little put-on.

"Sir, who would replace me here?" asked Captain Hardy.

"Why, I would, Captain. I would," Mr. Palmer replied with a smile. He sat down at the captain's desk as though the transfer was already made.

Stone had spent the morning near the hospital considering the Mississippi River Valley. He had been studying the fence, trying in his imagination to plan how he was going to escape and what to do about that final obstacle.

From inside the hospital, Ellen noticed Stone as she went by the window. She stopped for a moment and watched him, then she went back to her duties. She felt he was just a dreamer, a young man with an unrealistic outlook. She was trying to define him in her mind; would he take the bait and run? She wondered what he thought of the article in the newspaper she placed at his bedside while he was in the hospital.

Stone stood up and walked around the building and there saw Captain Hardy. Richard noticed he was prepared for a trip, with a long coat slung over his right arm and a large carpet bag on his left. He was standing at the bottom of the porch steps in front of the administration building.

Walking toward him, looking well recovered, but still with a slight limp, Stone greeted casually, "Hello Cap'in."

"Stone," acknowledged the captain, not able to hide his sadness.

"Suh, are ya goin on a trip?" asked Stone, treating the captain as a friend.

Mr. Palmer was watching from the window in the captain's former office. He was annoyed by their familiarity as the two shook hands.

"I'm being relieved of my duties here Stone. A man by the name of Palmer is takin my place."

"Ya know Cap'in, it's almost like we're on the same side," said Richard.

"Just be careful," warned the captain, to which Stone nodded.

The prisoner and the officer went their separate ways, leaving an irritated form standing in the window. Palmer's teeth were grinding as he stared at the now abandoned spot in front of the administration building. He slowly moved away from the window to the hallway and into the secretary's office. Here he looked through the files for new admissions and found a folder on Stone. He went back into the office, but left the door open for it was a warm day; and with the open office window, a cool and refreshing draft was created.

Stone stayed by the hospital entrance and waited for Ellen to step outside. He was a little impatient as time went by and Ellen had not yet appeared. This is not to say a rendezvous had been established, but Richard was just hoping. Cautiously he peered inside. There she was, sitting at the small desk that served basically as an admission's checkpoint, reading something. His constant, intense gaze seemed to make her raise her head and look toward him. When Stone caught her eyes, he waved and smiled.

"Hello, Mr. Stone," acknowledged Ellen with a smile.

"Hello, Miss Marshell," he replied cheerfully, as he made his way inside confidently and stopped at her desk.

"How are ya today, Ellen?"

"I'm fine, but a little bored."

"Yeah, it does git that way 'round here," he said, to which she nodded. "Um, I wuz jest wonderin. Ya don't live on the prison grounds, do ya?" She looked up at him, with sad eyes.

"I live just a mile outside of camp. The soldier you see with me picks me up in a carriage," she paused for a moment, then said, "So are ya still planning to ... go to New Orleans someday?"

Stone saw a lot more to that exchange in her eyes, at least he thought he did. She didn't seem to know how or what to ask him, Stone thought. He was hopeful.

"Well, Ellen if I could leave today er tonight er tomorra ... er whenever, I cert'nly would like ta take ya with me," he blurted out. "Oh I know ya have a job here an a man. I guess I'm dreamin, but there's a lot o hope ta people's dreams. Well that's what some people say." Stone couldn't help himself.

"Look, I'd like to meet ya during the noon mess. How about in front of this building?" she offered, as her eyes again seemed to have more to say.

Stone, with a serious look on his face, gazed into her eyes. She looked down at her paper and continued her reading. He turned and went back out the door, headed toward his barracks.

In his new office, Mr. Palmer had noticed something in Stone's admission and seemed to be angered about what he had read. "**Corporal, Corporal!**" he shouted to the male secretary in the hallway.

"Yes, sir, Mr. Palmer," answered the slim, almost skinny corporal.

"Do you know anything about this Richard Stone's work excuse for *three* days?" asked the heavily built Mr. Palmer angrily shoving the excuse into the soldier's hand.

"Well, sir," the corporal said, as he read the paper, "it seems he was wounded and is still recovering."

"*Let me have that*! Our drunken Captain Hardy signed this idiot a paper giving him three days to recover."

He slammed the paper down, but its momentum continued it off the desk and onto the floor. The quiet corporal gingerly picked it up and laid it in front of the man from Washington.

"Is Stone the young man I see wandering around the camp with seemingly nothing to do?" asked Mr. Palmer.

"He could be, sir. The one with the limp fits the

description on that paper. At least, that is the one I see walking around a lot. He seems to hang around the hospital quite a bit," informed the corporal.

"Yes, Corporal, we have the same young man in mind. Yes, for a wounded soldier he seems to fair pretty well," he paused to think. Then continued, "Corporal, send this note to the sergeant of barracks ...now let's see here, of barracks four." Looking at another paper, "Now that's Sgt. Doale. And Soldier, I promised our good captain that we would make some improvements here. Why, when I stepped in through the gate my head began swimming with so many ideas that I didn't know where to begin. Well let me assure You, Corporal ... by the way, what is your name?" preparing to write the corporal's name down.

"My name is Corporal Jonathan Cummings, Sir," he answered proudly, smiling as Mr. Palmer wrote his name down.

"Well Corporal Cummings, I repeat, I can assure you that we are going to make improvements here and I hope you will give me your full cooperation," said Mr. Palmer as he shook the corporal's nervous hand.

"You can count on me, sir."

"I thought I could. Thank you Corporal," he said with an insincere, but convincing look. He shook his hand again then dismissed him. The corporal, still elated left the office. After a few moments, Palmer took the unreadable piece of paper, crumpled it and threw it into his waste basket.

The line for noon mess was quite long, but Stone was only a few men away from his serving. Meanwhile, Ellen casually strolled from the hospital entrance and sat herself down on the front steps of the administration building. She was there for just a few seconds when Mr. Palmer walked out onto the porch. He stood there a moment looking at her. Placing his thumbs in his belt, he straightened himself and stepped up behind her.

"Well young lady, how are you on such a fine day?" opened Mr. Palmer.

"Oh. Hello, I'm fine. And yourself?" replied Ellen, surprised at his sudden presence.

"Oh, quite well, my dear, quite well. I don't believe we've met before, have we?" responded Palmer with an affectionate tone.

"No sir, we haven't. I'm Ellen Marshell," she said while offering her hand to shake. But Mr. Palmer, with what gentleman there was in him, turned her hand over and kissed it.

"My name is Palmer, George Palmer," he said while she smiled up at him. "I'm taking Capt. Hardy's place for a few months. He had to leave for some military business in Washington."

Just as he finished his introduction, a happy-go-lucky Stone appeared and had just been served mess. Ellen sat quietly and looked away as Mr. Palmer sternly made his way down the steps and silently past Stone. Palmer's eyes glared with an inner wrath as they briefly pierced Stone's. The new administrator headed toward the barracks.

"What's he mad about?" asked Stone and then smiled at Ellen. She returned his smile and made room for him on the porch. Richard sat down and offered her a piece of bread, but she frowned at it.

"I'm not too hungry today," she said sadly. Her eyes looked at the ground. Stone snuggled closer and looked into her face.

"Why so sad?" asked Stone warmly. Her eyes darted to his and he quickly looked back at his plate.

"Do you want to leave with me tonight?" whispered Ellen.

"What?" he responded as she quickly put a finger to his lips.

"Do you want to leave with me tonight?" repeated Ellen.

"Yeah," answered Stone with eagerness.

"I'm serious. John will pick me up around nine and it will be kind of dark here then. So when he does, you come out from under the porch and climb in the back. It will be a tool wagon, just hide under the burlap bags and tools. Do ya think it'll work?"

"I thought you said he comes for you in his carriage?

She answered shyly, "I was just trying to impress you. It's just a wagon."

Stone looked at the gate that was down across the entrance to Young's just past the slightly hilly prison grounds.

"How'd ya like ta go by riverboat down ta New Orlins? Jest you an me?" he paused, then continued. "Now *I'm* serious." Ellen smiled broadly. Stone took advantage of her close proximity and kissed her warmly.

"I won't leave without you, Richard."

"What about yer boyfriend John?"

"Oh, I figured you could take care of him somehow; but I don't want ya to hurt him too bad."

Stone was a little unprepared for the sudden abandonment of her soldier boyfriend. He smiled and gave her another quick kiss and then left. Ellen remained there thinking and planning with a satisfied look on her face.

The remainder of the day Mr. Palmer wandered around the camp, seeing where he could make his 'improvements', and unintentionally crossed paths several times with the amiable Richard Stone. This of course, only aggravated the stoic replacement for Captain Hardy; and if Stone remained, Palmer would have an excuse for something Stone might find to be very unpleasant.

The sun had not yet set at about seven thirty that evening and Stone was already spending his free time strolling around the Federal 'work' camp. His last free day of recuperation would be tomorrow, Thursday. But from the rumors going around camp about a man from Washington replacing Capt. Hardy, and his own observations of the one he had considered to be the same man, caused Stone to be enthusiastic about leaving tonight. He could see Palmer was not going to be as easy as the captain; he sensed the man's wrath. Stone knew he would never have received the excused three days for recuperation from him.

Richard could hardly wait for the escape tonight. But as he had more time to pass until the rendezvous, he tried to reason through Ellen's intentions for wanting to leave. Maybe he had seen into her far more than he realized. This thought pleased Stone. Maybe she was fed up with this whole scene. Maybe she wanted out as bad as he did.

On the administration building was a small clock that could just be read from Stone's position. It was eight forty-five. Richard, now a bit anxious made his way cautiously to the porch of the administration building. There he paused in the still warm, but fairly dark night, to catch sight of any of the guards. Only the tower closest to the gate could hold anyone in a position to spot him. Quickly, he slipped under the porch and took another look for anybody who could foil his and Ellen's escape plan. Finding himself so far clear, he crawled to another opening near the porch steps. From here he could with success, dart into the rear of the tool wagon without notice.

His anxiety was increasing as he waited for Ellen. What could be taking her so long? Where could she be? It must be about nine now he was thinking. Suddenly footsteps, just one set, walked overhead. He waited for some proof that it was Ellen. He was getting quite nervous. The plan's shoddiness seemed to be coming to light. He could not be sure who that was above him. If it was a guard, his death would be certain. If it was Ellen, she should do something to tell him. Stone was now sweating. He could do nothing but wait. Above him remained the unidentified person. Maybe, he thought, it was that new man from Washington, Palmer. If it was, he knew his stay here would be intolerable.

Sweating a little heavier but remaining still, he waited. The wagon had not come through the gate yet. Why hadn't he and Ellen talked over some kind of signal system? As he waited and waited his mind was racing. 'Why wuz I so quick an easy ta agree ta this whole thing?' he asked himself. The last couple of days had left him mentally exhausted and he wasn't thinking straight. He had too much free time ... time to think; and now his lax attitude showed its potential danger.

Suddenly, through the gate a wagon entered. It stopped and then continued toward the administration building. As darkness was now coming upon them, Stone could just make it out. From above him on the porch came a woman's humming voice.

"Everything's set. Are you there?" the voice whispered.

At first Stone kept silent, making sure it was Ellen's. Then he quietly responded as the wagon was slowly drawing closer, "Yeah." He could hear her humming again, but his anxiousness remained. He could not tell if she had heard him.

The wagon came to a stop. The woman, who Stone recognized as Ellen, came down the stairs. His suspicion of the nurse was based on his consideration of other women working here and the conversation he had had a few days ago with Silt. Richard's eyes darted about the waiting wagon looking for a path to silently and swiftly board. Not seeing anything but metal support rods underneath, he hurriedly crawled under the wagon and entwined himself into them. This miraculously coincided with Ellen's exaggerated struggle to board. Then without any suspicion, John drove her and a concealed passenger toward the gate.

The tool wagon was not a very comfortable mode of travel, either for Ellen or Stone. The ride got rougher as it neared the prison gate because of the increasing ruts and pot-holes in the ground near the roadway. The rods felt as though they were stabbing him in the back and every jolt felt worse. He found it very difficult to maintain his tangled position. The wagon suddenly stopped at the gate and almost immediately Stone could hear someone rummaging through the wagon's rear bed. He had slipped slightly but was able to reattach himself. His eyes caught the rough, worn boots of the guard as he stood at the side of the wagon searching the tools in back under the burlap. He could see another pair of boots at the front of the wagon where Ellen's boyfriend sat beside her.

His breathing was now so heavy he was afraid one of them would hear him.

"Everything looks alright. Have a nice evening Miss Marshell," said the guard in front of the wagon.

"Thank you; Good night now," responded Ellen. Stone breathed such a sigh of relief he almost fell out of his hiding place. The two guards moved away and the wagon continued on its rough course out of Young's Prison and into the more pleasant smelling, and even at night, inviting Illinois countryside.

After about fifteen minutes Stone was unable to hold on any longer and dropped to the ground. He really had no idea where they were or how far they had gone. The wagon slowly passed over him but his rapid descent had caused a light thug sound that aroused John.

"Whoa! What in the world was that?" he asked Ellen. She shrugged her shoulders in puzzlement.

"I'd better check," he said as he climbed down. Stone crawled to the other side of the wagon and there crouched trying to hide from John.

"There's not a thing here in the road. Can't be a rut, we're way past them. Besides, I can't seem to see anything of the like in the road at all. Now that is peculiar," he said, peering first down the road and then looking under the wagon. It was then almost immediately that he spotted Stone's very worn boots, ragged pants and his crouched form. John crept cautiously to the other side of the wagon not knowing that Stone was waiting there.

Rising to confront the dark form, John began, "Who-?" as he fell to the ground. Stone, breathing heavily and shaking, was standing above him with a pipe in his hand. He checked the unconscious man's neck to see if there was a pulse. There was, but it was weak. He was breathing, but it was shallow. He didn't mean to kill him, just stun him enough for the easy escape. Ellen climbed down and joined Stone. She was frightened and shocked.

"Ya didn't have to kill him!" she cried and knelt down beside him.

"He'll be alright. He's still breathin an he has a pulse," Stone explained.

"Yes, but ... well, I hope he'll be alright," she whimpered with a fretful voice.

"I was surprised they checked the tools in the back so fast. I thought ya said they didn't check the wagon."

"Now wait a minute, do you think I tried to trap you? Ya know I could have said something to the guards or John," she cried. Shaking she continued, "And you know very well I didn't say anything about the wagon *not* being checked. I didn't say any such thing at all and *you* know it."

She looked at him angrily and then softened

with a smile asked breathlessly, "You really don't trust me, do you?"

"Let's just drop it, Ellen ... 'course I trust ya. We better git movin outta here. I s'pose we're 'bout a mile from camp. This was a slow ride an the position I wuz in ..." Richard looked at her with a grin and tried to lighten the mood. He knew he was lucky to be on the other side of that fence ... and it was all because of her. She just looked at him with a guarded smile. It really disturbed her to think that Stone might not trust her.

Chapter VI

Stone, wearing a worn, but expensive looking dress-coat, ragged pants and well-worn leather boots, and Ellen, having traded her nurse's uniform for some comfortable old traveling clothes, made their way with the two-horse tool wagon toward the Mississippi River. It was now about midnight. They had ridden at a fairly decent pace, but there were times Stone went a little fast and this frightened Ellen a bit. Their journey of six and a half miles to the river was not tiring them at all. As a matter of fact, Stone was very enthusiastic about the trip and Ellen just seemed to be satisfied with the change of scenery.

"We'll be in New Orlins in a matter o days!" rejoiced Stone, to an almost tearful Ellen. "Hey, this is what ya wanted, aint it?" he continued tenderly as he put his arm around her. She hugged him closer and cried.

"Yes, yes, of course it is, Richard," she said tearfully into his chest. He held her tighter. She was very happy, thought Stone, happy to get out of that hole.

Morning arrived with the two of them sleeping under the burlap from the tool wagon. They were quite cozy as the warm morning sun stirred Stone. He wakened and looked down at Ellen who was still sound asleep. He looked up and before him was the Mississippi River. He recalled the ad in the newspaper just days ago and now could it be possible? He pondered as he peered through the willow trees at the mighty Mississippi. The sound of the rushing water was constant and relaxing. Ellen awoke, to discover herself in Stone's arms. She looked up into his smiling eyes as he kissed her deeply.

On this Thursday in June 1863 Stone was once more free. He wanted to be sure his renewed freedom and independence would last. While they huddled together, a riverboat blew its whistle as it steamed down the river, probably stopping in Cairo. On its side in fancy large red letters read 'ST. LOUIS RIVERLINE'. Stone's spirit soared as the large river steamer continued on its path. She blew her whistle again and he looked down at Ellen.

"We should git on one o those by tonight. 'Cause if we don't we'll hafta go ta Cairo by road an that might be dangerous," said Stone as he got up and moved toward the wagon.

"What're you doing?" asked Ellen as she stretched her arms to the sky.

"Well, we're gonna hafta make it part o the way by land. Ma'be there's some place close by where the boats stop."

"Hey, we haven't got any money."

"Do ya have a bank account?"

"Yes," she said, then paused a moment. "Alright, but I'll have to go into Hareley. It's a small town north of here and that's where my bank is." Stone looked down at the ground, then back at her.

"We'll both go ta Hareley. How far is it?"

"It's a few miles above Cairo," she said with a smile. Stone smiled and nodded.

Soon Richard and Miss Marshell were on their way toward Hareley. Almost all the way, Stone rode with one eye out for pursuers. No one, and no sign of anyone or anything could be sensed by Stone's eyes or ears.

They made it by early afternoon. Stone waited in the wagon as Ellen went inside the bank. The teller was surprised at her withdrawal.

"Miss Marshell, are you sure that you want to do this ... five thousand, five hundred and seventy-five dollars is a very large sum of money?" asked the bank teller, regretting to have to hand over so much money from his bank.

"Oh don't worry Mr. Jones, I'm going to pay some bills and maybe do some traveling. I will be back," responded Ellen innocently. To this the teller smiled and then with a hesitant look on his face, gave her the $5,575. Ellen smiled and thanked him, then placed all but five hundred dollars into her left boot. She then left the bank and climbed aboard the wagon to a hopeful Stone.

"See!" she said showing him the money. His face lit up as he took the money from her. She grabbed it back from his hands as he had begun to count it. He looked at her in surprise.

"Well, after all, it is my money. Don't worry, we'll get to New Orleans," she assured, while letting Stone be ignorant of the additional money she had hidden in her boot. Ellen did like him, but she was also a survivor and no fool. She kept telling herself that she really didn't know him. And after all, she did get him out of that awful prison. So it's up to him to stay out ... not her problem. Stone never thought to look at her bank book to see what she really had. He never considered what she could gain by holding any money back.

"Well, don't worry. I aint gonna rob ya. What kinda fella da ya think I am?" asked Stone, superficially insulted for the sudden slander of his character. He grinned, then drove the wagon out of the little town of Hareley to Cairo in the southernmost part of Illinois.

Stone drove the wagon almost continuously until it became too dark to see. Earlier that day, they had stopped at a farm and bought some bread and fresh vegetables for supper. It was about nine thirty that night when they finally stopped. He made a small fire and Ellen cooked some carrots and corn. She then prepared their burlap bed. Stone occasionally looked up and down the road for any sign of Federal soldiers, relieved none could be seen or heard.

"We'll be there by mornin, right lover?" asked

Stone. Ellen looked very content as she lifted her head and looked at him. She had just finished their bed.

"That's right, honey," she said. Her smile showed Stone that Ellen needed a change of scenery and a new life. He was pleased with himself that he was the one who had made her happy and not that soldier they left behind.

"Why did ya wanna come with me, Ellen? I mean really, why did ya wanna leave 'im, yer ol boyfriend?" asked Stone. Ellen's face grew serious, but the deeper feeling of happiness still shown through. Richard could read her pretty well, he thought.

"Oh, we weren't that happy together. I loved him, I guess, but I didn't want to spend the rest of my life at Young's Prison and married to him. I was ready to, because there was no one else around and no other way to make a living. But then I met you and thought I might have a better way out."

It wasn't long until they were both asleep. The night passed quickly and again the warm morning sun woke first Stone and then Ellen. He stretched, then dragged himself out of bed and prepared the horses and wagon for an early start. Ellen was awake but didn't feel like getting up. She seemed to be baking in the heat of the sun as Richard finally finished the necessary preparations.

"C'mon little lady. We're movin out o here as early as poss'ble. I figger we're only a little ways from Cairo," spoke Stone excitedly.

"Alright, alright!" returned Ellen as she now dragged herself from their bed. Slowly, she picked up the burlap and threw it in the back of the wagon, after which Stone helped her climb on board. He grabbed the reins and guided the wagon back on the road headed for Cairo.

The city of Cairo on this Friday morning was quite busy. The wagon and its two occupants were on top of a hill where they could see the remainder of the road disappearing into the city. Looking at the river, they could make out four riverboats and some assorted barges.

"Well Lady, we'll soon be on our way!" exclaimed Stone as he excitedly hugged her.

They continued on into the city and made their way through some narrow streets, finally coming to the docks. Stone pulled the wagon to a stop and looked for an office. He wasn't too far away from the *SOUTHERN LINES*; a sign over three windows issuing tickets and information was in front of them. There were quite a few people waiting to board, so in the meantime Stone read the river schedule while Ellen remained on the wagon. After a few minutes he returned to her.

"If we git on the Southern Lines' Queen at eleven this mornin, we kin be in New Orlins by Thursday night at ten," informed Stone excitedly.

"How much?" she asked.

"Oh 'bout sixty dollars fer the both of us," he

said, "course we'll be in a cheaper section. It's still kinda classy, I guess."

"All right. Here. But what are we going to do with the rig?" asked Ellen as she handed him some paper money. "I'm sure Young's Prison has reported a missing wagon with two horses."

"We aint got time ta hide 'em. If we don't hurry, we'll be picked up anyways, either by the Federals er the sheriff here. Remember, yer in pretty deep trouble yerself."

"Wait a minute, I didn't escape; I just worked there," she said angrily.

"Hold it ... ya figger yer all in the clear, huh?" Surprised at Ellen's attempt to save herself, Stone remembered how much she wanted to go with him to New Orleans. "Well, let me tell ya thet yer boyfriend aint too thrilled 'bout what ya let happen ta him."

"I will tell Mr. Parker you kidnapped me and made me do it! I'll tell him you had a knife!"

"Oh c'mon. Who da ya think ya are? Ya think yer pretty sly, don't ya?" Stone questioned her, looking puzzled himself.

Ellen looked down at her hands with such an innocent look. He angrily grabbed her leather purse off the seat. She tried to get it back, but he raised it over his head.

*"**What do you think you're doing**? Give me my bag … you have no right to look at my personal stuff!"* she wailed.

Now they were getting a little loud and starting to draw attention to themselves. Heads were turning toward the young woman, and as Stone began searching her purse, a large man approached.

"Young lady, is there a problem over here with this man?" he asked looking at a surprised and anxious Richard.

Ellen continued to struggle with Stone. "Give it back to me!" she demanded. He had already quickly slipped her bank book into his pocket unnoticed.

"Well, what're ya waitin for buddy?" asked the large man who appeared to be a dock worker. He put his hand on Stone's shoulder. He was twice the size and breadth of Richard. As the big man looked angrily into his eyes, Stone smiled back and noticed that many people were watching them; and that was a real big mistake. Still in the dock worker's grip, he placed Ellen's purse back on the wagon seat. She quickly grabbed it and wrapped the handles around her wrist.

"Ya wanna get rid of him, lady?" Stone was even more fearful now as he waited for Ellen's answer.

"No, no, he's my friend. We just had a misunderstanding," replied Ellen assuredly. The large man removed his hand from Stone's shoulder, gave him a disgusted look then continued on down to the dock area.

Stone gave Ellen an irritated look, then climbed up on the wagon. He drove the wagon down one of the back streets to hide it. They leisurely walked back to the dock area trying to blend in with everyone else. He nervously looked around for some sign of authority. He felt sure his escape with the Union's horses and wagon, not to mention the nurse, had been telegraphed as far away as St. Louis by now. Back at the dock area, they tried to mingle in with the crowds waiting to board the boat. They had gotten their tickets without any trouble, but he was still keeping an eye out for the authorities.

At about ten thirty that morning the 'SOUTHERN LINES' QUEEN', with its name painted across her sides, pulled into one of the docks. It was one of the most extravagant riverboats on the Mississippi. Stone and Ellen were awed by its outward appearance. Neither one was used to such style. This was a first for both.

"We're gonna be ridin in style; or are we gonna be ridin in style ... huh, my dear lady?" Stone was so excited. "New Orlins ... here we come!" Ellen just smiled.

Twenty minutes later, Ellen and Richard along with all the other passengers boarded the beautiful Southern Lines' Queen. Stone was so excited that he almost forgot to keep his eye out for any guards. He had registered them as Mr. and Mrs. Walter Blane. They were wearing the same clothes they had escaped in. This made Stone feel more uneasy as he looked at the other passengers around him. They were all very stylishly dressed. He caught some of the passengers staring at them with disapproval. There was a man at the dock end of the boarding walkway. He looked at Ellen and Stone seemingly interested in their appearance and lack of dress. Otherwise they passed through easily without anyone asking for identification.

After boarding, Richard and the young woman walked slowly to their room. They spent their time admiring the elegance of the boat, amazed at how some people lived and how relaxed they all seemed surrounded by such beauty. 'This is what drives Ellen. This is her desire, ta live this way', he thought to himself.

"Now, this is how I'd travel, baby, if I had the money," boasted Stone. Ellen looked at him. She was not the dreamer that he was and she really didn't care for a poor man's fantasy. She knew what she wanted and was willing to work for it.

"Richard, what are you going to do in New Orleans. I mean, you're just a farmer, aren't you?"

To this Stone was a bit insulted, but yet he couldn't disagree. "Well Ellen I never pretended I was anything else.

He really didn't know what he was going to do. He hadn't thought about that. His only desire was to get out of prison and on to New Orleans. The only work he had ever done was farming until he went into the army.

At about eleven that morning, the Southern Lines' Queen left the city of Cairo. Unbeknownst to the couple on board, Federal soldiers had arrived in Cairo just as the boat was leaving. Ellen and Stone had made their way safely out of Illinois. They could finally breathe easier.

It was three in the afternoon on Saturday when they reached Memphis. As they began to dock, Stone remembered the days he had spent at the reformatory near there. He looked down at the moving water, trying to find some kind of diversion. Ellen, standing with him at the rail, noticed his preoccupied manner.

"What goes on in that head of yours?" she asked playfully. He turned to her looking a little down.

"Oh, some ol mem'ries that I'd like ta fergit, but I guess I never will," he responded as the boat slowly moved into the dock.

"Well, if they weren't bad, maybe you wouldn't be like you are today."

The riverboat blew its whistle and came to rest at the dock. Richard and his accompanying lady were unaware of the Federal soldiers waiting at the edge of the boarding walkway.

"Hold it. We gotta keep our heads, at least till we get past here," exclaimed Stone. He was trying to find a place on board where he could observe the dock.

"What's the matter?" she asked.

"Take a look," said Stone. He moved away from the point of his view for her to see. They were peering through the ship's dining hall doorways from portside to starboard. He pointed quietly toward the soldiers.

"They're coming up the walkway!" Ellen gasped as Richard grabbed her. They found an under deck entrance that led to the engine room.

The Federal soldiers seemed to make a fairly decent search, but not thorough enough. They passed right over the open under-deck entrance several times. Soon they were off, satisfied the two they were looking for weren't on board.

Richard and Ellen breathed a sigh of relief as the boat slowly moved away from the dock. The two, now feeling safe, emerged from their hideaway. There was one witness who had seen them hide ... a drunk hanging on the ship's rail. In his condition, he didn't seem to care one way or the other. They passed him as they walked arm-in-arm. Stone stopped suddenly, letting go of Ellen.

"That guy's got some good clothes," Stone whispered to Ellen.

"Oh no! Don't get any ideas. We'll just be getting ourselves into trouble. And that's something we can't afford to do."

Stone turned to face her closely and firmly looked into her eyes. "Yer the one that told me not ta try ta escape," he said with a smirk.

"I just said not to 'get any ideas'."

Stone smiled and then motioned her to come along with him. They approached the man still hanging on the rail. Ellen was showing some doubts, but felt she had to go along with him. Richard went to the railing and slapped the man on the back.

"Uncle Dave, ya ol son of a gun!" Stone said loudly. The man almost fell to the deck. He was groggy, but still could communicate.

"I don't remember ya, Billy," he slurred. "Ya gotta beard?" He was exaggerating Richard's unshaven stubble. Stone smiled, rubbing his chin.

"Now Uncle Dave, I better take ya ta yer room." Stone was trying to keep his arm around the swaying man's shoulders. He was about forty-five and appeared to be worth some money.

"Ya gotta beard?"

"Yea, Uncle Dave."

"What's her name? She's sure good lookin." He winked at Ellen.

"That's yer niece. Ya remember, from the North," explained Stone.

"What? A traitor in my fam'ly!" shouted the man. Ellen and Richard now flanked him to keep him from falling. As they stood there, he looked into Ellen's

face, but seemed to be looking through her to something non-existent.

"Ya can't be a traitor. Yer so good lookin! I don't care what side yer on. Yer so good lookin! Does he ever tell ya that?" Ellen and Stone were trying to get him moving.

"Sometimes," answered Ellen, not really knowing what to say.

"Billy, ma boy, did ya ever consider marryin ma niece here?" Stone looked surprised, as well as Ellen. They stopped on the deck. He wasn't quite sure what to say or do next. She looked at him quite interested in his answer.

"Well, I've considered marryin many a young ladies Uncle," answered Stone as they began to walk along the deck again. They were nearing the passengers' quarters and the older man was nodding approvingly, as Ellen was all eyes and ears. "I think I'm not the kinda man the ladies, even my cousin here, would want ta settle down with," said Stone.

"Oh, ma boy, what could be yer problem? Money, charm, some ... nicer clothes?" the man said as he looked Stone over. Richard was at a loss for words and had that look of modesty.

"Here we are. Now here's ma key," the older man said as he fumbled with his key. Stone took it from him and unlocked the door. Once inside the room, Stone hit 'Uncle Dave' across the jaw and he fell unconscious into his closet. Richard started searching for some clothes.

"Hey, wait a minute!" Ellen whispered loudly. "We'll just be in more trouble. He'll have the captain and the crew lookin for us." Stone stopped and replaced a dress jacket and tried to straighten out the closet.

"Yer right, Ellen. Look, I guess we'll jest hafta dock in New Orlins lookin like this," Stone said sadly. He went over to her as the drunken man was still out on the floor. He placed his hands on her shoulders and said, "I jest wanted ta look better than I ever did. I never had clothes like he's got. Maybe we could'a got somethin really nice fer you too," as he looked softly into her eyes.

"Stealing will just lead to more running. And ... if you take his suit jacket, don't you think he would know you took it, if he saw you wearing it on the boat? When he comes to, he'll see his clothes are missing. Besides, I don't want to have that kind of life ... running. Don't get mad; I understand how you feel. We'll be alright till we get to New Orleans."

It was now about three thirty and the Southern Lines' Queen was leaving Memphis. It was Sunday when the luxurious riverboat, with her smoke stacks billowing, passed Vicksburg. By around seven that evening, Ellen and Richard hadn't had supper yet. They had returned to their room shortly after dropping off the drunken man that afternoon and had been in their room without noticing the time.

"Do you realize it's getting late, Richard?" informed Ellen as they both lay on the bed half-awake in their small, but ample room. Stone looked up at the door and could see little light penetrating the thin window shade that covered the small glass in the door.

"Wow, what time is it?" he asked as he slowly stood up from the bed.

"Well, it's about ten minutes after seven and I'm hungry," said Ellen getting the time from a small watch in her purse. Stone noticed her frantically searching inside her purse. He was suddenly ashamed of himself for taking her bank book, which was in his left rear pants' pocket.

"I can't find my bank book!" she said hysterically. Stone swallowed hard as he began to help search the room.

"It has to be in my purse, Richard!" She was so upset she began to cry.

"Now don't git all upset. B'sides, ya don't need it anymore if yer gonna do business with another bank. Right?" Stone offered, trying to calm her.

Ellen nodded, but continued to search anyway. He deftly pulled the small book from his back pocket with one hand, while not allowing Ellen to notice. He had already read it and knew that she was five thousand dollars richer than he first believed. He quickly threw himself across the bed and to Ellen's eyes, seemingly picked the bank book up off the floor.

He then gallantly handed it to her.

"Well, thank you. Do ya want to look at it?" she noticed Stone's look of humility.

"It aint none o my business, Ellen; that's yer bank book, not mine. I'm not the kind that puts his nose in somebody else's business. Ya should know me by now." Stone put one hand assuredly on her shoulder and one at his waist.

"No, I don't mind showing you," she said as she wiped away a tear.

"Now Ellen, that's none o my concern. I know yer not hidin nothin from me. There's no reason fer me ta know yer financial worth. I love ya an not yer money. See what kind o man I really am? No, my dear, ya don't have ta show me nothin," Stone said with a little too much drama and just a touch of sarcasm.

Ellen's eyes began to squint just a bit. "You took it when you grabbed my purse on the wagon, didn't you? *You've had my bank book for some time now, haven't you?*" she said with a loud voice. Stone turned away as though he was insulted.

"Now Ellen, what gives ya sech a foolish notion? Ya aint got any faith in me."

"If ya didn't have my book, then you have the uncanny ability to see through beds," Ellen shouted. Stone's face reddened and then he grinned as he tried to show her that her accusations were ridiculous.

"Now, now, my sweet Ellen."

"Don't sweet Ellen me! How could ya see my bank book on the floor when you were standing over there? I'm not stupid Richard," she came back, staring at him with suspicion.

"Aw, come on," he began.

"I know you Richard Stone. You don't trust me for one minute do you?" as she looked down at her purse.

"OK, I admit it! I took it from yer purse an read it. So what? An yeah, I wondered how in the world ya could have that much money. Ya said ya were an orphan. So yer family didn't leave ya any money. I can't help but wonder how ya got all this money. Five thousand dollars is a lot o money ... yer rich! Yer pay at the prison can't be much. How did ya get this money?"

Ellen's face put on the look of 'I knew it' mixed with anger. She stood away from the bed, nodding as she looked at him with disgust. When she calmed down she spoke.

"I guess you do have a right to know how I got this money. I know you're thinking I staged this whole escape so I can collect money off your head. No, Richard I'm not a bounty hunter. I didn't want to tell you this, but I once worked in a saloon, in Chicago. I did favors for men who came through there ... important men, high men of stature. I got paid well, but I didn't like the business I was in, so I trained under a doctor in the town to learn nursing."

Pausing a moment and regaining her composure, she continued, "A soldier was found shot outside town and he was brought into the doctor's office. I helped take the bullet out of his shoulder and became friends with him. He convinced me that I was needed at the hospital at Young's Prison. His name was John. He's the one that always picked me up and took me home ... the one you hurt and left behind. Anyway I accepted the job, because it was a way for me to do something good in my life after doing so many wrongs."

"Now Ellen, ya didn't hafta tell me yer whole life story. Don't be so hard on yerself. I wuz no angel myself. I'm sorry I took yer book, but ya did say ya had five hundred dollars. Right? Ya did a wrong ta me, so no wonder I had thoughts about you. An I was wrong too, 'bout you an in takin yer book."

They stood there looking around their small room and occasionally at each other, realizing they were a little bit alike; maybe more so, than different. Stone moved over to her and touched her cheek softly with his hand and an endearing look in his eyes.

She looked at him for a moment, then asked softly, "Let's get some supper, alright?" Gazing into each others' eyes just a little longer, they left the room together.

It was twilight and the riverboat with its twin smoke stacks not puffing as before, slipped down the river quietly. Its engines were chugging at an easy pace in order to aid the pilot's maneuverability at night. In the restaurant, Stone bought some large sandwiches and beer. He was politely informed that he and his lady friend were not appropriately dressed for dining inside the restaurant. Richard put up no argument, well aware of his appearance.

He left the restaurant without a scene and gave Ellen her sandwich. She was waiting outside the dining area fearful that they would be turned away. They went to the bow of the boat, and found some empty chairs. Stone moved a small table between them and placed the two bottles of beer on it. From there, the Mississippi River unfolded its winding course as they were passing through it. It was a warm, moonlit night. The moonlight dancing on the waters was a site to behold. A soft breeze stirred around them as they ate ... a breeze caused by the boat slowly moving through the warm water.

They looked at each other and Stone said, "This's much better than eatin in that dinin room."

Ellen fully agreed as she sat there experiencing such a romantic evening. A feeling came over her that she had never felt before ... maybe she should forget about her plan. Richard was nicer to her than anyone had ever been; and why ruin it all, just for some more money.

"Just think, Richard. We'll be in New Orleans by tomorrow night," said Ellen, looking very happy. Stone looked at her and smiled. The moonlight was highlighting her silhouette. She looked so aglow that he suddenly was overcome with his feelings of contentment.

"Ya know Ellen. It wouldn't take much fer me ta marry ya."

She was silent for a moment and then said, "I don't know Richard. Let's not think about it just now." She had deep feelings for him too, but wanted to make sure they both weren't caught up in the moment. "Ya see, I've never met a man like you before. You're sensitive, but strong willed. At least, that's how I see you. I believe you're sincere in your feelings toward me, but marriage is a big step." When she looked over at Stone, he looked dejected and sad.

"Then whatcha bin sayin an doin with me, wasn't out o love?" Stone was staring into the dark waters of the Mississippi.

"I don't know," she said as Stone got up quickly and disappeared down the starboard side of the boat. "*Wait*! Don't go, Richard."

She sat alone wondering why she had hurt him so. A moment passed and she got up from her chair and carefully walked down the starboard side looking for him. 'How did I think I could go all the way to New Orleans with him and not get my feelings involved?' she wondered.

As she walked, she looked into the gambling casino, dining hall and bars. There were three bars on board, each having its own type of clientelle. All the social rooms of gathering were the width of the boat. This enabled her to see the port deck in some places, for there were large openings designed for decoration through which she could view opposite sides of the boat; but she didn't see him. She continued on until she reached the stern and there stood Stone's lonely figure, hanging on the rail. He was staring into the dark Mississippi. Ellen slowly approached him. She didn't try to touch him, but just stood there for a moment. He turned and was surprised to see her.

"Well how long've ya been standin there?" he asked with a little hurt or maybe anger in his voice. Ellen didn't say anything, but looked down toward the deck. Richard looked at her and then walked from the stern rail that flanked the slowly turning paddle wheel to the rear bulkhead.

"I came to apologize, Richard. I'm just not sure of things." She paused a moment, "Would ya rather have me tell you that I love you and let you believe it was the truth, when I don't even know the truth myself?" she asked softly.

Stone turned from the white plank board bulkhead and looked at her apologetically. "I got a little hasty 'bout things. Only women're supposed ta do that," he uttered quietly.

Ellen smiled at him. "Let's go up front and watch the river go by. You didn't finish your sandwich, she said as she went to him. Stone put his arm around her as they strolled up the starboard side to the bow.

At about ten that night, while Richard and Ellen were sitting together on the bow, the Southern Lines' Queen passed a bend in the river that located the boat a couple of miles west of Natchez, Mississippi. Here the boat was between the state of Louisiana on its starboard and the state of Mississippi on its port side. Just after the boat made the bend, cannon fire rang out. It wasn't unusual to have rifle and cannon fire at times, but it usually occurred farther in the distant countryside. These shots were very close.

Chapter VII

As the Southern Lines' Queen continued on down the river, the rifle and cannon fire faded into the night's warm air. Ellen was nervous and Stone, being aware of her uneasiness, held her hand.

"What's that all about?" she asked him anxiously.

"That's jest a skirmish. I wouldn't worry too much about it. If yer gonna go, then yer gonna go, Ellen," Stone confidently assured her. She frowned at his acceptance of the inevitable.

"Somebody just died back there," she stressed as she sat up straight and pointed in the direction of the now distant and muffled gunfire.

"Yeah, isn't that kind o stupid?" Stone asked sarcastically. He laid his head back and closed his eyes. Ellen was puzzled for a moment and just stared at him.

"What do ya mean? That's it's ... 'kind o stupid'?"

"What're they dyin fer?

Ellen shrugged her shoulders at his short reply. "Well, I guess to reunite the Union," she said. Stone sat up to continue the conversation.

"That's what the Fed'ral gover'ment said. An they also said they're tryin ta free the slaves. Well, I think it's a big joke! It's all the Northern fact'ries who have the power in YER country! Unitin the Union an freein the slaves ... jest a big con," stated Stone. Ellen was now angry and sat back defensively, staring at Stone. He was surprised at her response.

"Wow, yer really a patri't," he said with some sarcasm.

Ellen looked at him straight in the eye. "You bet I am!" she said proudly.

"So am I," he said.

Ellen sighed in relief, then said, "What are you arguing for? We can't do anything about this damned war anyway!"

Richard sat back in his deck chair. Ellen's eyes darted toward him trying to watch his facial expressions. Stone felt her looking at him as he opened his eyes. "Now what's botherin ya?" he asked tiredly.

"You're right. The whole thing is kind of stupid. I mean all these men who've died ... for what, slavery? It's because of greed on both sides. The root of it all is greed. Slavery would die out on its own."

"Well, I see yer beginnin ta git the idea. Now that don't mean that fightin is all wrong, but I figger if two fellas have a disagreement, then let'em fight it out. What kinda man lets another man fight his battles fer him? I mean the rich an the big shots on both sides aint man enough ta fight their own wars. They don't like ta git their hands dirty, I guess. They're cowards, too. That's my 'pinion. So they git dumb, poor guys like me an give us a big con speech. They tell us that we're fightin fer our flag an that's the right thing ta do. Ellen, the North an the South do the same thing. That's why I'm jest livin my life. I got 'nough fights o my own than ta fight somebody else's battles fer 'em. B'sides, what're those rich people doin while we're fightin their war? Well, let me tell ya. They're drinkin wine, wearin fancy clothes, partyin an takin trips on riverboats. They're doin it in Washin'ton an they're doin it in Richmond. No diff'rence," lectured Stone.

Ellen was surprised at Stone's anger and resentment for the upper class. She actually felt the same way, but didn't allow her emotions to show. She wanted her piece of the pie and was willing to work for it. She longed for nice clothes and to party with the upper crust. Yes, some day she may even see Paris. She wasn't born into money, so she had to get it her way.

"I guess ya have a point, but wouldn't you do the same thing if you were rich an powerful?" she asked. Stone pondered her question, thinking that maybe she had a point.

"That's a good question. I never really thought o that cuz I never figgered on bein rich. Yeah, that's a good question. Yer real smart. Ya know that?" He looked at her, delighted with her way of thinking. She could argue, and always had a good point Stone thought.

"You're not too bad yourself. But, Richard don't

ya think you're pretty hostile toward rich people? And not just rich people, maybe, let's see ... people in power. I don't think you're against the rich as much as those with authority. That's it, isn't it? You can't stand anyone telling you what to do. I'm right, huh?"

Stone was taken aback by what she had said. She could really see right through him he thought. He tried to be truthful; he tried to answer those questions to himself before answering her.

"Yeah, I think yer right. But I got lotsa 'xperience with people who say one thing an do another. Ya know, hypocrites. I can't stand hypocrites. An 'specially when they're people that teach ya in school an at home ta respect 'em like they can't do no wrong. I think ya understand what I'm tryin to say, don't ya?"

"I guess I do. But ... I'm tired ... let's go to bed," Ellen said as she laid back in her chair stretching her arms over her head and yawning. Stone could see the outline of her breasts as she stretched in her tight dress.

"Yes, ma dear. I think that'd be a very good idea," he answered. Ellen brought her arms down and looked into his still gazing eyes, straightening the top of her dress. He grinned and she smiled as his eyes caught hers.

It was Wednesday, July 1, 1863. In three days it would be the Fourth of July ... and Ellen and Stone would be in the big city of New Orleans. A Federal detachment had been occupying the city since Admiral Farragut entered in 1862. Federal troops patrolled New Orleans, but the citizens still had the upper hand. Many

Confederates, missing-in-action or escaped prisoners-of-war like Stone, would wind up in New Orleans. Here in the warm climate and the great mixture of people, they could easily elude the Federal soldiers and officials that were after them.

Some came here with high hopes of somehow making it big; but for Stone, he was eager to carve out a new life for himself which hopefully would include Ellen. His plans were to get away from farming and seek out some other way to make a living. He felt sure it could happen here in New Orleans. Also, since it was a great sea port, many dreamed it would give them a chance to make their way to Europe for a change of life and sometimes a change of fortune. That is what Ellen was thinking. But, all in all, New Orleans had an attitude about life that made the problems of many disappear in its gaiety and eclectic nature.

In Baton Rouge, Ellen and Richard left the boat soon after it docked. As they strolled along the dock area, a black man approached her. "Mexican Weed?" he asked, using a term for marijuana. The small, dark, black man explained to her that it helps the musicians play better and a lot of slaves used it because it made them feel 'happy an full o life'. Stone said he had used it when he was in the reformatory near Memphis and he liked it. He noted how happy and lazy it made him feel, but that he hadn't had any in years. Ellen was cautious, but didn't disagree with Richard's purchase of it. There was about half an ounce of it in a leather pouch.

They returned to the boat and their room. Soon

an officer of the ship's crew knocked on their door. Stone opened it a little cautiously, not because of his possession of Mexican Weed, but because of the Federals he felt were in pursuit of him.

"I would like to inform you that our boat will be here for about three hours and will be leaving about six this evening. So in the meantime, if you would like to wander around Baton Rouge, you have three hours to do it." The officer smiled and tipped his hat to Ellen and left.

Stone shut the door and turned to Ellen," Well would ya like ta take a walk 'round the city er stay here?" he asked and she shrugged her shoulders.

"I don't care. Whatever you want to do," she replied. Stone smiled, grabbed the leather pouch and they headed out the door.

They walked into the city where Stone purchased some cigarette papers at a tobacco store and then went to a quiet park about a half mile from the dock area. It was a hot afternoon and there was a faint breeze. The heat was uncomfortable, but the willow trees offered some shade and the slight breeze made it very pleasant.

Stone removed his war-beaten coat and placed it on the ground. The grass was very plush and green, and the coat made a nice place for Ellen to rest. She sat down and was overcome with the attention and courtesy Richard showed her. She smiled as she thought how kind he was to her. No one had ever treated her with such consideration.

He sat down beside her, opened the pouch, took the cigarette papers and 'weed' to make four joints. Swirling it in the flame of a match for an even light, he took the initial drag, then passed it to Ellen. She awkwardly held it, took a puff, then coughed. Stone grinned.

"Didn't ya ever try weed b'fore?"

She shook her head and said, "No, I never really had the desire."

"Well, with this ya breathe it down real deep. Ya'll git used to it."

It was around five o'clock and they finished three of the joints. He had just lit the fourth as Ellen was contentedly lying on his jacket, enjoying her first take. Richard also experiencing the high was blissful. He breathed in every bit of the joint's trail that he could. The only thing good he remembered about the reformatory was the 'weed' he could get there.

At around five forty-five as the couple made their way back aboard the luxurious Southern Lines' Queen, they went to the rear of the boat and watched the paddle wheel turn as it began to leave Baton Rouge. As the boat left the port promptly at six o'clock, she bellowed out the old calliope song. Oh, what a grand feeling it gave the passengers as it majestically slipped down the Mississippi River, her smoke stacks streaming smoke and playing her song.

The allure of the paddle wheel boats touched just about everybody. People would stand in the street and by the docks to wave goodbye to the passengers as the steam ship slipped away. All along the river's length, many people of all ages enjoyed watching these slow moving, luxurious and beautiful riverboats. They were entertainment centers that would stop in otherwise quiet and almost boring towns and liven them up.

As the evening passed, Stone again bought some sandwiches and beer which had become their staple diet of the trip. They sat at the front and watched as they continued down the river to New Orleans.

At about nine o'clock that night the lights of New Orleans were just visible. Stone grabbed her hand and kissed it excitedly.

"We're almost home baby! We're almost home!" Stone exclaimed as he began to kiss her with passion. Ellen wanted to bring him to reality, but not enough to spoil their fun.

"Um ... Mr. Stone ... I'd like to ask ... you a ... small question," she said through his kisses. He moved back with his face glowing like an excited kid at Christmas.

"Yeah, ma dear, lovely lady?"

"What are we going to be doing here?" she asked. "One of us has to be a little practical."

"Oh, don't worry 'bout it. Hey, in this place ya

kin do anythin ya want, without gittin into any trouble." Stone assured her, as Ellen gave him a look of playful suspicion.

"Anything, huh?"

"Well, ya know what I mean. We kin be free here. I mean really free. There's a diff'rent view of life here. Nobody worries 'bout nothin. They have parties here all the time, like the Mardi Gras. Everybody gits drunk an has a lot o fun. Ya know there's a lot o Mexican Weed here too."

Ellen was slightly worried. "Yea, but good times don't last forever. Where are we going to get money?" She was less jovial and a little more serious than Stone.

"Hey c'mon now, don't spoil the fun," he said a little irritated and wished she wouldn't be so practical.

"I like to have fun, too. I'm just being realistic. Where are we going to get the money to have our fun? I refuse to pay for everything," she insisted, a little irritated at that thought.

"Oh, no; cert'nly not. I wouldn't do that to ya. Look, I'll find a job right after the Fourth o July, alright?" Stone tried to assure her.

"Why not Friday, the day before?" Still a bit peeved, she thought to herself, 'Isn't he ever going to grow up?'

"Well, alright … Friday. But I thought we'd

spend a little time havin some fun b'fore we git into the more serious stuff. Don't ya ever let go?" he asked.

She looked even more annoyed at him now. Stone stood up from her, irritated with her attitude and now more determined than ever to set out to have some fun, with or without her

"You have a bit of a selfish streak in you, don't you?" she asked.

"*What?*" Stone returned with surprise.

"I said, you have a selfish streak in you."

"Ya better explain that one, baby," Stone retorted, now really getting angry.

"All you think about is yourself. Isn't that right?" Ellen was getting a little loud.

"Now wait a minute!" Stone began.

"All you think about is fun and freedom. Just *your* fun and *your* freedom," Ellen accused.

"Ya got me all wrong!" Stone said furiously as he was struggling to understand her reasoning.

"I'm not like you. I can't live from day to day. I'm more responsible than that. I can't be like you … I tried. Where are we going to stay? Have ya thought about that? What about food? What about these clothes? Grow up, Richard! *You* aren't going to use me … oh no. Is my money all you really wanted?" Ellen's

---

voice got louder, "I worked hard to get what I have; and *you* or no one else is gonna take it away!"

"Well, if it's a rich man ya want, why did ya leave Chicago? Ma'be ya should go back there an hang out with those rich men, huh? Ma'be that's where ya wanna go. Is that where ya belong Ellen? Do ya really think I'm usin ya? If ya remember it was *yer* idea ta escape. *You* asked me!"

Stone paused and Ellen looked at him with piercing eyes; he waited and when she seemed to calm down a bit, he continued, "I bet ya'd make a real good actress. Here all the time I thought ma'be, jest ma'be, ya loved me. Well Ellen, I do love you an it's not fer yer money. It's you. I love the way ya walk, the way ya talk, an when ya look at me with those big blue eyes, I wanna take ya in my arms an protect ya from all the bad in the world. Yer slowly changin me Ellen. I want ta make somethin o myself ... fer you Ellen! Ok ... I'm a little irresponsible, but who aint? I won't ever be president. I won't ever be a success like that. I jest wanna have the chance ta make ya happy."

"I'm sorry Richard! Sometimes I get the feeling by the way you talked that you brought me along for my money. Well maybe for some fun too, you know?" She was feeling so confused by now. She was wondering how in the world she thought she could go all the way to New Orleans with him and not get her feelings involved. He had treated her kinder than anyone ever had.

"Ya keep thinkin I'm after yer money. Ya don't

know how many times I wish I never seen yer bank book. Then ya couldn't accuse me o wantin yer money." He was beginning to get angry again, but with himself. He walked up to the bow away from her, and for a moment neither said anything. Then Stone turned around and looked straight into her eyes. She bowed her head as a tear ran down her cheek.

"Ya know, Ellen," he said softly, but still struggling with his feelings, "that really makes me feel bad. I mean really bad. I don know what ta say. I'm not after yer money. I don't care that much about money. I guess I'm too busy tryin ta be free. Kin ya try ta understand that?"

"Ya see," he continued, "I wuz in a war that I thought at one time had some purpose. That made sense. I lost friends ... real friends. An then I came ta the conclusion that it made no damn sense at all. I didn't ask ta be in it. Why should I git killed fer somebody else? Even if we did win, it wouldn't do me no good. What would it do fer me; make me a rich man ... a world trav'ler ... happy; would it put a lot o love in my life, give me a lot o friends? Well baby, I won't get nothin! Just a hole in the head er a shot off leg an a piece o paper sayin I did a fine job. Now go back ta yer farm an make a livin. That's all. I'm not a coward either. I'll fight if there's somethin worth fightin over. So, ma'be there's somethin worthwhile ta this war. If I was on yer side, I could say that I'm freein slaves er bringin the Union back together; but on this side, I really don't know what I'm fightin fer. As far as I'm concerned, we're gettin some kind o mean swindle in our part o the country; I jest don't understand the politics of it. So, why shouldn't I try ta make somethin o myself. I came ta New Orleans ta start a new life. Excited, yes! I wuz in prison an now I'm free! I guess that's why I'm anxious ta have a little fun." He sighed after his tirade was over.

Stone was trying to explain himself, even though he wasn't sure what he was actually trying to say or do. Ellen had stopped crying and was listening, and feeling a little embarrassed about her jumping to conclusions. She had made a mistake about Richard and opened her mouth before she thought things through. She was sorry and understood him more now. It's a wonder he didn't just leave her after the accusations she had made. Her respect for him was growing into a relationship she wanted to avoid.

Richard continued with his explanation after an awkward silence. "I liked ya at Young's, an I wuz thinkin o askin ya ta escape with me. But when I really wanted ta say somethin like that, I felt foolish. I mean, not every prisoner-of-war asks the nurse he likes ta escape with 'im. Ya thought I was crazy, right?" he asked as Ellen shrugged her shoulders. "Well, I didn't take ya with me so I could use yer money. I didn't really think 'bout how much ya were worth till we were on our way ta the bank. Actu'ly, that's the first time I thought 'bout the cost o gettin ta New Orlins. I figgered I'd work ma way down river somehow. I mighta turned ta stealin. Yeah I know it's wrong, but I wuz that desp'rate. I do love ya, Ellen," Stone paused for a just a moment then continued, "I'm really surprised … no, that's not it. I'm … disappointed; not in you, but … well, a bit in you; but more in the suspicions we have of each other."

Stone was standing by the railing near the bow. Ellen was silent and just looked at him, and then stared at her now folded hands in front of her. Slowly, he moved away from the railing, straightened his coat and quietly walked away. She felt that he must be terribly disgusted and disappointed in her. 'He's right', she thought, 'They were suspicious of each other and both felt maybe they should never have left Young's. They both would have been better off if this whole thing had never happened.'

The Southern Lines' Queen arrived in New Orleans at ten minutes after ten that night. Ellen went to their room and packed the few belongings they had into a small carpet bag she had found in the closet. They had been carrying their stuff in his pockets and her purse. She had no idea where he was. Ellen left their room and waited on the starboard side of the boat. It was on this side that the riverboat docked.

As Ellen waited alone wishing Richard was with her, she wondered where he was and if he was still angry at her. Stone, after walking around the boat and thinking about their conversation, went to their room only to discover everything gone. He began to swear to himself as he figured she took his personal stuff and was going to leave the boat without him. He angrily left the room, slamming the door so hard he almost knocked it off its hinges. He made his way to the starboard side looking for Ellen.

The crew lowered the wide gangplank getting ready for the passengers to disembark. Soon the

Southern Lines' Queen was almost empty. The dock area was crowded with about eight horse drawn hacks waiting to carry the passengers into the big bustling town of New Orleans. Ellen waited off to the side watching for Richard. She was afraid he had somehow slipped past her without her seeing him. He was still on board when he saw her. He felt ashamed of himself, as he thought about having left her at the bow a half hour ago. Seeing her waiting like that for him made him feel a little remorseful. He came toward her, "C'mon. I wasn't gonna leave ya all alone," he said as he took her bag and put his arm in hers.

"I'm sorry Richard, I really am," she said apologetically. They stopped and she looked into his eyes. "I love you very much." They were now alone on the gangplank. Stone smiled and guided her, moving along toward the dock. He put his arm around her as they made their way into the streets of New Orleans.

Coming up a narrow street, they noticed a variety of people. Near the docks they saw a large number of unfriendly dock workers, bums and two old women arguing about something in broken French. They seemed to be drunk. As they came out onto a wider street named St. Charles Avenue, they looked for a room, stopping by several hotels that lined the street.

It was about eleven that night when they finally found a room at Chez Louise's. It was a four story, red brick structure and looked old and a little dirty on the outside; but when they entered their room they found it affordable and quite comfortable. It was clean, had a nice soft bed and a wash stand. It was just the two of them and all they cared about was a place to sleep and a roof over their heads. Their room was on the fourth floor, room twenty-three. Each floor had six rooms, but only seven in the hotel were occupied. The remainder were available by the hour. They had no idea that Chez Louise's had that kind of reputation, until they were there for a couple of days. They soon realized what was going on after a few nights of men coming and going. 'Oh well', thought Ellen, 'the price is right and who cares what goes on in the other rooms?'

Ellen and Richard were in bed by midnight and slept until nearly eleven the next day. Stone awakened and laid quietly listening to the church bells ringing out the quarter hour. He looked over at Ellen who was still sound asleep, and felt a bit more ashamed of himself for not trying to fully understand her. He had hurt her and she him; it was a wonder it hadn't ruined their relationship.

Stone was watching her sleep; then after about fifteen minutes he got up out of bed and looked out the room's two windows. As he gazed at the street below, he felt content with his accomplishments and situation, and pondered over all that had happened. Last week at this time, he was lying in a prison hospital bed, being inspired by the riverboat's advertisement in the paper.

He found it hard to believe that he had actually escaped from a prison camp. He was amazed that the escape had worked and he was here in New Orleans, a place he had dreamed of, but never thought he would really experience. The nurse he then liked and now loved had come with him.

Turning from the window he glanced at Ellen, still not stirring. She must have been exhausted. He was looking around the room; it actually wasn't just one room, but two … a parlor and a bedroom, and quite nice. He quietly got dressed and decided to take a morning walk. He left her a note saying *'Back by noon. Went for a walk. Love Richard.'*

As he strolled down the street, he noticed how quiet a morning in this part of New Orleans was. In two days, he thought to himself it would be the Fourth of July. Of course, as New Orleans was not part of the United States, there would be no celebration here.

Stone was becoming concerned about how he was going to make a living. He hadn't any skills for the city, so he thought maybe he could try working at the docks. He was leaving St. Charles Ave. and heading up Jackson. He wasn't going anyplace in particular, but was walking around trying to think things through.

As he continued on, he came upon a group of slaves sitting on the sidewalk. All were chained to the lamp post. He looked at them, but tried to ignore their condition, moving on past. It was just noon and he could hear church bells ringing again. It was, even for the Southern born Stone, a strange picture of hypocrisy. Rich men sitting in church, restaurants or their businesses, while their slaves sat on the sidewalk chained outside. He began casually looking around for other noticeable injustices of society.

When Stone was a child living in Tennessee, he

had seen slaves ... human beings owned by other human beings ... whether right or wrong, never really occurred to him. It was an accepted part of life. The slaves were 'different' and that seemed to make everything alright. Richard's attitude toward slavery hadn't really been challenged until this morning. 'For a freedom lover', he thought to himself, 'I don't seem ta have many opinions on the subject. The only reason those blacks're slaves is so a rich fella doesn't have ta work.' He thoughtfully concluded, 'everybody's tryin' ta enslave somebody else jest ta make their own life a little easier.' He continued to walk and think.

From what he had heard, the North's factories were just as bad. Both blacks and whites were slaves to a rich man there. He heard they even had children working in factories. 'I guess there's a point ta all the fightin goin on, but who has the answer?' he thought.

Walking on, up ahead he heard music. It was coming from some kind of street band made up of some poor black men and a couple of poor white men. There were about ten of them playing on homemade instruments and a few guitars and banjos. Some had sticks hitting bricks, some had spoons. There was one playing a harmonica, another one playing an old concertina, and one blew an old, dinged bugle. It was a foot tapping, sweet rhythm in the middle of such otherwise quiet and discouraging surroundings.

Stone stopped and listened. The music made him smile, but he unexpectedly noticed the men were all blind. There was a white man with them who appeared to be a minister. He too seemed poor. Their music was lively and very melodic, but with a different type of rhythm. Stone liked what he heard, but it sure wasn't like the music played in the hills of Tennessee. Soon one of the black men started to hum, then the rest of them joined him. He broke into a song and the verse was broken French and English that surprisingly matched the rhythm.

People were now gathering around them and one of the black men in the band began to play fiddle. Stone watched as the minister put out a tin can and people began to throw coins in it.

"**Brothers an sisters!**" shouted the minister as the band continued to play. "You can see these men are poor in body, poor in money an poor in ways that you take for granted. Even though these men are blind an lack the *necessities* of life, they are still happy an full of joy in their spirits," he paused and a couple of the men would shout 'Amen' every now and then.

"Many of you are lookin for somethin an ya can't seem ta find it. What is it ya want ... freedom, pow'r, money?" he looked into the eyes of everyone on the street. Some of the people watching grunted or moaned; some said nothing; and some walked away. Stone wasn't walking away; he had nowhere to go and he liked the music.

"Well, don't worry about such things, brothers an sisters, let the Lord guide your life. What you need will be *provided*. Yes sir, I'm not kiddin," said the minister fervently. He turned to the band and they sang a gospel song having the same rhythm as the other songs that had already caught Stone's ear.

Back in their room Ellen had just finished reading Stone's note. Going over to the parlor window, she tried to spot him on the street below, but didn't see him anywhere. She went to the bedroom to get dressed. Ellen put on the dress that she had been wearing for days and tried to straighten it a bit, then went to the mirror to fix her hair. She was pleased with herself, as she was attractive without doing too much fussing. She only wished she had a change of clothes. Looking at herself in the floor length mirror, she whispered audibly, 'Ah, you shapely thing'. Her hands slowly caressed each side of her waist and down her hips. She had a very seductive look on her face as she entered the parlor to wait for Richard.

The band that Stone had been watching just finished and he enjoyed every minute of it. He wandered around this part of the street trying to gather enough courage to approach the minister. He finally went over to him.

"Rev'rend?" Stone said quietly, wanting to say something more, but didn't know what.

"Rev'rend?" he continued a bit louder, "**Suh ... Rev'rend, *suh*?**" Stone was standing by him, but he had just begun to speak loud enough for the minister to finally hear him. Slowly, the minister stood up. He was taller than Stone and looked at Richard sympathetically, noticing his ragged clothes.

"**Brother!**" the minister's voice boomed, embarrassing Stone. "I can see a question in your eyes; a question that's been worryin you for a long time. What is it brother? What's brought you here? What do you want to know?" asked the minister, putting his hand on Stone's shoulder. The band had now gathered around them making him feel self-conscious.

"I wuz jest wonderin ...," Stone said softly.

"**Speak up**! Don't be afraid to speak what's on your heart." His hand was still on Stone's shoulder and his eyes stared directly into Stone's. The poor blind men from the band, mostly middle-aged and older, said another 'Amen' to the minister's words to Stone.

In his mind, Stone was thinking about his freedom, but decided not to say anything.

"Where's yer band from?" asked Stone with a forced smile. The minister removed his hand from Stone's shoulder disappointed in his question.

"Over yonder near Lake Charles, brother," answered the minister, in a softer voice.

"I like that kinda music; never heard it b'fore. What's it called?" asked Stone, a little embarrassed.

"That's from the Black an French people in this part of Lou-s'ana, called Cajun. Well, Cajun with some Black. I learned that it's mostly French from the ones that came down from Canada. Now, you have to excuse us, 'cause we're goin to another part of town. Would you like to come along? Maybe we could find some better clothes for you," said the minister, more personal than before.

"Oh, no! I'm in from the river. Um, ya see, I'm lookin fer a job an, uh- well, I couldn't let ya do that. I mean, I kin work, an b'sides ya'll probably meet somebody 'long the way who needs clothes more'n me," Stone said with a smile. Surprised at his kind generosity, the minister put out his hand and Richard shook it.

"Praise God, brother! Praise God!" the minister said with a smile. Stone nodded back as the minister led his band up the street.

"Praise God," Richard said softly, wondering how men in that condition could go around singing. Their music wasn't forced; they were sincere. And you could tell they enjoyed their playing and singing. It was different and entertaining; as lively as the music in the Tennessee Hills.

Chapter 8

Stone headed back to his room whistling one of the tunes with every step. When he got there, Ellen was sitting on the sofa reading a newspaper.

"Where did ya find that?" he asked.

"Oh one of our neighbors brought it over," she answered, giving Stone a strange look. "She's blonde, young and quite pretty." Stone acted surprised, but quickly became disinterested for Ellen's benefit.

"Well, what're ya readin 'bout?" he hastily asked. Ellen just looked at him and then showed him an advertisement for ladies wear in one of the New Orleans' expensive stores.

"Yea-a-a. Well, ma dear, ya'll have ta dream awhile longer. I gotta find some kind o work first," Richard said.

"Hold it lover, I've got money. I think I'll go down tomorrow and take a look at some of those dresses," she said, showing him her independence.

"Well, what 'bout me? I'd like some other clothes too. Ya think I feel great goin 'round lookin like this?" Stone returned with an irritated voice.

"What's the matter, Richard? Don't you like me

being and doing what I want to be and do?" she asked sarcastically.

"What're ya sayin? Oh-h-h-h, ya think it bothers me that ya got somethin ta hold over me, huh? Well, let me tell ya somethin, little lady. I happen ta *want* ya ta be independent," he said now a little loud.

"Oh, come on Richard. It bothers you. It bothers you that I've got money and you can't do anything about it. You don't like being dependent on me for your own ... um, it bothers you that you're dependent on me for your freedom. That's what's killing you. You need me ... for clothes, for food, for a roof over your head," Ellen laughed at him. "You're jealous because I have the money and I control it."

"It don't bother me at all. What's so funny? It bothers you, 'cause I'm the one who's got the brains an figured out how ta be free an end up in New Orlins with you payin fer it. There, what d'ya got ta say fer that?" smartly returned Stone.

"Then get out of my room," softly ordered Ellen. Stone pretended not to hear her.

"Richard, you're not wanted in this room. Get out," she said a little louder.

"Awe, c'mon, ya can't be serious," he paused, trying to see some light of humor in her eyes. "I'm jest bein prideful 'bout this. Yer kiddin aint ya? No-o, I guess yer not," Stone said trying to look sorrowful.

"I think you finally admitted what your real intentions are, and I don't like them. You best leave," she ordered softly.

Stone couldn't believe what he was hearing. He began to walk to the door, then turning nervously and feeling awkward, he loitered with his hand on the knob.

"Once I open this door an walk out, I won't be back," Stone threatened with a sorrowful look. Ellen never looked up from the newspaper.

"Alright, I'm leavin now," Stone said as he slowly opened the door and then paused. He was hoping Ellen would tell him she didn't mean for him to leave.

But Ellen just said 'Goodbye Richard'. Her tone was cold and serious.

Richard closed the door and wondered what had gotten into her. He knew he shouldn't have made such comments to her. But by the way she acted, he thought she may have been trying to figure out a way to get rid of him. Stone walked down the hallway and paused at the top of the stairs. He waited there a moment to see if she would call him back, but the door remained closed. He figured he would take advantage of the moment and go for another walk. Maybe he should go back and apologize. How could Ellen believe that she was being taken advantage of, when *she* was the one who offered aid in his escape.

Stone went on downstairs and outside, all the while feeling that perhaps he should apologize to her. He slowed down his pace, as he considered going back, but his pride stopped him. He quickly moved on down the street until he came to a saloon and went in. As he opened the door, all eyes were on him and they weren't friendly eyes either. He again became aware of his clothes and wished he had something better to wear. He should have accepted the preacher's offer this morning. He ordered a drink and kept to himself. Once in a while, he would carefully scan the room and found that most were just minding their own business.

There was one man, probably about his age, sitting with three others at a table on the other side of the room. He was slim, but appeared tall even as he slouched in his chair. The other men at the table took a quick glance at Stone, but seemed more interested in their poker game. The tall man watched Stone. His unshaven face and deeply set eyes didn't make Richard feel too comfortable. Stone remained facing the bar and would look through the corners of his eyes for anybody walking up from behind.

As he sipped his beer, he felt something hit his back, but he acted like nothing happened. He continued enjoying his beer when he felt something hit the back of his head. This time, he slowly turned and saw two shelled peanuts on the floor. He looked up and saw the slim man at the table. He slowly picked up another peanut, hoping Stone would notice and tossed it at him, hitting him in the chest. The other men at the table were still minding their own business and even seemed irritated that the slim man would throw peanuts at a stranger, interrupting their poker game.

Stone could hear one of them say, "C'mon, John. Just play, will ya?"

"He thinks he's pretty tough. I hate his guts," John said to the others at the table.

Stone finished his beer, and started to leave. The slim man moved from the table and stood in front of the door.

"You're goin nowhere, boy," said the man called John. He was chewing on an old, dead cigar butt. Richard stopped and looked at him with a cool, stern face. At first the man seemed as though he was going to move to the side, but he didn't. His pride wouldn't let him. He began to act tough again and remained in front of the door.

"I hate your guts, boy," John said defiantly chewing on his cigar butt. It was quiet now with the whole room watching. The sweat was trickling down their faces and you could feel the heat of the Louisiana afternoon.

"Ya get out o my way er I'm gonna move ya out o the way. Ya hear me *boy*? I'm goin out that door." Stone now staring straight into the man's eyes, began moving straight at him.

The slim man didn't say another word, but slugged Stone in the stomach. Richard didn't expect anything so fast. He was caught off guard and doubled over, as the saloon became alive with excitement. Stone was hit again … this time in the mouth, causing him to fall backward into the center of the room. As John came at him, Stone tripped him and they began to wrestle. Tables and chairs fell over, and people even in the street began to watch from the door. The bartender left for the sheriff. Richard was hit again, but didn't fall. He was now returning blows and his opponent found he had more to handle than he realized. Stone and the other man were having it out, without either one gaining over the other. It was a good fight and by the excitement they stirred in the saloon, the people around them thought they were having some good entertainment.

Suddenly two deputies came in and broke them up. By this time the crowd had grown quite large. People were around the door and inside the saloon. The deputies broke up the crowd. "**Alright, alright, move on … clear out!**" shouted the deputies. "If you wanna have a beer an be peaceful, then stay. If not, **out!** You're not gonna bust up the place." Stone and his opponent were separated and the crowd began to leave.

"Take 'em down to the jail," the one deputy said disgustedly. "Don't appear to be too much damage, Henry. You wanna press charges?"

"Naw, jus keep 'em away from here. The tall ones always startin somethin, "said the bartender. The deputies took Stone and the other man outside. The one deputy that dispersed the crowd and gave all the orders, talked to the two men.

"Now, there's no charges against you and neither of ya are drunk, so the only thing ya done was disturb a quiet Friday afternoon. So, I'm jus gonna tell ya, stay away from this place. Ya got that?" he pointed his finger into the tall man's face, who nodded.

"You stay away from here, too. Do ya understand?" as he pointed to Stone, who nodded. "Alright, both of ya get away from here and I never wanna see either of ya again," the deputy said.

Stone and John walked down the street together and the deputies walked the other way, each pair taking a quick glance at the other, making sure they left the area.

"Ya know, yer pretty tough fer a little guy," John said, looking at Stone with some respect.

"Well, had a lot o practice," Stone grinned.

"I'm John Caulfield," and he offered his hand.

"I'm Richard, Richard Stone. My buddies call me Stone." He shook John's hand and they talked as they walked away from the saloon.

"Haint seen ya roun b'fore. Mus be new ta New Or-leans, huh?"

"Jest came down from Illinois; got here Saturday night."

John stopped in his tracks, turned to Stone squinting and spat out, "You a Northerner?"

"Aw, no-o! I'm from Tennessee. Ya see, I was in

a Federal prison camp in Illinois. No, I'm no Yankee." They were walking toward the Chez Louise's Hotel where Stone had left Ellen, and hopefully where he would be staying again, too.

"Oh, that's all right! I'm glad yer no Yankee. You know they're jus mean killers. That's all they are."

"Well, everybody's a mean killer in war, John."

"Yea, but not like them Northerners! Why, Stone, you oughta know," said John a little emotional about the Union Army's methods of fighting."

"Both sides fight the same John."

This conversation made Stone think of how his friends were killed, and how they killed Capt. Orrey McDonald. 'Cynthia's dead, my friend O'Reilly's gone, the poor old doctor dead. All fer what?' He was in deep thought. 'Why did they have ta die? Dr. Grant took the bullet outta my leg an they killed him.'

"Stone, ya hearin me?"

"Jest thinkin I seen some pretty mean things alright. Things happened that I'll never fergit. An now an ag'in they creep into my mind."

They were in front of the hotel where he and Ellen had spent the night. "Well John, I'll be seein ya. This's where I'm stayin." He put out his hand for John to shake.

"Oh! Hey buddy, we'll see ya. Ahh, where ya hangin around at?" asked John.

"I don't rightly know yet. Like I say, I'm new here an I really don't know my way 'round."

"C'mon down ta Bourbon Street. There's a place called Lovin' Lillys. Jus the place if you're lookin fer some female company," John said as he began to laugh and twist up slightly, which he did when he laughed.

"Thanks. I'll be there," Stone said as he looked up at a certain hotel window.

"When ol buddy?" asked John, wanting a definite answer. Stone looked down at the sidewalk, then at John.

"Prob'bly tonight. Where'll I meet ya?" asked Stone. He had a feeling Ellen was serious and didn't want him around anymore.

"How 'bout here ... 'bout eight or eight-thirty?"

"Okay, see ya then."

The two men went their separate ways; John disappearing farther down the street and Stone into the hotel. He went up the stairs and stopped at the door. He hesitated to open it and considered knocking, but decided to listen to see if he could hear anything. He heard nothing, so he knocked softly. There was no answer, so he knocked a little louder and still there was nothing. He tried the knob and it was locked.

'Where the hell could she be?' he said angrily to himself. He tried to open the door again with some force. He stopped himself, knowing she was getting the best of him.

He went downstairs to talk to the man at the desk. "Did a young woman by the name of Ellen Marshell check out this afternoon?" Stone asked a little nervously. The proprietor didn't recognize Richard, for he hadn't check him in.

The man looked at him inquiringly. "What is your name?" he asked with a New England accent. Stone didn't like the man and was becoming angry at having to give his name and still not finding out where Ellen was.

"My name's Richard Stone an her an me checked in Saturday night."

"Sir, do you mean to inform me that you shared a room with the young lady?" asked the proprietor.

"Look, jest tell me if she checked out," ordered Stone, leaning over the desk with a threatening look on his face.

The man moved back away from the desk and looked a little frightened. "Sir, I am not supposed to give out that kind of information."

"Ya tell me er I'll break yer neck," Stone hissed as he grabbed the register and turned it around so he could see the names. The proprietor tried to stop him, but Richard shoved him and he fell to the floor. Stone gazed at him lying on the floor; he looked quite frail, and frightened.

"Thanks!" Stone said disgustedly to the man. She had not checked out. Maybe she took a walk. He thought he might meet her coming back. He waited for three hours under the uneasy eyes of the manager.

It was about six o'clock in the evening when Ellen finally entered the hotel lobby. She noticed Richard immediately, but chose to ignore him. He was reading a newspaper when she finally approached him. He slowly looked up at her and with no feeling asked, "My dear lady, jest where've ya bin all afternoon?"

"Well, my dear sir, I've been enjoying the afternoon. Probably like you. What happened to your face? Were you in a fight?"

"I went fer a walk an ran inta a little trouble, that's all."

"Well, I went for a ride this afternoon with one of our neighbors from the building."

"Who'd ya go with? What's her name?"

"I didn't say it was a she. His name is Donald and he took me into the city in his carriage." Then she walked toward the desk.

"Ellen, are ya serious 'bout splittin up with me?" He walked over to her. "All those things we said ta each other, were they jest lies?" Stone asked softly. He tried to put his arm around her, but Ellen refused his affection.

"I don't think you were lying to me; but I didn't say I didn't like you," she said nonchalantly. This hurt Stone. Her love seemed sincere. He let go of her and swallowed hard.

"Let me git my things," he said to Ellen. He went over to the desk and asked if there were any rooms available.

"Richard, where are you gonna get the money to pay for it? You don't have any money," she said.

The man at the desk coughed and kept looking at Ellen. He didn't quite know how to handle this.

"Sir, we do not have any other rooms. I'm sorry." Stone was disappointed, actually shocked at Ellen.

Then, through the door of the hotel came a handsome, almost dashing man. He was a little taller than Stone and far better dressed. He was carrying a gown in his left arm, took Ellen with his right and walked up the stairs. The man completely ignored Stone, probably thinking he was another boarder.

Stone went up the stairs after them and Ellen introduced the two men before they got to the room. She gave Richard his comb and razor, and handed him thirty dollars. The man thought Stone to be a little odd and wondered what Ellen had to do with him.

Richard left the hotel and started walking. 'She must a met him while I was out this mornin. Wow', he was thinking to himself, 'that guy really moved fast.' He wondered if maybe they had known each other before. He didn't know what to think. Ellen certainly wasn't the person he thought she was.

Stone's stomach began to ache. Was it from hunger or a broken heart? He didn't know. He had a lump in his throat wondering how she could dump him and find someone else so fast. It didn't make sense. How could her feelings for him change so fast? 'Oh well', he thought, 'she helped me git ta New Orlins. I do owe her that.' He turned his thoughts to John and what tonight may bring for him. 'Maybe I'll meet someone tonight an forgit about Ellen.'

He met John at about eight thirty that evening in front of the hotel. He hadn't had anything to eat all day and his stomach felt hollow.

"John, do ya pal around with anybody?" Stone asked as they walked down the street.

"Aw, jus a few guys, an 'course, anythin I can pick up," John said with a laugh, showing a missing tooth that Stone hadn't noticed before.

As they got closer to town, they could hear some of the music coming from the bars that lined the street.

"Ya know where I come from, they don't have so many bars in one town. That's back in Tennessee," said Stone.

"Aw, if that haint somethin. Ya know, I haint really been nowhere 'cept Mexico ... some good lovin women down there."

They just got on Bourbon Street and the two men smiled at each other as they approached Lovin' Lily's. As they continued on down the street, they came to a place called Madeleine's Belles. John didn't seem to have known about this place and they couldn't decide whether to go there or Lovin' Lily's.

"Well, Rich, it's up to you. Where'd ya rather go, here or Lovin' Lily's?" asked John, leaving the decision to Stone.

"Don't know. What's Lovin' Lily's like? Is it like this?" asked Stone, as they stood in front of Madeleine's Belles.

John shuffled slightly, "Well, this place's a little more expensive lookin. Lovin' Lily's like a cellar club, ya know b'low the sidewalk. This place's got lotsa well-to-do fellas, an the women here haint gonna look at us twice. Do me an you look like the guys ya see in there? Take a look."

Stone went to the front window and looked inside. It was quite classy, but the women inside were just irresistible. Richard, having champagne tastes on a beer budget, knew it was an impossible place to consider. But after being so tempted by the beauties he saw through the window, all reason was lost.

"How much money ya got?"

John was a little taken aback by Stone's question. It wasn't any of his business. "Wait a minute. How much money *you* got?" John retorted.

"Yeah, I got about, let's see …," Stone looked in his pocket and pulled out ten dollars. He kept the other twenty hidden.

"Well, what're ya worried about *my* money for?

"I jest wanted ta make sure ya could pay yer way. Jest bein friendly. That's all, John."

"M'be. I don't know ya very well buddy, but I don't think ya were worried 'bout me not havin 'nough money, were ya now?" asked John. He was a little irritated at Stone wanting to go in there when the place was clearly out of their reach.

"Well, alright. I was wonderin if me an you could get some real fancy clothes an catch a couple o rich ladies," said Stone.

"Wow, I don't know. Ya gotta have a style … a manner fer that. Do ya think we got it, Richard?"

"Aw, everybody's got some of it. Ya jest gotta use it, John."

John took off his boot and pulled out a hundred dollar bill. Rich's eyes lit up as he tried to look at it, but John made sure he didn't get too close.

"I think we can find some nice clothes, my good

Buddy. But we hafta wait till tomorrow mornin when the store's open."

"I'd sure like ta know what ya do fer a livin," Stone said with a grin. "Maybe I could get in on it. "

"Aw don't worry. When I feel I can trust you an I think you'd be interested, I'll let you know," John said with a note of caution in his voice, "'Til then I haint sayin."

"Let's try Lovin' Lily's tonight then."

"Yea, lookin at us, that'd be the best place to go," John agreed.

They made their way back up the street to Lovin' Lily's. It was a small room below the sidewalk and outside it was marked 'CLUB'. It wasn't as nice as a saloon. The floor had some wood planks, but most of it was hard clay. The bar was nice. It was made out of mahogany and Stone couldn't help but wonder where it had come from. There was a mirror above the bar. None of the chairs matched. Kerosene lamps were on the tables for card playing.

Madeleine's Belles wasn't much like a saloon either; it was more a cabaret and music hall. Stone had seen pictures in novelettes. As he had peered through the window, he saw beautiful pictures hung on the walls, pictures of faraway places. That alone had intrigued him. The girls were dressed in colorful, fancy dresses. He could see the bar and it was hand carved with a huge mirror behind it. All the furniture matched.

Stone wanted a taste of the good life and he couldn't wait to get there. He never saw anything like it. He wondered what the brothel area looked like. These short, but exciting memories of Madeleine's Belles were occupying the forefront of Stone's thoughts. He was determined to get there in any way, shape or form. For the moment, Ellen was forgotten.

They entered Lovin' Lily's. The name was decoratively written with red paint on the dirty glass window of the club's small door. On entering, Stone and John were surprised to find it crowded. Smoke filled the air and they could hardly see. They went to the bar where the dance hall girls were lined up drinking with the men. Stone saw one standing alone and he tried to talk to her. Deciding she was about fifteen years old, he walked on. The two men looked at the waiting women and some looked back at them.

"There's sure a bit o v'riety here, aint there?" Richard said to John. John smiled as they gazed over the room. Some of the women were already sitting at tables with their men drinking and laughing. There were all different sizes, shapes, ages and colors of women. Stone noticed that two were Oriental. He wondered where the brothel was.

"They even got some Chinese in here," said John.

Richard was so fascinated that he hardly knew where to begin. He had never experienced anything like this before. And since Ellen had dumped him, he was anxious to find another woman. He'd show her, he thought. 'She got a man so fast; well I can get me a woman.' But what he really wanted was someone who would stay with him; someone who would be with him through thick or thin. He knew he wouldn't find anybody like that in here. So for now, one of these women would do just fine.

Stone spotted a woman who appeared to be about thirty and he went over to her. He stood by her, admiring her, and she looked up at him, asking, "Ya got a ten?" He couldn't afford her. "Well if ya don't have a ten, leave me alone."

Richard went back to the bar. She watched after him and shook her head slightly with a bit of interest showing in her blue eyes. She wore a red dress that showed off her small waist and complimented her blonde hair and cherry red lips. He wondered what she was doing in a place like this. She belonged at Madeleine's Belles if she was going to live this kind of life. He wondered why she wasn't married. She was as pretty as Ellen.

Stone rushed over to John. "Ya got ten I co'd borr'w? There's a beautiful woman over there an she wants twenty!"

"Hey, buddy. I ain't gonna pay fer everything. Is she what ya really want?"

Stone nodded, "She's sure good lookin."

"All right, but jus this once. Here," John said slapping Stone on the shoulders as he headed back to her table.

He paused, took a deep breath and continued on to her. Stone offered her ten. She looked at him sadly and stood up. She had a pretty face. He decided he already liked her. They went to the back of the club. There were several rooms. 'Sure is busy', he thought, 'men an women, comin an goin, in an outta the rooms.'

"Business seems ta be good t'night," Stone commented awkwardly. She looked at him as though she was tired of it all. He closed the door behind them and she started to take off her clothes.

John was still at the bar looking over the women. More men were coming in and the place was getting uncomfortably crowded. 'Aw, this's unbelievable!' John said aloud to himself. A small Mexican woman approached him saying something in Spanish, which was completely unknown to him.

Stone and the woman named Marcy, were now lying on the bed. "Marcy's a nice name."

"Ya think so too, huh?" said the woman with indifference.

Stone began to get very affectionate and she responded. She suddenly sat up and seemed to be sick to her stomach.

"Are ya alright?" asked Stone.

"Aw, c'mon! Go get somebody else. I can't go on like this. Here's yer ten dollars."

He moved toward the door, but stopped and looked back at her; she seemed to be better.

"What's the matter with you? Why don't you force your way?" she asked.

Now at the door, he had his hand on the knob.

"Well, if you're going, then go!" she ordered. Stone just stood there and looked at her. "Well, what's the matter with you. Go on ... git out!"

"What're ya doin here, lady?" He asked as she looked away.

"I'm waiting to die. I wanna leave here so bad. Boy, do I want to get away from here." The pain in her stomach seemed to have gone. Now she was just sitting there.

"I'm not a hustler, lady. I'm jest lonely."

"So what do you want me to do? Cry for you?"

Stone didn't know what to say. But her wanting to leave New Orleans was like him wanting to leave Young's Prison, he thought. He could feel in her what he had felt there. Oddly, this was where he found his freedom, but she would have to find a different place for her freedom. He was concerned for her, but not in much of a mood to get involved; yet his need for affection was strong. He remained at the door.

"Where would ya go?" he asked, his concern

was obvious.

"Boy, I'm thirty-five. There's no man for me anymore. I'm gettin near middle age. I think you're a dreamer, but I'm not. I had a chance once for marriage, but I didn't want it then. So I'm paying for it now. There's nothin left for me. Go find yourself a nice sweet girl an marry her."

Stone picked up his shirt and coat. She sat on the edge of the bed, watched him as he opened the door and started to go through the doorway. Both his concern for her and his innocence was obvious to Marcy. She saw his sincerity.

"Hey!" she said, and Stone stopped. "I'm really never gonna change. You're too nice a guy to put your time in me. Go an get married or somethin."

Stone slowly closed the door and went back to the bar. He didn't see John and figured he had found a girl. After a few minutes, Marcy appeared. He looked over at her. She was sitting where she was before, at a table near the back wall. Men and women were still going in and out of the rear hallway. Richard kept his eyes on her as she stole glances at him.

"Hey, buddy! How'd ya do?" shouted John, laughing. He gave Stone a slap on the back from behind. He was clearly drunk.

"Fine ... real fine!" Stone said smiling. He took a glance at Marcy and then slapped John on the back playfully, spilling John's drink all over both of them.

"I guess ya did. Ya seem a little down though. Didn't she do right by ya?" John was laughing and he slipped a little off the bar he was leaning on.

"Yeah, yeah," smiled Stone.

'Yea, yea," John said in a serious tone mocking Stone. "Jus don't git involved with 'em. Ya oughta know that."

"I guess I jest gotta weakness fer women," said Richard.

"Ha! Who don't?" laughed John. He realized Stone's seriousness over one of the girls. "Look, take some advice. If your're gonna pick up these kinda women, don't fall in love with 'em. Ya understand? Don't fall in love with 'em … don't do it. Ya can't win with 'em." John so drunk was trying to advise Richard who was now really feeling low.

"C'mon, you need a drink," insisted John.

John put his finger on the bar and the bartender placed a glass there and filled it up

"Yea, that's jus what you need," John said as Stone began to drink it. Stone went to pay for the drink but John motioned him to stop. He had already paid for it.

"I guess I do look a little down," Richard remarked.

"Yea, you sure do. What happened to ya anyway?"

"Oh, I don't know," Stone returned sadly. John looked away realizing he wanted to be alone with his thoughts.

Chapter IX

Ellen and Donald were at Madeleine's Belles drinking. They were at a table for two, sitting in a corner off to themselves. She didn't seem too happy and her new man seemed to be in the same mood. She wondered if maybe she was missing Stone. Everything was such a whirlwind the last couple of weeks she didn't know what she felt.

"My dear, why don't you and I go for a long ride out and around New Orleans?" She hesitated for a moment, wondering what he really thought of her; but she agreed the ride would be nice.

Stone and John were now getting more drunk and each had finally made an all-night pickup. As they left Lovin' Lily's, they walked arm in arm with their two women down Bourbon Street; while Ellen and her new man just happened to be in a carriage parked across the street from them. Stone didn't recognize the carriage, but thought he knew the woman inside. He was plastered and his vision wasn't the best. He was anxious to spend the night with this woman, but his emotions were still with the one inside the carriage.

"Hold it! **Hold it!**" Stone shouted. The four stopped on the sidewalk directly across the street from the parked carriage. By this time, he was sure Ellen was inside of it.

"Hey John, have ya gotta gun?" asked Stone acting as though he was going to play some kind of game, while he was trying to hide his hatred for Ellen and what she had done to him.

"Ha! What d'ya want my gun for, Buddy?" asked John laughing. He thought Stone was finally enjoying himself.

"See that light on the lamp post over that carriage?" said Stone.

"Yea, I see it. Ahh, I think I see it." His vision was blurred from so much liquor. "Stone old buddy, ya might hit somebody. C'mon, let's find a place to treat these ladies." John and the two women began to laugh excitedly as they thought about the fun they were going to have.

Stone was getting mad; he wanted revenge for what Ellen did to him. He forgot all about the woman he was with. His thoughts were on Ellen.

"Lemme have yer gun, er don't ya think I kin knock out a damn light?" Stone demanded. Now John was getting a little irritated at his impulsive need to prove that he could shoot out a gas lamp from across the street.

"Look ol buddy. I'm not gonna let ya take my gun ta prove some half-assed stunt for us. Nobody cares if ya can hit that light from over here or not. Now why don't we forget the gun an take care of these ladies as only a man can do?"said John laughing. He and the two women were trying to divert Stone's mind to something less dangerous. But Stone wasn't laughing.

He grabbed John, and as he did, he pushed his woman and she fell to the sidewalk.

John pushed Stone back and tried to talk some sense into him. Ellen could hear the disturbance across the street from inside the carriage, but she was too occupied with Donald's affections and didn't realize it was Stone causing the ruckus.

"**Look Stone**! Stop being stupid an get yourself acting normal." John, beginning to sober up, was coming to his senses. "You're crazy drunk! Now c'mon, take it easy."

Then speaking easily, not wanting to disturb an already troublesome area, "Let's jus move on an take these ladies away from here." Drunks always hung around this area at night. Stone seemed to quiet down and John put his arm around him thinking he had relaxed, but by now both women were fearful of him.

Ellen thought she heard Stone's name, but considered it too much of a coincidence and continued to enjoy her evening.

Suddenly Stone hit John in the stomach making him double over in pain. He hit him again and John fell unconscious onto the sidewalk. The two women hysterically ran down the street away from them. Stone went for John's gun ... a small derringer. Holding it in his hand, he considered firing into the carriage, but realized that would be a bad idea.

'What am I doin?' He was still drunk and

confused, but was reasoning with himself a bit.

Inside the carriage Ellen began to wonder what was going on across the street. She became anxious and stopped Donald from his lovemaking.

"Now, what's the matter with you? They're just a couple of drunks over there. That's all. Now come on," Donald said.

Ellen relaxed and answered, "I guess you're right; they can't hurt us." She didn't want Donald to know she thought she knew one of them.

Stone was now standing across the street aiming the gun and nervously in debate with himself. 'Should I pull the trigger er shouldn't I?' He was sweating profusely and shaking. His alcohol-filled brain was battling with itself ... hatred and hostility versus reasoning. He didn't know why he wanted to fire into the carriage, while feeling an almost overwhelming desire to do so.

Slowly he brought the weapon down to his side. Ellen and Donald were totally unaware of the danger across the street. Richard had collected himself and replaced the pistol back on John Caulfield's unconscious form. Thunder rumbled on this humid night, as he placed John across his shoulders and tried to carry him. But Caulfield was too heavy for him and Stone fell to the sidewalk causing John to roll off.

A light sprinkle started while Stone tried to waken John, but he didn't respond. As he kept trying to arouse his unconscious friend, the carriage moved away on down the street. Each party would never be certain of the other's identity. Stone tried to pick John up again and place him across his shoulders. Thunder and lightning rumbled and flashed as the rain came harder.

Stone stood up looking to find some refuge for the two of them and spotted an alleyway nearby. He struggled with John on his shoulders and made his way to the alley. There he found an outdoor stairway where they would be dry from the rain that was now pouring down. The thunder was loud and lightning flashed, and the rain wouldn't be stopping soon.

As they found shelter in the stair well, Stone heard the sound of somebody singing. It sounded like a black man, then it sounded like a lot of black men singing. He didn't hear any instruments though, as the singing continued. He looked down the alley with the rain now drenching his head, wondering where the singing was coming from. He didn't see anything, couldn't tell of its direction. At one moment it sounded like it was coming from his left, then from his right; and then it seemed to surround him. Stone was feeling a bit strange. It was a sensation that he had never felt before and he was scared.

"Hey, John. Are ya hearin the singin?" asked Stone over the sounds of the storm, as he tried to wake him. But John just laid there.

"Hey, ol buddy. What's wrong with ya? Listen to that singin," now shaking him, he tried harder to waken John. Stone had an awful feeling inside.

"I hope ya didn't hit yer head," he said softly, then felt the back of his head for bleeding. He pulled his hand up and it was covered with blood. Stone put his head on John's chest to listen for a heartbeat, but he couldn't hear anything. He was getting very frightened and panicky.

"What the hell's goin on?" he asked angrily moving John's limp form closer to the wall of the building that supported the stairway. Stone went back over to the sidewalk to see if he could find any blood. He was getting drenched in the heavy rain. He didn't see any blood anywhere, 'but ma'be the rain washed it away', he thought. Stone went back under the stairway and tried to dry off. He looked at John and tried to find a pulse. There wasn't any and he knew he was dead. He couldn't fully comprehend his actions tonight. He just listened to the almost ghostly singing.

'Now where the hell's that comin from?' he asked himself, becoming very frustrated and beginning to doubt his sanity.

There seemed to be so many loose ends to everything ... almost as if there was no real purpose at all. He tried to love and it was taken away from him, in one way or another. He tried to find himself and that was beginning to be more difficult than he thought. He wanted to be free, but now was wondering from what. What would he gain by this freedom? The storm was raging and it seemed as though it would never end. What really is freedom anyway? He tried to reason the night's happenings. 'Freedom', he thought to himself, 'is something, er a state er condition where ya aren't under anythin er anyone's power er rule. Is there such a place?' He began to realize there can be no absolute freedom, not even when you are truly alone. 'That kind of aloneness is the saddest thing of all. Where is God?'

The singing now seemed to be fading and soon it was gone. He listened hard and could not hear it. He thought it sounded like what the slaves sing in the fields and the one's he saw all chained up on the street. They were singing about freedom. So, it's not freedom that's bad, Stone concluded, but ... maybe independence. Maybe too much of both, or too much of anything could be bad. He continued to think, as the rain slowed to a light shower, that the freedom and independence he sought, is what everyone was searching for, but each had been doing it in their own way.

Stone had not considered himself as the personification of freedom, for he had struggled so hard to attain it. Despite himself, he had influenced others and they had the right to choose their own way.

But Stone hadn't considered that, especially in the case of Ellen. While she was wrong in her method of dropping him, she had that right. He thought maybe she used him to get out of that hole. Or was it that bad for her? What was she really doing there? He began to wonder what her real motives were for helping him to freedom. He couldn't help but wonder if this whole thing was a plan to lead him into a trap. How did she get all that money? She lied about her feelings toward him; maybe she lied about how she got all that money too.

Stone noticed the rain had stopped and the air smelled fresher. Remembering that John had money in his boot and realizing someone would take it anyway, he quickly removed the remaining money. Stone didn't want to add more to his problems, so he left John's body and walked away from Bourbon Street. He walked across town and found himself at the city park. He went in and feeling tired, looked for a place to sleep. He wanted to escape to somewhere peaceful and this was just right, but the grass was so wet that he left the park regretfully and went to look for a room in a hotel.

He came to a small boarding house. He stood in front of it for a minute and thought he would try every boarding house and hotel in New Orleans if he had to; there wasn't anything else to do. He opened the door quietly and found no one at the desk. A small oil lamp was lit, so someone must be up, but he couldn't see or hear anyone. Seeing a sofa near the desk he sat down to wait. It wasn't long until he fell asleep. Soon he was awakened by a large man who probably belonged behind the desk. Stone was wearing the same clothes he had on since he had escaped from Young's and they were deteriorating. The clerk didn't seem to mind his appearance. Stone was afraid that he would be thrown out, but the large man was quite friendly.

"What's your name boy? Are you alright?" he asked.

"Yeah, I couldn't find a place fer the night an I been wanderin all over town." The large man nodded as though he understood.

"Well for two you can have a room here. That sure is strange you couldn't find a room in this whole town," he said scratching his head.

Stone gave the man the two dollars and he got the key to a room upstairs. He was still feeling a bit strange from the strong drink he'd had, but the man at the desk didn't seem to pay any attention to his condition. The clerk looked and felt sorry for the thin raggedly clothed man. He didn't even ask Stone to sign the register. Stone thought that to be odd. Maybe he didn't want to get involved if he was some dangerous criminal, or maybe he saw that Stone was so distraught and tired, he didn't bother with his name.

Stone slept well and awoke the next morning quite refreshed. He remembered John and some of what had happened last night; he felt miserable about his death, but it was an accident. 'Why does something bad happen everytime I find a friend? Ma'be I was meant to be alone.' He realized he could have been in real trouble if he would have used John's gun. Stone really didn't want to kill Ellen or anyone.

The sun shined through his window and he thought about where he'd look for work. Having not eaten since Saturday night on the riverboat, his stomach ached. His lack of concern for food hadn't surprised him, for he usually didn't feel like eating after losing a woman ... especially a woman like Ellen. He couldn't get her out of his mind.

He sat up in his bed and looked around the room. For two dollars he thought his room was comfortable. There wasn't much furniture, but all he cared about was a bed. John's death began to bother him again. So much had happened in so little time. He thought of Cynthia, O'Reilly, and the old doctor. They died for what? For him to be free. Nothing seemed to make sense. Life isn't fair. He thought of Ellen. He couldn't understand her sudden change. Why would she risk helping him escape? Stone knew someone had to be hunting him, but what about her? Would she be considered a victim? Stone shook his head, trying to understand his situation.

Swiftly pulling himself together, Stone got out of bed and put his dirty, torn clothes back on. 'Whatta tramp. I'm jest a small tramp of a man. I'm nothin ... really nothin ', he said aloud to himself. His pants were stained and ragged. His shirt wasn't much better, but he wished he had something else to wear. He threw on his coat, which was not in too bad of shape, except for being a bit dusty and stained in a couple of places. Otherwise, it was the best piece of clothing he had. He had not spent a dime last night ... thanks to John. He still had the thirty dollars that Ellen had given him and the money from John.

'Well, I won't starve fer a while anyways', Stone said to himself. He left the boarding house. He was cautiously hopeful on this sunny morning, whistling and walking briskly, with his hands in his pockets. He looked like a tramp with his scruffy beard, for he hadn't shaved since Saturday morning on the riverboat. He continued down the street and came to a small restaurant. In the window he could see the menu.

'*Bacon 'n eggs with tea*' 'Now, that don't sound too bad ... only fer two bits. Yea, that's alright,' he said to himself and then went inside. The cafe was small, but not crowded, with just him and another man inside. There were a few tables and a counter. Stone sat up at the counter and waited for the woman to finish pouring the other man's coffee. She looked to be in her forties and seemed pleasant.

"H'ya, what would ya like this mornin?

"Oh-h-h I'd like some bacon an eggs an tea," he ordered.

She smiled, "Comin right up." Stone returned the smile and looked around for a newspaper, something to occupy his thoughts until his food came.

As he was looking around, the other man about in his sixties kept watching him. He watched Stone with almost unblinking eyes. He felt the stranger's glare and turned to him and smiled, hoping the man would be satisfied and stop staring. But he kept staring. Stone buried himself in a newspaper he found on one of the tables. Then occasionally looking up from it he always caught the man's constant stare.

It became very annoying. As Stone was reading, the other man mumbled something about boats. Stone made no reply as he wanted to avoid conversation with him.

"Hey, are ya from da boats?" he asked a little louder. He couldn't ignore him, so Stone just turned his head toward him and nodded with a smile.

"Workin on da boats are ya?" asked the man still with a mumble.

"Yeah, workin on the boats," Stone said hoping the conversation would end. The man must have been satisfied for he stopped talking and he quit staring at him. Stone was relieved when his breakfast finally came.

"Thank you," Richard said cheerfully, as the woman stood there.

"That'll be two bits, sir. Twenty-five cents." She stood there smiling at Stone with an extended hand.

"Oh! There ya go." He handed her the money and began to eat. As he turned the pages of the *New Orleans Carrier,* he noticed a reward by the Federal government for the arrest and conviction of Union deserters and escaped prisoners-of-war from their prison camps. He was surprised at the extent of the Federal government's influence in New Orleans. The bounty money was usually thirty dollars.

"Well, I'll be. Did ya see this?" he asked the woman behind the counter.

"Yea, that's the Union tryin to make traitors an ratters on our own. Ever since they come in here, they been postin those bounties an rewards around."

Stone was startled by this. He couldn't understand why Southerners would turn in their own kind.

"Wow. Them Federals are really smart. There's sure enough poor folks 'round that would try ta collect the money," replied Stone.

"Well, don't worry; nobody's doin it! It's just some Northern scheme ta try an split the Southern cause!" She continued with her work.

Stone was a little taken by this, though after thinking about it, he wasn't surprised. It was a good way to entice disloyalty among Southerners, as there were many poor and desperate who might consider it. But their loyalty to home and family in most of the cases would be too strong and the plan to divide the Southern cause wouldn't pay off as expected. There were some who tried to collect, but usually those around them put an end to their plans one way or another.

Stone wasn't worried, for he didn't consider it a threat to his freedom. Anyway, he saw it as a psychological ploy rather than a military one. He suddenly thought of Ellen. 'Did she know 'bout this bounty money?' he asked himself. He became more suspicious as he thought about her. Then looking around him, he saw many Southerners in need and decided there probably were many trying to collect bounty.

One man, as yet unknown to Stone, was Allen D'Amore. He was a part owner in a slave trade business and didn't have any real allegiance to either side. His loyalty was based on where he could acquire the most profit. His slave trade business, D'Amore and Haynes, profited well. It was a functional cover-up for his work for the Union in the capture and return of Federal deserters and escaped prisoners of war, many of whom, like Stone, were in the New Orleans area. His amount of reward and bounty monies was not large, but he did acquire a substantial profit from it and had been doing so since the Union forces acquired New Orleans, just a little over a year ago. D'Amore's influence in the reward and bounty game was not very great, but he had enough informers and men to do the job.

His one method of operation was to find out about new arrivals to New Orleans and see if they would be of any benefit to him. If not, he wouldn't do anything about them. But if they had bounty on their heads, he would send a couple of men to find them and capture them any way they could. After acquiring a certain amount of 'freight', a boat would leave New Orleans and meet up with a Union boat, neither with flags up. The men would then be delivered with the proper amount of payment exchanged.

Stone went back to his room carrying the newspaper. He decided that would be the best way to find work. As he looked through it, he saw a small article about a body found on Bourbon St. He began to get nervous about being a suspect for the crime. The article said '... *the body, identified as John Caulfield, seemed to have been brutally beaten about the head.*'

'Aw, c'mon, who wrote this? It can't be the same guy; it didn't happen that way!' Stone said to himself. He was anxious about the two women being questioned. He began to wonder if he should get out of New Orleans.

'I jest can't seem ta escape trouble. Well by now, I guess I should expect it, but not ones this serious', he said to himself. He had come here to escape the injustice of the world. He thought he could blend in and find work in New Orleans; that this would be a safe place for him to survive and begin a new life. He was realizing what he should have known all along. There is no perfect place free of troubles. Now that he had some knowledge of the reward and bounty game, he wasn't so confident of his safety anymore.

That afternoon Ellen Marshell and her new gentleman friend, Donald Doyle, were at the office of D'Amore & Haynes, the former being his cousin. They were just discussing the weather and making small talk. Doyle had no idea of his cousin's sideline. As they talked Allen D'Amore wondered what had brought Ellen to New Orleans.

"Miss Marshell, you aren't from around here I take it. What brings you to New Orleans?"

"I knew, and had worked with a William Elliott. His office was on Bourbon Street, but I went by and found it vacant. Do you know where he is? He was in the same business you are in. He spoke of you from time to time," Ellen said smiling.

"Well now, Mr. Elliott left here about six months ago. He moved north to Chicago. I would be happy to have you do business with me, Miss Marshell."

Donald was quite surprised at Ellen and asked, "How long have you been in business? And what business are you two talking about?" Ellen ignored him and continued her conversation with D'Amore.

"Well Mr. D'Amore, I guess if we're going to do business together, I should give you some information about myself. I am a nurse at a Northern prison camp and, well, sometimes I help prisoners escape. In this case, I helped a young man from Tennessee. We caught a riverboat in Cairo, Illinois and came down here. We arrived Saturday night," she explained as his eyes lit up and he was all ears.

Doyle, listening to their discussion was confused. He couldn't figure out what they were talking about. Ellen turned to Donald and said, "That was that ragged man that was after me in the hotel. You know, the one I kissed and gave thirty dollars to?"

"Ah yes, I do remember. He looked like a tramp. I'm sure he's gone my dear. You won't find him now. Not in the middle of New Orleans." Doyle was shocked at her. He couldn't believe a woman would do such a thing. He was actually feeling sorry for the man and questioning her motives.

D'Amore sat at his desk listening with a smile and said, "Well Miss Marshell, you certainly are in a good position for this business and I am looking forward to working with you."

His office was on the riverfront, not very elaborate, but it had style and Ellen was impressed. She was happy she had found Doyle; without him she would not have met D'Amore and the trouble she had gone through would have been for nothing.

"Well Mr. D'Amore, if we are going to work together I must ask what you are paying before I lead you to anyone," she said smiling.

D'Amore smiled back and said, "Miss Marshell, you are quite the young business woman. You don't waste time; you get right to the point, don't you? Call me Al and may I call you Ellen? I like to be on a first name basis when I work with someone, especially a pretty woman like you."

Donald was beginning to wonder about Ellen. What kind of woman would lead someone on, making him think she was in love with him and provide an escape route, only to turn him in ... to collect what?

"Ellen, I pay a percentage of the amount of bounty on the deserter ... in this case an escapee. Has he killed any officers? How dangerous is he? It depends on how badly the North wants him. The more he is worth, the more I will pay. What did Elliott do to make it worthwhile for you? How did you meet him anyway?" Allen D'Amore had many questions for her.

"Well I was living in Chicago when I met Bill. It sounds like he went back to the hotel and saloon business he was in when I met him," mused Ellen.

"Yes, he bought another hotel there and is doing quite well. He wanted to get out of this 'business'. He made his share I guess. He owns two hotels now and a saloon."

"I was paid well. He gave me forty percent and the cost of my food and room while here".

"Now that is quite a deal and I guess if I want to do business with you, I will have to match it. I do business with a hand shake." Smiling, he reached out his hand to her and Ellen, smiling, took it.

"Now Ellen would you know where this man might be staying?"

"How are you going to approach him? Are you going to offer him a job?" she asked.

"That would be one way to get to him, but I have to find him first." Allen smiled and kissed her hand. "You are going to go through with this aren't you?"

"Of course I am. Why would I change my mind? I have no feelings for him. We split up Friday. I know he's still in town because he only had thirty dollars."

All this time, Doyle stood by listening and was stunned. He *never* met a woman like Ellen. 'How could she do this?' he thought to himself.

D'Amore excused himself and left the room for a couple minutes, then returned. "Could you give me his name, where he's from and just some type of description?"

"Isn't this going a little bit too far to pick up some tramp? Who in hell knows or cares where he is? Ellen hasn't seen him and we've had nothing to do with him." Doyle said, agitated and still not understanding completely the 'business' deal that was being negotiated.

"Look, cousin, I'm just doing the poor guy a favor. It won't hurt anything. I'll offer him a job of some kind."

After obtaining the needed information, Allen again left his office. Two rough looking men, probably from the docks were waiting outside. He handed them the paper with the description and other details about Stone and they left. They did not know where he was, but they usually didn't have any trouble finding anyone that D'Amore wanted. He paid well and the job wasn't that hard. Al returned to his office and the three of them had a couple of drinks.

Stone went back to the same restaurant and was having lunch, a couple of ham sandwiches and coffee. He wasn't too worried about anyone after him in New Orleans; he was more concerned about finding work. It was a bit more crowded in the place that afternoon. Lunch time was busier than breakfast.

Still in the same ragged clothes, he was scorned by some of the customers. They didn't say anything, but every once in a while, he would catch one of their glances. He was becoming very self-conscious of his appearance and decided to purchase some better clothes that afternoon.

It was about four o'clock and the two rough looking men from D'Amores' office were standing by Chez Louise's, the hotel where now just Ellen was staying.

Stone was on the other side of the town buying

new clothes. He bought a stylish twenty dollar suit for a night at Madeleine's Belles. The clerk seemed bothered by his presence. He did have an unpleasant odor, and his unshaven face and less than eloquent speech did stand out. It was one of the finer shops in New Orleans and the clerk's slight embarrassment was shared by some of the other customers.

"Sir, please do not take offense, but why don't you ... perhaps you should get yourself a shave and bath. It would really help your appearance," said the clerk with a slight French accent. Stone took his suggestion as an insult, but as he looked into the mirror, he had to agree.

"Yeah, that sounds like a real good idea. 'Course, I intended ta do that," he said with a polite, but sarcastic tone. The clerk coughed slightly and Stone paid for the clothes and suit. They were the less expensive line, but he couldn't afford the better. He just wanted out of the filthy clothes he was in and maybe people wouldn't stare at him. He left the store and went next door to the barbershop for a haircut and a bath. He changed into his new clothes there too and when he came out he looked very different than the man Ellen had described and far different than what D'Amores' two men were looking for.

Stone was still carrying his old clothes in his left arm and some other new ones in his right. He found a trash can and was going through his clothes deciding what to keep. He threw away his shirt and pants, but kept the old coat. He was also wearing a new pair of black boots. He was a totally different man and it felt good, clear down to his clean skin.

He went back to his room, packed a new carpet bag and checked out. He hadn't intended to leave this hotel, but decided he wanted something a little better. He was feeling good about himself and wanted to be able to make a good impression.

Stone had a little money left, thanks to John and took a room in one of the most luxurious hotels in New Orleans. He bought some cigars and strutted around like he was some important visitor. While walking down the street, he practiced a French accent. He was trying to mimic the clerk in the men's store. As he strolled, he noticed the better dressed ladies would smile at him now and respond to him when he tipped his hat. He had purchased a black hat with a brim. He was full of confidence and enjoying himself. For the first time in his life he felt well-to-do and no one around him knew any better. He thought he might change his name, but then decided that might be going a bit too far; no one knew him anyway.

He returned to the lobby of the luxurious Alexander Hotel of New Orleans located right in the heart of the city. He placed his bag in his room and then returned to the lobby. He wanted to watch the people and learn the mannerisms of the more 'pure bred' people coming in and out of the hotel.

Little did he know two men were combing the back streets looking for a dirty, raggedly clothed tramp. And here he was, a changed young man strutting around the better part of town looking as though he ran a business.

Stone certainly did not fit in completely. He did leave the old dirty coat in his room, but some of his actions weren't socially accepted by the people coming and going. He flicked his ash off his cigar onto the hotel desk. The clerk frowned at his actions and pointed to an ashtray on a side table nearby. He would use eccentricity to hide his lack of social grace. Stone wasn't really comfortable with the people around him as he knew his own shortcomings. He was beginning to get nervous, hoping not to make a fool of himself. Not having any job prospects was playing on his mind as well.

He thought he saw someone approaching him, but then he didn't see him anymore. Suddenly, an important looking man tapped him on his shoulder, startling Stone. The man motioned for him to follow. Stone diplomatically obliged. They went over to the register desk and the man motioned to the desk clerk.

"Mr. Stone?" the man with him finally asked.

"Yes indeed", replied Stone with a fair French accent. The man didn't seem too charmed by Stone's accent, causing him to become a little anxious.

"Sir, it's not that we are untrusting here; but I'm the manager, and we require a deposit for your room." The desk clerk seemed a bit edgy as the manager looked at him.

"Well," said Stone, "I am expecting within the day a payment for a cotton purchase. I can certainly assure you that I will pay the deposit and any other costs of my stay here. Now I am a very busy man and I could stay at the French consulate, but that would just upset my very heavy schedule." Stone was acting a bit disturbed by the insinuations made by the manager. His French accent added to his continental and important manner.

"I'm sorry, but I too have a business to run and I can't change our policy." He seemed determined to get his money.

Stone smiled and with his best French accent replied confidently, "Pardon, I am quite sorry for my irritation. Of course you want your money; you have a duty to perform. I assure you that you will be paid in the morning."

"I thought you said you would have the payment by tonight," reminded the manager.

"I said 'within the day'. I am usually finished with such transactions by seven. Now certainly, you are well aware that there are no banks open at night. You will have your money tomorrow morning," Stone said fervently.

The manager, not knowing how to handle the irregularity, reluctantly agreed to wait until the morning. He didn't know if he could trust him, but didn't want to cause a scene in front of the other guests. Stone smiled, bowing slightly and returned to the lobby.

Chapter X

An elderly man, apparently a business man, was talking to a couple of women, one in her twenties and the other middle aged. The man was English, and if one could hear them, the ladies were too. They appeared to be a family.

"My dear Leslie, we will surely have to find a young man for you tonight," said the smiling elderly man.

"Oh father, please do not embarrass me. You do this all of the time and it never works out. I do not want nor do I need an escort," replied the daughter.

"Now Leslie, he is right. You cannot go out without an escort," her mother cautioned her.

"Why do you not just go without me? It has been a long time since you two have been alone; having an evening out together would be nice," Leslie suggested. Her father was not really listening. He was scanning the lobby for an eligible gentleman of his daughter's age.

"Ah, look Martha, there is a young man. He

seems quite the gentleman for Leslie! Do you not think so?"

"Oh father, please do not! Mother, stop him! This is so embarrassing," she cried. Her father dashed off toward Stone.

"Now dear if you were married, your father and I would not have to find you an escort."

"I do not want to be married. Not unless it is with the right person; and you keep trying to match me up with anybody you see and I am just not interested," the young woman replied.

"Excuse me young man. My name is George K. Howles and my wife, daughter and I are planning to go out this evening. Our daughter has no escort and I was wondering if you would like to join us for dinner?"

"Why, thank you, Mr. Howles. Merci, I would love to join you and your family for dinner. I just have one meeting with a cotton broker and then I will be free for the remainder of the evening." Stone was enjoying his new found French accent and his dashing appearance, as he lingered in the hotel lobby nodding and smiling at the other guests. Richard was thinking of all the advantages of meeting this man's daughter when he appeared again with her at his side.

"Sorry, what is your name sir?" asked Mr. Howles. "I did not think to ask you."

"Pierre LeBon, sir."

"Well Monsieur LeBon, this is my daughter Leslie." 'Pierre' bowed slightly, looked at her with approval and smiled.

"Enchantéz." She looked up at him, smiled and then looked away. He couldn't tell if she was shy or just didn't want to be with anyone. She was a pretty young woman with blonde hair and hazel eyes that were highlighted by her pink dress, trimmed with lace around the neckline that exposed a single diamond necklace. She looked very feminine.

'Looks like I really fell inta somethin pretty good. Ma'be my luck's changin. Sure glad I was able ta pick up a few French words from that store clerk', Stone thought to himself.

"Well Miss Howles, you are from England I see."

"Yes, I am and you seem to be from France, but your accent is a little unfamiliar. What part of France are you from?" She seemed to be a little suspicious of Stone from the beginning.

This made him feel uneasy, but he thought it better to continue the charade. It really didn't matter, this was just going to be one evening and anybody could pretend for one evening. Besides he was just having fun with his new role, acting like he had style and class. After all, he thought, 'I done pretty well so far.' His new clothes, boots and hat gave him confidence. 'This is the kinda life I wanted ta live an even if it's jest fer one night, it's worth it all', thought Stone smiling.

"I am from the south side of Paris," replied Stone easily as he led her to a pair of empty chairs on the other side of the room.

"Oh, I see," Leslie responded, looking at him questioningly. Stone was fearful that Leslie could see right through it all, and that his accent and name was fake.

"Well, where is your father planning to spend the evening?" asked Stone as he tried to keep from feeling any more nervous. He wanted to divert her mind to something they could talk about. He didn't know a thing about France or its geography and wanted to get away from that subject.

"My father has been talking about a place called Madeline's Belles. Have you heard of it?" Leslie asked.

Stone's face became aglow with enthusiasm thinking he could intrigue her with his familiarity of New Orleans and Madeline's Belles. He had not been inside, but his brief view through the window allowed him to charm Leslie with the evening ahead.

On the other side of town, Ellen and Donald were preparing for another evening at Madeline's Belles. The couple had grown very close, but she still felt a concern for Stone. She wasn't comfortable working with Allen D'Amore. Ellen felt no remorse telling D'Amore she got forty percent from Elliot when it had been much less. She almost wished she hadn't told him anything about Richard. Doyle had class and money; that was what she wanted. The feeling of being double-crossed came over her. Ellen didn't really know how he got his money and really didn't care. He was somebody for her while she was in New Orleans.

Donald Doyle was a gun runner. He was involved with the transport of guns to and from Bermuda. No one knew this. Not even his cousin D'Amore. He was in and out of New Orleans several times a month and never had any close friends; and he didn't want any. Relationships were dangerous during this time and Ellen was the first woman he had had a close encounter with. She was easy and never asked any questions. He enjoyed her company. She intrigued him.

"My dear Ellen, while you were resting this afternoon I slipped into town and bought you this."

Ellen looked at the black velvet box. Her eyes widened as she opened the lid. It was a beautiful sparkling stone embedded in a fleur-de-lis design in gold on a chain.

"Oh Donald, it's beautiful. I am so surprised; I am at a loss for words."

"Darling, we are going out this evening and I wanted you to have something nice. You are a beautiful woman Ellen. This will look nice around your neck." Donald put the necklace on her.

"Oh thank you Donald. Is it a real ruby?" she asked feeling and touching the stone as he closed the clasp.

"Why my dear Ellen, it wouldn't be anything else." He smiled and looked at her with approval, pleased with his purchase.

The evening dinner hour came and Stone was riding with the Howles' family together in a carriage toward the popular Madeline's Belles. Across town at the same moment Ellen and Donald were coming in his carriage.

At Madeline's Belles a crowd had formed as it did every night. The Howles' and Stone arrived at about eight o'clock.

"Pierre, my dear man, what do you feel like having tonight? I think I will have a Delmonico steak," Mr. Howles said.

"Oui, I believe I will have the same," Richard agreed with Howles. Leslie and her mother decided on duck for dinner.

"Oh, waiter! We are ready to order, please." Mr. Howles motioned to the waiter. "We would like two Delmonico steaks, rare and the ladies would like duck. Oh yes, and bring us a bottle of your best wine, too." He was smiling, feeling good about LeBon as Leslie's escort. He had chosen the right man for Leslie he thought.

Soon a band began to play and when dinner was over Mr. and Mrs. Howles, Leslie and 'Pierre' began to enjoy an evening of dance and wine.

Donald and Ellen made it to Madeline's Belles at

eight thirty, about a half hour after the Howles' party was seated.

"Donald, that looks like Richard. If you think your cousin has a job for him why don't you go over and introduce yourself and tell him about your cousin's job offer?" asked Ellen. She recognized Stone on the dance floor.

"Aw, Ellen. I can't go over and offer him a job. Besides, he seems to be doing pretty well for himself. He's with someone and I don't want to interrupt anything," Doyle replied uncomfortably.

Just then D'Amore stopped at Ellen and Donald's table. "Well Don, nice to see you. How are you enjoying the evening?" He smiled at his cousin, as he raised Ellen's hand to kiss it.

"Fine, Mr. D'Amore. Oh I'm sorry, Allen," Ellen replied with a smile.

Doyle nodded and said, "I'm surprised to see you here cousin.'

"Oh, I figured if my cousin was going to be charming some beautiful young lady, why should I be sitting in that lonely office by myself," Allen chuckled aloud. "So here I am. I thought you might be here."

Doyle tapped D'Amore's arm and pointed to Stone who was dancing with Leslie. "Well, Allen. There's the man you wanted to give that job to," Doyle said. "He surely doesn't seem the material for a deck hand."

"Who said I was looking for deck hands?" Allen glanced over at Ellen with a doubting look.

"And my dear Ellen, if that's Stone out there dancing, he sure doesn't look like a tramp to me. He doesn't match the description you gave. What do you think he did? And where do you think he got the money to make himself over like that? You weren't trying to trick me were you?" smiled D'Amore.

"Well, he has certainly changed, but that is him." He looked at her and just shrugged his shoulders at her answer.

"He is dancing with quite a pretty lady. Do you think he'd mind if I would cut in?" Allen asked.

"I don't know. I never saw her before. I don't know where he would find a woman like that," Ellen answered with indifference.

Allen approached the couple dancing and politely cut in. Stone was puzzled as to who this man was, but politely gave Leslie to him.

"My dear, I hope you don't mind my cutting in?" asked D'Amore trying unsuccessfully to charm Leslie. "I can't help noticing the young man you are with. I'd like to say hello, but I can't remember his name. He used to do business with one of my partners." He smiled as they danced across the floor.

"His name is Pierre LeBon," she said softly. Allen acted charmed by her accent.

"Ah, an English lady," Allen smiled but knew he was not charming her. She was putting up with him, anxious for the dance to end. "Could you tell me where he's staying? I know I shouldn't be asking you all these questions. You dance very well my dear."

"We're staying at the Alexander Hotel. Mr. ...?" Leslie questioned.

"Allen D'Amore, my dear, call me Allen." He smiled and waited for Leslie to offer her name then continued, "You said you both were staying at the Alexander Hotel. Are you two married?"

Leslie stopped dancing and looked up at him in surprise. "Sir, we are not married. And I do not see where it is any of your business. You are being rude, Mr. D'Amore."

"I'm sorry my dear, you are right, and I apologize."

Leslie then smiled and said, "That is alright Mr. D'Amore. Excuse me please. I must return to my party." She moved off the dance floor in search of 'Pierre'.

As she was walking away, D'Amore smiled and said, "Call me Allen." His voice trailed off as she left. Allen slightly embarrassed, returned to Ellen and Donald's table.

"Didn't charm the lady, huh Allen?" Doyle asked smiling.

"Don't let it bother you, cousin!" Allen shot back.

Doyle kept his grin as D'Amore wandered away from their table and went to the bar to exchange conversation with a tough looking well-dressed man. They seemed to know each other and both of them kept glancing at Stone. Soon, Allen came back to his cousin's table, while the man he had just talked to, along with a couple of other rough looking men, left Madeline's Belles.

It was about an hour later when Stone and Leslie excused themselves from her parents' table. They went out onto Bourbon Street for some fresh air and privacy. The only privacy you could find on such a warm night on a crowded street like this, would be around strangers and uninterested couples, as the sidewalks of Bourbon Street were full of people.

From Madeline's Belles, Leslie and her escort walked about two blocks. They came to an old, abandoned church that seemed to have a sense of sanctuary from life, and from a large, but heavily impersonal town.

Ellen seemed to be drifting away in thought as Donald looked at her. "Ellen, my dear," he said bringing her back as she smiled.

"I'm sorry," she said quietly and apologetically. Her soft voice and feminine features brought a thankful smile to Doyle's face.

"I'm a very lucky man, Ellen. A very lucky

man," he said softly, now holding her hand. She looked down at his hand on hers and the smile left her face. Donald's smile also disappeared as he sensed all was not well between them.

"What's on your mind, love?" Ellen quickly drew her hand from his and placed both of her hands on her lap.

"Your cousin is interested in Stone; too interested. And I don't think I want to do business with him. I don't trust him."

"Oh he just wants to give him a job. There's nothing to worry your pretty little head about," he said as he tried to pick up her hand. Ellen suddenly stood up and hurriedly moved toward the front entrance where she had noticed Richard had been a few minutes ago with the young woman. She desperately looked up and down the street. Doyle joined her and was irritated at her behavior.

"Ellen, what are you doing?" he was losing patience with her.

"I came out here to get some air. That's all."

"Or Stone," said Donald.

"Oh don't be silly," she returned and took his hand, but Doyle knew she was not being sincere. He knew she was concerned about Stone. They walked back inside Madeline's Belles and sat down. He ordered them another drink.

Inside the dark and abandoned church, 'Pierre' and Leslie were kissing intently when two men silently entered through the half opened door. Stone heard the wooden floor creak and opened one eye toward the door. While Leslie was totally unsuspecting, he could see two large figured silhouettes standing there. The men then slowly moved toward the young couple near the altar. It was dark and that door was the only possible exit. The windows, though without glass were too high for a quick escape from their place on the floor. Leslie now saw the approaching figures and screamed. Suddenly, Stone felt a whip crack and wrap around his shoulders as the other large figure covered Leslie's mouth. He struggled, but was unable to remove the entwining whip. And just then a fist slammed into his mid-section causing him to lose his wind and fall to the floor.

Leslie was terrified as the other man threw her to the ground where she pretended to lie unconscious, acting as though she had hit her head. Stone was quickly gagged and bound, and placed in a burlap sack. The two large figures, totally silent, removed 'Pierre' by one of them placing him over his shoulder and carrying him out of the church.

The young woman peeked and saw the two men and the sack leaving the church. Leslie looked around for her escort, thinking they were robbed and he might be lying somewhere. She couldn't find him anywhere and soon realized she was alone in the dark, deserted church. 'Oh no', she moaned to herself as she ran from the abandoned church back to Madeline's Belles.

Her dress was soiled and torn, and tears were

running down her cheeks as she ran through the doors of Madeline's Belles and to her parents. The band had stopped playing and couples close by were watching.

"Oh, my baby girl! What happened to you and where is LeBon? What did he do to you?" Howles was trying to comfort his daughter.

He wiped her tears and she cried, "Oh Daddy they took him away. We went for a walk and wandered into an abandoned church. Two men came and took him. They knocked me down and I ... I pretended to be hurt."

"We will have to contact the sheriff. Now stop crying. We will find him. Everything will be alright."

Ellen saw Leslie run to her father without Richard. She watched intently and could almost hear her father's words.

"Ellen, what's going on?" asked Donald.

Ellen gave him an 'I-told-you-so' look and said, "I know your cousin did something or had someone do something to Richard!"

"What? How the hell do you figure that? You don't know him!" Doyle was getting angry with Ellen. But he really had no idea what his cousin was involved in, or what Ellen was really doing in New Orleans. Each was deceiving the other.

"I just know. I know how his kind works," Ellen answered with fear and concern.

She felt betrayed and angry that this had happened without her knowledge. Elliott didn't work that way. They worked together and then after the capture was complete, she received her pay. She had a strong feeling D'Amore wasn't giving her a cut in this. She was sorry she had ever told him anything!

An empty sack was now laying on the side walk about a block from the abandoned church, without a trace of Stone or the men that attacked him.

Ellen could no long contain herself. She jumped from their table and darted over to talk to Leslie.

"My name is Ellen and I know the man you were with. What happened?"

"They took 'Pierre' away. He is hurt and he is gone and he was such a nice man," cried Leslie.

"Dear, his name was not Pierre. His name is Richard Stone."

"Well, he told us his name was Pierre LeBon, from Paris." Leslie stopped crying and began to wonder what was going on. Still sobbing she continued, "They had a whip, used it and then they hit him and put him in a sack. It was terrible." She began to cry again, turning to her mother for comfort.

Ellen was now absolutely positive that Allen had swindled her all along.

She left Madeline's Belles to go look for Stone.

She didn't know that Doyle was following her. With a hurried step, Ellen walked toward the abandoned church. Donald caught up with her and placed his hands on her shoulders and tried to calm her.

"Alright! Alright! I believe someone is after Stone, but it can't be my cousin. Al wouldn't do such a thing. And why are you so worried about him? I thought you were in love with me."

"You don't know all the businesses he's in. You don't really know what he does here. You only know what he tells you," declared Ellen. "In fact, none of us really know what the other is here for. Don't you think I wonder how you got the money to buy this necklace? You don't love me, Donald and I don't love you. Let's face it. We are both using each other. I learned a long time ago. You don't ask questions. I don't know what you're doing here and I don't care. We are all three playing a game; a survival game. And when I leave New Orleans, I will never see you again, so it doesn't matter."

She looked at him intently, "Oh come on Donald, we both know. It's a tough world out there huh?" She softened and smiled at him. "Honey, you don't know it, but Allen's a double crosser and I'm telling you, don't ever do business with him."

Inside Madeleine's Belles, Leslie and her family were preparing to leave. The sheriff and some of his detectives were still questioning Leslie. Mr. Howles had given them their names and where they were staying. He also told them that the missing man introduced himself to them as Pierre LeBon, but he found out later his real name was Richard Stone. They questioned Leslie for about ten minutes and then the Howles went back to the Alexander Hotel.

Ellen and Donald left for their room at Chez Louise's. Ellen realized Richard was gone, and she had been double crossed and there was nothing she could do about it. She silently decided that when she left New Orleans, she would head for Chicago. Ellen knew Bill Elliott. He would help her get a new life. Maybe she could work for Dr. Welky. She helped him before. He had taught her everything she knew about nursing and medicine. Yes, she thought, Chicago was the place for her.

Chapter XI

It was Saturday morning, the Fourth of July, 1863 and Richard Harold Stone found himself chained and bound, tossed in the back of a wagon. The wagon was crowded with black and white men, all shackled, just as he was. They were cramped together, some semi-conscious.

What a disgrace to humanity that nine men would be transported to a ship's hold in such a manner. It appeared that cocaine was used to keep them groggy and quiet on the docks, or somebody would have suspected something of this and the other four wagons covered with canvas filled with the same type of cargo.

This was a very efficient and neat operation Allen D'Amore built. He was quite cunning and a man without conscience. He would stop at nothing to get what he wanted. He laughed to himself thinking of how easy it was to swindle Ellen Marshel.

At about one o'clock that afternoon, a cargo ship left New Orleans with its freight to meet a Federal vessel somewhere near the Florida coast. It was later, about midnight on July 6, when the cargo ship dropped anchor off the coast of Florida.

Stone started to come around and was becoming aware of his surroundings. He knew he was on a ship, but not sure whether the rocking that he felt was in his head or from the wave motions of the water. He felt as though he had been drugged, but had no idea what it was. He had no experience with cocaine or any other drug for that matter. He did try 'Mexican Weed' a couple of times. He tried to figure out where he was and what was happening, but fell back into a semi-conscious state.

In the hold, the stench of sweat and human feces began to get to him. He felt sick to his stomach and wanted to vomit. He knew he had been captured with all the rope bounds and chain; somebody wanted him badly. Would they go to all this trouble for a prisoner of war? 'Wait! Bounty money … Ellen! I sure did fall into a trap this time. I should've known better', he muttered to himself.

He was more aware and conscious of his surroundings than his captors supposed. He didn't know the time of day, the hold was closed and it was pitch black.

It was still dark when the nine men were brought to the deck. The boat was anchored, but Stone couldn't figure out where they were. The air was fresh and his nausea began to subside. Some were asking questions and those who did got roughed up; so Stone learned quickly to keep his mouth shut.

Tuesday morning the escaped prisoners-of-war and Federal deserters were transferred to a Union cargo ship. Their destination was the New Jersey coast. They were shoved down to the hold. Stone could see immediately this ship was made especially for the transportation of prisoners. The only difference between this ship's hold and the one from New Orleans, was that this one had chains fixed into the wall so one could sit and stretch out.

It was very early Thursday morning July 9, when the prisoners were told they would be leaving the ship and be put on a train. They had reached the New Jersey coast not far from the Delaware Bay.

Soon they were taken by smaller boats and delivered to guards and Federal marshals who were waiting for them on the beach. Their leg irons were removed and they marched into a nearby town to await the train. It was before noon when the prisoners, all forty-five, were led to a freight car ... destination, Harrisburg Federal Prison.

By the following evening the prisoners found themselves in Harrisburg, Pennsylvania being processed into the Federal prison system. Wearing the dirty clothes they had arrived in, they had supper in the large dirty mess hall. 'This sure ain't Young's Prison', thought Stone. 'Young's was much better. I shoulda never left there with Ellen.'

From his cell, Stone could see the prison yards and the wooden framework of the new, unfinished gallows. He felt empty inside ... not disappointed or frightened, just empty. It was not a surprise, but it was unexpected. Stone sat in his cell and at times went to his window and looked out into the yard with its gallows staring back at him. He waited for some feelings to come over him, but he was numb and empty. After getting up several times, he looked out at the yard, then would sit on his bunk and stare at the floor and walls around him. He was waiting for the cold stone walls to make him laugh or cry, or the bars in the windows and door to make him scream. Stone wanted to die ... to die a quick and silent death ... maybe the sooner, the better. Again, he stood up and looked through the bars in his window. He started to grin, looking at the ever present gallows, and then broke into laughter. He laughed so hard it was hurting his stomach. Stone had never known himself to laugh so hard for so long. It scared him. He began to laugh and cry hysterically at the same time. The pain in his stomach was unbearable. He had stopped laughing and was crying ... crying so hard he couldn't see for the tears. He was choking now and slumped down on his cot. A very sick feeling came over him ... a depressing, lonely, hollow feeling.

Stone went to his cell door and shouted out for the guard, but nobody answered. He screamed and shouted, but nobody came. He tried to pull himself together, but was beginning to think that it was fruitless. Holding tightly to the bars of his cell, he thought, 'I gotta git outta here. But how? I'd only git captured again.'

He was really feeling hopeless. There were multiple charges against him, but he didn't know what they were. He looked at the gallows again; that would be his end if he stayed in this place. 'I bet Ellen got a lotta bounty fer me', he muttered to himself.

Stone was lying on his cot quietly sobbing. He sat up, looked at the three dirty walls and the bars in front. '**Hear this**!' he shouted, 'I'm gonna beat ya at yer own game, bastards! **I'll win**! *I will*! I'll git outta here. *Nothin* er *nobody* holds me. I'll get outta this place!' He was shouting to empty walls. He laid back down exhausted and slept.

The following morning at about eight o'clock, a guard opened Stone's cell door and led him down a long hallway of empty cells, up a flight of stairs and down another hallway and more empty cells.

"Where's everybody?" Stone asked the guard.

"Around."

"Where?" asked Stone, but the guard was silent. This gave Stone an eerie feeling. Walking down all these halls past more empty cells made him realize how nearly impossible it would be to escape. 'Too many hallways an too many guards', he thought.

They soon arrived at the office of a Union Army officer, Major Paul Webb. The guard knocked on the door, then a voice from inside said, 'Come in.' The guard opened the door and shoved Stone roughly through the doorway.

"Sit down, Stone," ordered the major. Webb had a very stern look on his face adding to Richard's nervousness.

"I'm Major Paul Webb and I'm the warden here," he said introducing himself as he was reviewing the records of the newly captured men. "Now your name is Richard Harold Stone. Is that right?" Stone swallowed hard and nodded. The Major was intimidating. Young's Prison sure was different.

"I don't want a nod, Stone. I want an answer. I can't hear you Stone."

"Yes suh," Stone replied aloud this time.

"Stone, you escaped from Young's Prison in Illinois about a week or so ago. On June 28th, is that right?" asked the major with a firm voice. Stone looked down at his chained hands and then looked into the officer's face.

"Yes, Suh," Stone said loudly.

Maj. Webb smiled, "That's better. We know all about you Stone. A young woman by the name of Ellen Marshell helped you escape, didn't she?" To this, Stone did not answer.

"Why are you remaining silent about her? We suspect she's in the bounty hunting business and we'd like to find her. She is costing us money. We feel sure that she has helped several escapees, and then collects her share of the bounty when the men are caught. What do you think of that Stone? That should make you angry to think someone would help you escape only to turn you in to collect off your head. Now that makes me angry; why doesn't it make you angry? Now tell us where she is?" Major Webb finished loudly.

"I don't know where she is. We split in New Orlins long before I wuz captured. She went with someone else an I don't remember his name."

Major Webb stood up from his desk and told the guard to get Mr. Palmer. Palmer came in and regarded Stone, who was very startled to see him here. He saw him at Young's Prison and he knew Palmer didn't like him then.

After the major left, the guard remained standing at attention near the door of the office.

"Remember me Stone?" asked Palmer with a sly look. He hadn't changed his demeanor since their last confrontation at Young's.

"Yes suh, I do," replied Stone with a clear, loud voice.

"Good. Let me assure you that from *here* you will *not* escape. There is no way out ... and there are no Ellens! I guarantee it. Now we know all about you Stone. If there is anything we don't know, we will find it out, won't we?" Stone didn't answer, but just stared at him.

"Stone, you answer me!" Palmer demanded loudly.

"I'm sure ya will, Suh," said Stone with a note of slight defiance in his voice.

Palmer's face grew red with anger as he remarked, "You still are an arrogant little bastard, aren't you?"

"Suh, I'm just me."

The man's irritation with Stone was increasing. He stood up from behind the major's desk, leaned forward and with forced control, stared straight into Stone's eyes. "Why you little bastard, I'm going to break you. I can't stand that arrogant attitude of yours. When you leave here, you will be a changed man Stone. I promise you that!"

"Suh, all I done was ta escape from my enemy's prison. I done what any man woulda done under the circumstances. The only dif'rence is ... I got caught."

"Your response shows nothing but defiance and insolence to authority! There are several charges against you Stone and I am sure you are aware of that. Guard, get Major Webb. I have no more to say to this ... this prisoner."

Mr. Palmer, still standing by the side of the desk and Stone sitting in front of it waited in silence. Webb came back into the room.

"An arrogant little bastard, wouldn't you say Major," asked Palmer. The officer nodded in agreement and dismissed the guard.

"Alright, Mr. Palmer. Stone get up!" ordered the major. "No one told you that you could sit down."

Stone quickly jumped to his feet and Palmer left the room.

Looking him eye to eye, Major Webb said, "Stone there is one way you can save yourself a lot of problems, and that is to swear allegiance to the United

States of America. Right now you are an enemy and a prisoner of the Union. Think about what I've said. Think about it real hard. Mr. Palmer takes over tomorrow and I don't think you two get along very well. So make it easy on yourself, Stone."

"Yes suh, I will," Stone replied with unfelt duty, "I'll think about it." The major looked at him surprised at his answer. He thought Stone meant he would swear allegiance.

Stone was then led back to his cell. On the way, they passed another prisoner and guard going toward the major's office, still bound the same way he was.

Once back in his cell, Stone was thinking about how he was found in New Orleans. It had been more than a week and so much had happened in so little time. He was amazed at the efficiency of his capture and how quickly he was returned to prison … a Federal prison in Pennsylvania at that. He feared he would be here a very long time.

He hadn't really thought Ellen was involved until now. He didn't want to think she was capable of stooping so low as to con prisoners into escaping. He thought of their lovemaking and all the sweet words said to each other. He would rather think she made her money the way she had told him, in the brothels of Chicago. He laid back on his bunk. Maybe one of those men who captured him was Ellen's new boyfriend. Donald Doyle could have been one of them. Stone could only see two forms in that dark church. It all happened so quickly, he didn't see their faces or how they were dressed or anything. The thought of Ellen's deceit made him sick to his stomach. He rolled over in his bunk waiting for morning to come as he knew this would be a sleepless night.

Chapter XII

Stone had been at Harrisburg for three months and the conditions of his confinement had not changed. It was October and the damp, dreary fall weather was affecting Stone. His morale had been going downhill ever since his capture; and it seemed to him that the use of an intelligent, clever means of escape had given way to hostile means.

Stone was unwilling to accept his predicament and though down trodden, he ran scenarios of successful escape plans through his mind. He drew a little map on the back of a piece of paperboard he had gotten in the mess hall. He had it tucked in his pocket. He had already memorized the hallways and doors to get to the outside of the mess hall and to the officers' rooms. 'Even if I died tryin, it'd be worth it.' He knew the half-built gallows outside his window were for psychological fear to the prisoners. He never really believed that a death sentence was awaiting him. He would get out ... somehow.

For the last three months, Stone surveyed the stone walls and buildings. This was a much more secure prison, with the barred windows and doors. An escape like the one from Young's would be insane here. He would have to have the cooperation of other inmates in order to help in a tunneling project. Climbing the wall, which was well guarded, would be suicide. He constantly looked for weaknesses in the supervision -- where the guards were located, the number of guards in the hallways. 'Yes', said Stone aloud to his cell, 'I will get outta here. I'll prove that Palmer wrong!'

Stone was not in solitary confinement, but he was alone most of the time. The cells were filling up with prisoners from Gettysburg. There were so many the Union didn't know what to do with them all, so they were brought to Harrisburg. He heard it was quite a battle, but didn't know which side won; only that President Lincoln had been there.

The only time Stone saw or interacted with other prisoners was during mess. He just figured with his record of escape, they didn't want him around others. Most of the other prisoners were alone too except for mess time. This kept them from working together to plan a way out, he thought, and it would prevent riots.

One of Mr. Palmer's new rules was 'a prisoner was not allowed out into the compound'. He was clamping down on other things, too. Palmer's interrogations had stepped up, and over and over he would ask the prisoner to pledge allegiance to the United States of America. Once the prisoner gave his pledge, he was moved to a section where he could mingle with the other prisoners. Otherwise, they were kept as Stone was, chained by his feet and hands when out of his cell.

A Bible, a pad and a pencil were Stone's only companions. His bunk was hard, but after a while he had gotten used to it. The only visitor was a guard who carried a sawed off shot-gun and Stone envied that gun. The guard was talkative at times, but not really friendly. He would stop at Stone's cell and make a comment or two, and then walk on. Stone wanted that gun.

'The weakest point in this place is the doorways an gates. If I could get enough ... no, that wuz really a crazy idea', he muttered to himself shaking his head wildly. 'They prob'bly thought o that; I'd get really killed, that way!' As he ran more ideas through his head, he'd say, 'Nope, not that way neither, nope!' and 'Well, I don't know if I could git enough ammunition' and 'Ma'be, I better play it day ta day.'

Stone's rambling thoughts were continually on how to escape. He decided the best way was the way he did it at Young's ... 'right through the front gate!' What held Stone back was the idea that 'ma'be it was too simple'. He became intoxicated with the idea of fleeing from this place. He dreamed about it, talked about it, planned it over and over in his mind. 'WOW! This seems so easy! My Lord, what an idea', he pondered, smiling.

His spirits lifted every time he thought of the escape. He was well aware of the odds against him. Every gate had a guard and every gate, door and cell was locked at all times. His next step was to observe the guards and find out how many different keys they had. He figured he had to have a key to the front gate as well. Stone made up his mind a long time ago, that this time, he would do it alone.

'A strategy, a procedure, a good solid plan …
that's all I need.' As usual, he had been thinking and
talking to himself most of the day. It was a weekday
and he would be in evening mess in a half hour. He
laid back on his bunk and closed his eyes waiting for
the guard. 'Tonight is not the time; too soon.' He
decided to spend the next couple of days watching the
guards and figure out how to get their keys. He had
been studying the layout he had drawn of the hallways
and doors. He needed to figure out the most efficient
and fastest route from his cell to the front gate.

He was obsessed with leaving this place; it was
continually on his mind. During supper, surveying the
hall, he thought of taking a hostage. He would not take
the guard though, that would be too dangerous. Who
could he take as a hostage? Well he would have to think
about that. Taking another prisoner wouldn't work at
all; they wouldn't hesitate to kill them both. 'If I take a
hostage, it'd hafta be a guard.' He had the lay-out of
the prison memorized and was concentrating on the
guards. How well equipped were they? Stone kept a
close eye on the one guard he had seen most of the day.
That sawed off shot-gun would really help him escape.
'In fact, I can't leave here without that gun! I have ta
have that gun ta git outta here without gittin m'self
killed.'

Stone had no one to talk to, so his thoughts were
all fixated on escape; it was all that was on his chaotic
mind. With that gun, he couldn't miss. And the heavy
barrel would be useful if he had to crack some heads.
It was that shotgun that Stone based his escape around.
'That gun an keep it simple. Yep, keep it simple. Down

the hall as fast as I can an out the front gate.' He knew if he messed it up this time, there'd never be another chance.

Much planning laid ahead for Stone, for he had to have some idea of the number of guards that were at the prison, how they armed and whether to make his move at night or during the day. He had decided against a hostage or escaping with another prisoner. He was afraid to reveal his plan to anyone. 'What if they'd squeal on me ta make their stay easier?' He knew Palmer and his tactics. He would do about anything to get the prisoners to talk. 'No, sharin ma plan with somebody'd be too dangerous.' He would have to do this himself. He knew he was on his own. He had one chance and if it failed ....

October passed and Stone had not made any attempt. He appeared to all to be a 'good prisoner'. He was still studying the prison's lay-out to the guard's stations. He drew a map of his escape route on a back page in his Bible.

His plan was to strangle the guard in his cell with the chain that connected his handcuffs. That was step one. Then he would switch clothes with the guard. He could use the keys and carry the shotgun without question right out of the prison. The last phase of the plan, walking out the front gate, would be the most dangerous. He didn't know what to expect from the guards on the wall. This plan would have to be played out moment by moment, and maybe with the use of another prisoner. Stone decided that that might prove to be quite dangerous.

Stone wanted to escape before the cold weather set in. Pennsylvania could get very cold, colder than Tennessee. His plans were to escape sometime in the next week or two. But, maybe if he felt good enough and the conditions were right, maybe even in the next couple of days. His plans after that were vague. He would probably head for New Orleans. He liked it there and it was a place like no other. Even after all the problems he had there, he still liked the city and was anxious to see the Mardi Gras. He would start anew and the problems he had before, well … he would just accept as experience. New Orleans and the way of life there, still best represented freedom to him. It was a kind of place a man could be himself and still feel a kinship with everybody else. His idealistic notions about the town, the romance and his independence were all that kept Stone's spirits alive.

The problems he might encounter walking out the front gate in the daytime bothered Stone. Those guards on the walls could surely see him well enough to get a good aim; and one shot at him would be fatal. He steered his thoughts more to a night escape, thinking his face would not be so recognizable and the guards would not be as accurate with their aim. Stone had watched the night guards for a couple of weeks now and they seemed to be lazier than the day guards. Night shift was boring and after being up most of the day, the night guards would be drowsy and Stone felt he had a better chance at night. 'Yep, a night escape it's gotta be!'

The days passed and one night in November, Stone called from his cell getting the attention of a semi-awake guard just outside the door of his cell block. He still had the whole cell block to himself. The prisoners from Gettysburg were held in another section of the building.

"Alright! Alright! Keep your mouth shut. Hold it down," as the drowsy guard walked the hall to the shouting and moaning Stone. He unlocked the gate to the cell block and entered, then he shuffled to Stone's cell.

"What's the matter with ya? **What d'ya want?**" shouted the guard. He was a large man, in his late thirties. Stone was doubled over on his bunk, trying to talk through his moaning. This guard was also carrying his shot-gun. As Stone looked at him, he noticed the row of ammunition on his belt.

"Somethin's wrong in ma chest," he moaned as the guard opened the cell door keeping his gun aimed at Stone.

"Ya better not be havin a heart attack on me boy!"

"I don't rightly know. It hurts so bad," Stone moaned convincingly.

"Alright, try to get up an walk. We'll go to the dispensary," ordered the soldier. The prisoner stood up and went ahead of him to the dispensary. The guard held his gun to Stone's back all the way there.

Stone didn't know whether to attempt the escape

tonight or not. So, as circumstances were not with him, he used the occasion to see how the prison looked at night. The way to the dispensary was on the same route to the front gate, relative to Stone's place of confinement within the prison. The guards had never held their shot-guns on him before, so if this guard used this method, Stone would have to take that into consideration, too.

After about a half hour wait, the doctor finally examined Stone. He put his stethoscope down and said, "You've got gas my boy. That's all; just gas. Get him back to his cell Charley." The doctor seemed disturbed by Stone's malady. And with the guard's shotgun again at his back, the prisoner was returned to his cell. He still moaned a bit, after all, he had to have his gas attack.

It was on this night that Stone decided to make his escape within the next three days. He felt the time had come and that the circumstances and conditions seemed right. His morale was high even though he realized the danger involved. Stone was ready and he would succeed!

The following day, Stone was building up the courage within him. He was also reflecting on the way he had lived his life ... always struggling in search of a better way of life. But somehow, he always felt cheated. There had been days when he didn't have anything to eat. He always had hand me downs for clothes, except for the time he went all out in New Orleans. He smiled as he recalled that one afternoon; how much fun he had had, and then to end up captured. He didn't want to be involved in the war, he wouldn't gain a thing by it, win or lose. But somehow he found himself right smack in the middle of it all. It seemed like more times than not, he was always in some kind of trouble. From the time he was small, in the orphanage, always in trouble. He didn't look for it, it found him. He thought over his life and said aloud, 'I gotta stop feelin sorry fer m'self; I gotta stay focused on the task ahead. Freedom!'

During Stone's stay, he had been taken back to Mr. Palmer's office and questioned several times; trying to get him to admit to some kind of spying or espionage against the United States of America. Palmer wanted him to admit to something, but Stone refused. They didn't want to believe that Stone was just a foot soldier. He didn't even consider himself that; he had never been involved in any real battle, not even a skirmish. Mr. Palmer once offered an ease of sentence, which had never been determined, for an admission. But Stone continually refused to cooperate. He had nothing against the democratic system; it was the methods he disagreed with. He resented being held captive, when he didn't feel he had done anything wrong. Any of the conflicts he had been involved in were results of being captured. He was imprisoned before he ever had a chance to experience a battle. This last capture instilled a disgust in Stone. Who was responsible for it? He would never know.

The 'interviews' with Palmer happened about two or three times a week. And for the last few times it was without handcuffs or 'lock-irons' as sometimes referred to by the guards. His ankles were without chains as well. The meetings were mainly about Mr. Palmer detesting Stone's attitude and his refusal to cooperate. Stone hated Palmer's sarcastic and belittling interrogation sessions, but was able to keep his hostile feelings to himself. He would then be escorted back to his cell, supposedly to await the end of the war, which was the only clear objective to his untried case. The charges against him were unclear to Stone. He knew one charge was escaping from a Federal prison. And all the meetings he had with Palmer centered around his supposedly 'subversive activities'. Palmer felt sure Stone had information the Union needed and he let him know that. Stone repeatedly said he knew nothing, but he knew Palmer didn't believe him. His escape from Young's Prison never came up again since its mention on the day he was brought to Harrisburg.

It was Friday night, November 6th, 1863 and Stone sat on his bunk, preparing to make his way to freedom ... or death. It had been raining throughout the day and now at ten o'clock, it was bitter cold outside. The rain was heavy with thunder and lightning all around. Stone was nervous and for the first time, felt unsure of himself. The moment of truth had arrived, and once he started, he knew there was no turning back.

The palms of his hands were sweating and he rubbed them against his pants, the same ones he had bought in New Orleans. His prison uniform, like the other inmates, had never come. Stone figured the money was spent for the Union soldiers. The prison was secure and well-guarded, and they never had had anyone successfully escape. Therefore Palmer felt it was a waste to buy uniforms for the prisoners. All the prisoners were dressed with the same clothes they had on when they arrived.

Stone was unsure of how to even begin his escape. He had to go tonight. The weather was perfect for it. He wondered how the guard would react to him. Would he do anything different than he normally did on his routine checks? Stone thought about the 'gas' attack. The same soldier was on duty every night except for weekends. He had had occasional attacks so anyone would think it was 'normal' for Stone. The guard was getting annoyed at his moaning, but he didn't know what else to try. He had to get his attention somehow. It had been four nights since Stone had a good attack. All the ones he had, except for the first one, had not been severe enough to warrant a trip to the dispensary. Stone decided to have a really bad attack tonight.

First there was a low moan; then Stone began to moan in earnest. The regular guard outside began to listen and tried to ignore it. The prisoner's attack got worse; the loud moans and groans annoyed the guard until he was unable to overlook it.

"Hey, Stone!" the guard called as he paused to hear an answer. Stone's response was a louder groan and he began to wail and cough. This was the most severe attack he ever had. The soldier was becoming alarmed, but tried without success to quiet Stone. He tried to ignore him, but Stone's wails became so intense the guard had to respond.

"Hey, Stone. Shut-up! You got gas. That's all; you aint gonna die." The guard didn't really know how to respond. Stone was never this bad before.

"Alright, alright! I'm comin'! **I'm comin'!**" shouted the guard. He unlocked the gate and went to Stone's cell. He didn't unlock his cell, but stood looking at the prisoner to try to determine how bad the attack was.

"I gotta go ... ta the ... 'spensary," Stone choked, as he struggled from his bunk to the bars, collapsing onto the floor. Though a bit melodramatic, his acting convinced the guard. He unlocked the cell and laid his shotgun against the bars. Stone seemed barely conscious as he laid on the cell floor.

"Look, I'm gonna go get the doc," the guard said to the supposedly unconscious man. Stone noticed the placement of his shotgun. It was an almost miraculous moment of carelessness on the part of the guard. But Stone didn't take advantage of it yet. He was concerned about the guard bringing the doctor, and he didn't want to contend with both of them.

"Wait. Wait," cried Stone weakly, "I'm feelin a little better; I'd rather go down ta the 'spensary than ta have ya bring the doc all the way down here. I kin make it."

"Look, I'm not stupid. I'm not gonna take ya outta your cell in the state yer in. Besides, ya might try somethin," said the guard.

"Even if I had the strength ta try somethin, I wouldn't. I know I'd never git out o here alive," Stone tried to reassure the soldier.

"Are you gonna be alright now or what?" asked the weary, disgusted guard. He bent down and picked up his shotgun and shouted, "**See that**? I got so damned scared, that I left my gun in a real good place for you to grab. You almost had my gun, you little bastard!" The guard was fuming. "I'm sick an tired of your constant *gas* problem! Now keep your mouth shut and let me do my job!" The guard was muttering to himself as he started to walk away.

"Hey, don't leave yet. Um okay. Huh? Do ya like women?" Stone asked softly. He was frantic to try anything and this was the first thing that came to his mind. He had to get that shotgun and out of his cell this night.

"What? **Are you nuts**?" shouted the guard.

"You know what I mean," Stone said as he half-crawled back over to his bunk.

"You gotta be nuts!" The soldier left the cell block slamming the gate behind him and making sure every door was locked.

Stone felt embarrassed for he had never done such a thing before. 'I must be more desp'rate than I realized', he said to himself. 'I can't believe I said that.' He laid back on his bunk thinking of what a stupid move he had made. 'Well, I ruined all chances of escape tonight, that's fer sure.' His cell was dark except for light from the kerosene lamp near the gate.

As Stone lay there, he heard the cell block gate slowly creak open and then he could hear heavy, slow footsteps creeping toward his cell. The footsteps came faster, almost a run. It quickened his pulse and a cold sweat began to come upon him. The guard was apparently responding to his offer and he didn't know exactly what to do! He remained in his bunk and pretended to be asleep.

It was too dark for the guard to notice Stone's eyes were open and that he was watching him. The light from the lantern made it possible to see the soldier's form at the cell door. Stone had whittled a slat from his bed two days ago and he was now gripping it.

"Hey, are ya asleep?" the guard whispered loudly in a raspy voice. Stone could see the soldier lay the shotgun on the floor just outside the cell door. He quietly unlocked the cell and laid the keys beside the gun. Slowly the guard walked in and began his move on the sleeping prisoner. Stone shoved the sharp weapon he had made into the soldier's belly. The man moaned gruesomely and fell to the floor in severe pain. Stone quickly went out the open cell door, grabbed the shotgun and keys. He checked the gun, found it was loaded, went back into the cell to check the guard. He was deathly quiet, his pulse and breathing were weak.

Stone hurriedly removed the guard's uniform and put it on over his own clothes. He now had the keys that he needed, the shotgun and all the guard's ammunition. He walked confidently out of his cell, and left through the still opened gate of the cell block.

'Well, this is some night, ain't it?' Stone asked himself proudly as he paused and looked back at the open cell block gate. He knew he had to act fast. He glanced down the corridor toward the gates to other cell blocks and the guard at the other end. Stone decided there must not be any soldiers close by or his guard wouldn't have taken him up on his offer.

He looked at the gun. It was the same type that the night guard carried. Stone confidently walked toward the tired looking man on duty at the end of the corridor. If Stone got through this gate he would be in the hallway that went to the dispensary. The guard looked suspiciously at him, but didn't make any move toward Stone.

"I gotta get the doctor. That prisoner down there's got gas again," Stone said gruffly, trying to make his voice sound like the guard's. He apparently did a good job of losing his Tennessee accent. The guard grinned at him. As he unlocked the gate, Stone struck him in the head with the butt of his gun. He quickly slumped to the floor. He then took the keys in the lock and finished opening the gate. He was not taking any chances. As he hurriedly made his way down the hall, he saw three guards talking.

Stone moving swiftly, aimed his double-barreled shotgun at the closely grouped soldiers. They were laughing about something. As Stone got nearer, he pretended to fix his belt. And in so doing the gun 'happened' to be pointed at them.

The guards noticed Stone as he got closer. One called over to him. He didn't bother to ask what they wanted; he fired both barrels into the men. The three fell to the floor in a pool of blood, and some of their remains were splattered on the wall behind them. Stone with silent determination, quickly tried different keys to open the gate. He could hear shouting from down the halls. The blast had wakened up half the prison. Stone soon found the right key. While kicking the gate open, he reloaded his gun. He went through the gate and came face to face with another guard. He was so stunned, he didn't move. Stone hit him with the butt of his gun and the soldier fell to the floor.

Stone took the key he had just used and opened this gate. He was relieved to find that one key had opened all the gates. He looked down the hall behind him and saw two guards running toward him. But since he was in a guard's uniform, they didn't suspect him; they just looked confused and ran on by. The two split up; one went down the hall Stone had just come from, while the other, now realizing that this man was the one trying to escape, aimed his gun at Stone. Just happening to catch the rise of the gun from the corner of his eye, Stone spun around firing. This guard fell dead in his tracks.

He continued running down the hall and through another gate with several guards chasing him. Stone was out of the building and running across the open grounds with the soldiers not far behind. He could hear them shouting. The prisoners were now awake and watching from their cell windows. It was chaos.

Stone didn't stop to unlock the front gate. He quickly reloaded his gun, and with both barrels, blasted the lock off the front gate. The power of the blast swung the gate doors open and Stone ran through. He slowed down to reload his gun and took a quick look behind him. It was still raining and fog had set in. The guards who had been chasing him across the grounds, were now at the front gate. They were shouting and firing into the foggy rain at the running figure. Stone fell as he caught some shot in his right shoulder. He winced, but quickly got up and kept running.

Once outside the prison gates, Stone was now a free man; but it was still moment to moment. He knew the Pennsylvania authorities would be on the hunt. He made his way down the road, as guards telegraphed a nearby army post and soldiers began to mount and ride. Stone was never so desperate in his life. He did it! He really had escaped! This was what Stone had racing wildly through his mind. He was terrified, while at the same time euphoric about his accomplishment. Realizing he was the first to ever escape from that prison, he couldn't help but smile with pride and relief. He knew the storm had been a big help to him and he had made the right decision to escape when he did.

"**Yee-oow!**" he shouted as he spotted some trees for cover. The rain had stopped, but the fog laid low. He was now coming into the city limits of Harrisburg. Stone had two shells left and this concerned him. He was within two miles of the main part of town. He stopped and took a look at his shoulder. It wasn't as bad as he thought. It felt like there were a couple of shots, but not that deep. The shoulder needed attention, but that would have to wait. He wanted to get out of the area and head south as quickly as possible.

He came upon a river as he passed the clump of trees. There were two horses tied and what looked like two men fishing. 'Jest what I need', he said to himself. 'I'm gonna git me a horse.' He couldn't believe he would find anyone out, let alone fishing at night. He quickly mounted the horse closest to him.

"Hey, what do ya think you're doin?" shouted one of the men who looked to be around fifty. Stone waved obligingly and took off down the road. His route went along the Susquehanna River where the men were fishing. The river route took Stone into some beautiful country. He continued on at an easier pace, resting the horse when he could. He came to a granite sign post that said 'Baltimore 64 miles'. This meant he was not far from the Maryland border. He wanted to avoid Washington; and if all went well, he figured it wouldn't take him long to get to Richmond.

It was three o'clock in the morning and Stone looked around in awe of the beauty of the countryside that welcomed him. The rain had stopped, the fog lifted and it was a clear fall night. The moon shone brightly and he could see the mountains. He was free and all was well.

Stone rode on about an hour more. He felt it was safe to stop awhile and rest. As he looked to the eastern sky he could see the beginning of dawn. He was worn out and scared. He knew his pursuers wouldn't be far behind and the fishermen would certainly tell anyone that came by what had happened. Stone remounted the horse and headed in the direction of Baltimore. The road he was following was now taking him away from the Susquehanna River and into some hilly countryside. If he continued the pace, he figured he could be on the outskirts of Baltimore by afternoon. Today was Saturday and the early morning was a bit chilly. As a matter of fact, Stone thought about Thanksgiving which was only weeks away.

As he rode along, he thought back on how Thanksgiving was at his Uncle's home in Parkinson, Tennessee and all that had happened since that last Thanksgiving. Stone shook his head to keep his wits, and not get caught up in thinking about home. He had to stay on track and think about here and now. If he wanted to see Parkinson, then he would have to keep alert about his surroundings.

As a tiring Stone continued, he came across another sign that noted the Pennsylvania and Maryland border. He sighed deeply; Baltimore lay ahead. He stopped and dismounted to remove the guard's uniform he was wearing. He bundled it up and tossed it into some brush. He winced as his left arm propelled the clothes. The wound was bleeding, but not bad. He had to get home before he could think about treating the wound.

Palmer had telegraphed Union Army troops of Stone's escape and issued them orders to shoot on sight. Only seven miles behind the escapee, were Federal troops making their way on horseback checking every place Stone could possibly be hiding. Thankfully he had no idea how close his pursuers were, but he knew they would be following him; and he had to keep moving on no matter how badly his shoulder hurt him.

As the day continued, Stone felt a headache and a weakness coming on him. He figured he was tired, but when he felt his shoulder, blood covered his hand. It had been running down the back of his shirt and he didn't realize it. He was concentrating on getting as far away from Harrisburg as he could.

His injury was throbbing and painful. Every now and then he found himself slumped forward on his horse. He must move on. He knew the Federals were on his trail, but he was unaware there were more in front of him combing the countryside. The guards from the prison had turned back at the state border and the Maryland authorities were his closest danger.

Stone didn't know who was out there chasing him, but he knew he was a hunted man and he had to keep going. He was exhausted and he could hardly keep his eyes open. It was now about ten o'clock in the morning. He didn't have the luxury of resting; he had to keep moving.

Following the road into higher ground, he was soon approaching the periphery of Baltimore. It was about one o'clock when Stone could see the city; and in the near distance were Federal troops.

"Well, I'll be ...," Stone drawled as he observed about five of them making their way toward him. He paused momentarily looking down at his horse. The Federal troops were moving toward him slowly and he had just a short time to think. He patted the saddle firmly as he concentrated on his predicament.

"I can't jest sit here an wait, an I can't ride right past 'em. Bold things like that don't always work," he said to the horse. He looked at his wound and gave in to the weakness that had been slowly coming on him. Each time he looked at his shoulder it was worse. Stone was concerned for the loss of blood and if he was leaving a trail of it for someone to follow. He was losing time; the sooner he could get to the Virginia countryside the better. If he had to use a Baltimore doctor, he might have to kill him and he didn't want that; but Stone was desperate. He had enough blood on his hands and he didn't want to kill again unless he had to. Stone had no justification for the deaths of so many Union soldiers, except to rationalize them as an incident of war, and a necessity for his freedom. He didn't want to kill any more.

Stone turned his horse to the side and he rode swiftly into a wooded area off the road. As he continued, now unable to see the road, he began to make a wide arc, keeping Baltimore in sight and staying away from the Federal troops who were still combing the nearby hillsides. His physical weakness was overtaking him as he circled about, trying to stay out of view from the road. He decided to make his way into the city, realizing the gamble he was taking; but his need for medical attention was too great. He had to take the chance.

Entering Baltimore, he tried to appear as healthy as possible; trying to keep an eye out for a doctor's office. He rode down the street fearing someone would notice him, but no one seemed to pay much attention. As he searched for a doctor, he tried to think of a story that would erase any suspicion the doctor might have. He turned a corner and there it was: a sign that read: 'Dr. Pales. MD'. Stone rode up to the doctor's office, tied his horse to the hitching rail, dismounted gingerly, and holding his shotgun, entered. Both barrels of the shotgun were loaded with his last two shells.

As Stone entered, the nurse stood up from her desk and moved toward him. He had become so weak it was difficult for him to stand on his own. He asked to see the doctor. The nurse led him to the exam room and it took both of them to get Stone up onto the table.

"It seems, my boy, you've lost quite a bit of blood. Who shot you?" he asked, probing the wound as well.

"Um ... some Rebels jest north o here," winced Stone. "They spotted me an fer no reason that I know of, started firin at me."

"Well, it isn't as bad as all the blood makes it look. You caught a couple of shots and it's not that deep either," explained the doctor. He began to wipe the blood off and had Stone lay on his stomach. "Now this'll sting. I have to clean the wound before I can remove the shots; and all I have is whiskey." Stone's face twisted in pain, but he remained silent. It took about twenty minutes for the doctor to remove the two small lead pellets and sew him up.

"You're lucky today isn't Sunday," said Dr.

Pales as he finished.

"Why's that?" Stone tried to make a little conversation with the doctor. He knew if he said too much, the doctor would know he was a Confederate.

Pales smiled, "On Sundays, I go fishing. There is a nice fishing hole north of town and that's where I go to get away for a while. I've caught some pretty nice fish there. Yea, tomorrow I'll go up there, build a fire and throw my line in, lay back and take a little snooze." He had stopped working on Stone and was lost in his thoughts of tomorrow for a moment as he gazed out the window.

Stone just smiled. He didn't want to get into much of a discussion with him. The doctor seemed nice enough, but Stone didn't want to take any chances.

"Now you don't have to stay in bed or anything like that, but I wouldn't do any heavy work or extraneous activity."

"Ex-train-e-us …?" Stone didn't know what that meant.

"Don't run too hard for too long, son," the good doctor said looking at Stone, who got the feeling he wasn't fooling the doctor. He put his blood stained shirt back on and was preparing to leave.

"What's the charge for this Doc?" asked Stone. "I don't have much money."

"No charge, son." He looked at the nurse as she was leaving the room. "Sally, don't charge him anything." The nurse nodded knowingly and shut the door.

The doctor turned to Stone and in a low, firm voice said, "It's in the newspapers this morning ... If you head directly west, you will run smack into the Potomac River. You'll miss Washington. Virginia's right on the other side."

Stone looked at the man in appreciation and with outstretched hand said, "Much obliged Doc," and smiled.

As Stone walked toward the door, the doctor said after him, "Watch out for those Rebels! Hear me?"

Stone laughed easily, "Yeah, I will" and shut the door behind him.

Out in the street, Stone mounted his horse and headed west. He believed the doctor was sincere. He had no reason to think otherwise. After all he took care of his wound without charge. 'Yeah', he said to himself confidently, 'Doc wuz a nice ol man. He could be trusted.'

He knew Washington lay south and the Potomac ran from the northwest to the southeast of where he was. The doctor sure had given him the right information. 'But why did he help me?' This question kept popping into his mind as he traveled along. Stone was surprised at the newspapers having the story and was thankful that Doc Pales let him know. Now he would be more cautious than ever. Stone was still puzzled about why the doc would help him escape. He pondered that question all day long.

Stone figured if he could keep his pace, he would be at the Potomac River by night or early morning.

Chapter XIII

Back in Baltimore, Dr. Pales hurriedly leaped into his buggy, headed straight to the Marshal's office and quickly ran inside. There he found an Army officer and the marshal discussing the morning's big story. The newspaper said it was *'a daring, single-handed escape by Richard Harold Stone shooting his way out of the Harrisburg Federal Prison to freedom'*. The article went on to say it was something no one had ever attempted.

"These newspapers ... they do more harm than good. They're makin a hero outta him," said the angry officer.

The marshal agreed saying, "Not only that ... they're helping him get away."

Just then the doctor pushed through the door and into the marshal's office shouting, "**Gentlemen! Gentlemen!**" He stopped to catch his breath.

"Doc, I never saw ya run so fast. What's wrong with you?" asked the marshall.

Gasping for breath he shouted, "**I just treated him!** *I just treated him!*"

"Slow down Doc. Who'd you treat?"

"The man who escaped from Harrisburg! He had shot in his shoulder. I removed it and told him to head west to avoid troops near Washington. It's him. I know it was him!" he finished breathlessly.

"**You did what**? Why'd ya let him get away?" shouted the marshal. "Why didn't ya send your nurse over here while ya were workin on him?"

"I've gotta get goin, Marshal. We'll get on his trail an get him," the officer said as he left in a hurry.

The marshal looked at the doctor with disgust. "I can't believe it. He was so close."

"He came staggering into the office and asked for help. I didn't know what else to do," the doctor said apologetically.

"Alright! Alright! Tell me exactly what happened. Why didn't ya knock him out or do somethin to keep him there?"

"Well, he had a shotgun and I knew he wasn't about to let me do anything like that. He wanted those shots removed as fast as possible. He wasn't going to let Sally leave the room. I couldn't afford to try anything with him holding that gun. He held it even while I had him lay down to remove the shots."

"Sounds to me like he was weak enough ya could have taken it off of him without any trouble. Why didn't ya try somethin?" The marshal was surprised at the doctor's decision to help him. "Okay, Okay. Where west did ya tell him to go? How bad was he hurt? Did he lose a lot of blood? Doc, you really haven't told me anything!"

"I directed him west to the Potomac River."

"Well, now that's quite a long ride for a wounded man, don't ya think?"

"Yes and he lost a lot of blood and was quite weak." They sat in silence for a few moments and then Dr. Pales asked the marshal if there was a reward out for him.

"I think they're workin on it; especially if he isn't captured soon. Why?"

"Well I was just wondering ... I came in here and turned him in. I mean I gave you information so you could apprehend him," the doctor smiled sheepishly. "I thought I would get a reward for that."

"Why would you think you deserve anything? Hell, Doc, you let him go, and now you're askin for some reward? I bet you got your money for diggin the shots outta him, huh?"

"No. I didn't charge him a cent."

"If there's gonna be a reward on his head, you'd have to capture him to get it."

Dr. Pales got up from his chair and said, "Marshal, I'm sorry if I let you down; but I did what I thought was right. You know we doctors take an oath and I try to abide by it."

"Thanks for comin and reportin this Doc. No hard feelings. If I'd been in your shoes, I'd probably have done the same thing."

Stone was a few miles out of Baltimore, but was anxious to put more distance between himself and the doctor. He knew Palmer would have telegraphed far and wide to alert as many troops as possible. And he had to keep moving on. His horse was tired and he decided that if he came upon another he would have to take it. He would trade. Stone was tired and hungry. He hadn't slept since the night before his escape.

As he was planning his strategy, Stone noticed in the distance what looked like a village. It was Unionville, a small town where he hoped he could get food and a horse.

He rode his horse slowly down the main street looking for some place to get some food. At the end of the street on the left was a store front that said 'Harding's General Store'. Beside it was a livery stable. He smiled and said to himself 'jest what I need.'

The old man who ran the general store also owned the stable next door. Inside the store Stone noticed a map on the wall. He went over and studied it and found he could make the Potomac in far less time by going southwest instead of the advised west. Stone became suspicious of the doctor and wondered if he had reported him already. Then he looked around the store for the things he needed. He hadn't eaten in a long time and he was getting sick from hunger. He picked up a pound of bacon and some beans, beef jerky and he picked up some matches and shells. Oh yeah, he needed a horse.

Stone was smiling as he said to the old man, "This sure is a handy set up ya have here."

He went next door and discovered a nice, spirited horse that was much stronger than his. He left his horse and took the one in the stable. As Stone wandered through the store and stable, the old man remained behind the counter watching him. Stone was the only one in the store, but he knew he had to move fast. He thanked the old man for the grub and the use of the horse. The old man nodded and waved him on. He was secretly sympathetic toward the south, but no one in town knew how he felt. He ran a store and didn't want his business to suffer, so he kept his thoughts to himself.

Stone took one last look at the map and said to the old man, "He wuz tryin ta git me captured, that son of a-."

The old man never answered, but slowly walked over to a shelf and quickly sorted through a stack of shirts and handed him one that was blue plaid. "Take that bloody shirt off boy and be on your way. You don't have much time. They probably aren't far behind you. I read about you in the newspaper."

Stone took off his old, torn, blood-stained shirt and put the new blue one on. He was shocked that anyone would be so kind to him. He met so many deceitful people, he forgot what kindness was. Stone looked at the old, white-haired man, his blue eyes still sparkling, and said, "Mister, I don't know yer name; but as soon as this war's over, I'll surely be back ta make this right."

"Just be on your way." The old man turned and said, "By the way, my name is Sam Harding. Be gone with ya now."

As Stone was rushing out of the store, he turned and smiled, "and my name's Stone, Richard Stone. See ya."

He quickly mounted his new, brown, frisky stallion and headed southwest. Already Federal troops in and around Hagerstown were preparing to meet Stone, as they headed toward the eastern part of the state. Stone was aware that his course of escape was now taking him closer to Washington. He would be about thirteen miles from it.

Around six thirty on Saturday evening Stone was only twenty-five miles from the Potomac River and hungry. He approached a hill and rode to the top where he had a panoramic view of the area below him. He dismounted and walked a few paces to an apple tree. He gathered some withered apples from the ground for his horse. There was an old pear tree that still had some fruit on it. He took one; it tasted pretty good to a fella who hadn't eaten for a long time.

He walked a little farther and saw a shack, part of the roof had fallen in. There was a chestnut tree with lots of chestnuts on the ground. This was once somebody's place thought Stone, an abandoned homestead. As he began to gather chestnuts he decided this was a perfect place to rest. He allowed himself an hour.

Stone sat down on the ground under the pear tree. There was a pile of fallen leaves that made a nice soft place to rest his head. Soon he was asleep. When he awoke, he was looking at the night sky. It was a clear, cool night and the stars were out. He sat there and thought how wonderful it would be just to be able to have a fire; but he wouldn't dare risk it. He smiled as he thought of a nice warm fire with a soft, lovely woman to hold and call his own under the beautiful star studded sky.

Then Stone thought to himself, 'it sure is too bad … all the fightin, men dyin, cotton fields destroyed, homes burned, over what? … some men's greed fer power This war's forcin one man's way of life on another. Why can't men with different ideas, workin or farmin, live in one country together peacefully? An me … always runnin. I'm so tired of runnin. None of it makes sense.'

It was getting late and Stone knew he couldn't afford any more time to rest. With regret, he got to his feet and mounted his horse. It was dark and he couldn't see very far in front of him. Remembering the map on the wall in the store, he knew he couldn't be far from the Potomac. He slowly moved down the hillside and continued in a southwesterly direction using the stars to guide him.

Federal troops had stopped in Unionville, but no one had seen a Richard Stone. The soldiers now had a face drawn on a paper to hang at the sheriff's office. 'Mum' was the word in Unionville; the town never heard of the man. The Union soldiers moved on and the Federal troops near Washington turned back.

There were some soldiers riding along the Potomac, but none had seen Stone or even the tracks of a lone rider. He made sure he stayed away from the main trails and it was night. Most of the soldiers went back to their posts.

Stone was not going very fast for he still suffered from dizzy and weak moments. He was sure he had lost more blood than the doctor had let on. Stone proceeded slowly but surely, toward Virginia.

It was late and he felt himself dozing off now and then, but he and the horse kept moving on. Stone reached into his bag and pulled out some jerky. He thought chewing on it would keep him awake.

The stars disappeared and rain moved in. The road became muddy and this caused the few soldiers still on his trail to slow down, but the grassy fields Stone moved through made his travel easier. He was glad to see the rain; his spirits were lifted and his pace increased. He was soaked, but his enthusiasm pushed him on. He could almost feel the Potomac nearby. The feeling of exhilaration overcame him as he thought of how he had over and over again been able to escape his captors.

Meanwhile, the soldiers were grumbling. They had ridden all day and didn't see anyone. The rain was coming down hard and the men were soaked, hungry and tired. They argued over whether to turn back or go on.

"Ha! Ha, ha! **I'm free, so free!**" shouted Stone. He was not far from the Potomac, but not yet close enough to see it.

'*Dead or Alive*' were the orders the troops had as they chased through Maryland after Richard Harold Stone. He had made headlines in some of the Richmond newspapers. The officials and authorities in the North were reading of Stone's miraculous escape and how he had managed more than once to free himself from the enemy. He had become a hero; and in fact, any more publicity would have made him a legend.

Palmer and the Pennsylvania prison officials were furious and embarrassed as they read the southern papers, making a mockery of the Union's ability to handle its prisoners. They wanted to get this story out of the news and fast. The North never published the number of guards who lost their lives that night. But Washington was very aware of what had happened in Harrisburg.

Morale was low after Stone's escape and several of the guards had asked to be transferred to other prisons; some even wanted to be placed on active duty.

Washington quickly relieved Palmer of his assignment and plans were being made to close the prison.

Only about seven miles from the Potomac River, still out of site, Stone continued on. His fatigue, loss of blood, and the lack of sleep were taking its toll. 'Dead or Alive' was the only thing that kept him moving.

He had picked up more shells at Unionville, but if he did run into a skirmish, there would be only him against many. He knew it would be his death. He was fighting for self-preservation and fighting it alone. It was a battle ... a battle that he had been fighting for a long time; one he had fought most of his life, he reasoned ... a battle for freedom and for individuality; and his pursuit of it had caused much of his trouble. He would not, nor could not change. He was searching for peace. He wanted left alone to pursue his dream. His dream was simple ... a life without running; one that he could settle down somewhere with someone. 'Was that askin too much?' he wondered. He didn't want to kill anyone, but what choice did he have? It seemed as though throughout his life he was always fighting his way out of some situation he had no idea how he had gotten into in the first place.

It was midnight and Stone was only two and a-half miles from the Potomac River, the South, Virginia and freedom. The rain had stopped, leaving the roads very muddy, full of holes and puddles. Most of his pursuers had turned back; only a few were wandering the roads leading to the Potomac and they too were about to head back. Stone was at the top of a hill and as he rose up in his saddle, he could see below the

Potomac River. Oh the excitement that rose up in his soul to see such a site. The beautiful Potomac! He would soon be free, but he had to find a way to cross it.

Still sitting in his saddle thinking over his life as he often did, Stone decided he would go back to New Orleans. 'Yep, the place they took me from. I'm not there yet,' he said to himself. 'There's gotta be a bridge near here.' He decided to head west. If he headed in that direction he wouldn't run into any Federals.

As he continued, he came upon a muddy road. He stopped, looked at it and smiled. 'Lord will ya lead me to a bridge?' Crossing without a bridge or boat would be plain suicide. Riding at a slow pace, he came upon a deserted house. It was just off the road, near the river. He got off the horse and led it to the opened front door. He eased his head inside and looked around. It looked like a good place to dry off and get a little rest. Stone wanted to be in Virginia by morning.

Inside there was a table and a couple of chairs. The table looked okay, but a leg was missing from one of the chairs. As he looked around further he could see there was a pump for water by the sink. A bed was in the corner of the room. Not much else was there. A picture laid on the floor ... a picture of a man and woman. He had a suit on and she a dress. 'Hmmm, ma'be their weddin pi'ture', he thought. 'I wonder what drove 'em away from here?'

Stone curled up in the corner of the room. He picked up a cushion that was by the bed. It had part of the stuffing out, but he could lay his head on it. So for about half an hour Stone and his horse found refuge.

"Let's go friend. Ya gotta git me ta Virginia by mornin", he said to the horse. Stone found himself talking to the horse often. He would tell him his plans and how they were going to cross the river. The horse's name was Thunder ... at least that's what Stone called him. Once outside, he mounted his stallion and continued down the side of the road. Thunder liked the grassy vegetation. He would stop once in a while and graze a little. Stone didn't mind. That gave him time to think and plan. He knew he was almost free; and because of the rain that night, his tracks would have been erased. He made sure he stayed away from traveling the roads anyway.

After riding for about an hour, Stone spotted a bridge. The road that he was on led right to it. So with a feeling of great relief and satisfaction, Richard Harold Stone was now safe in Virginia. "*Hurrah!*" he shouted; he couldn't help himself. Even Thunder reared up on his hind legs and then galloped toward the bridge.

He was about one hundred fifteen miles from Richmond. He knew being in Virginia didn't guarantee him safety. There were Federals here too, but it was much safer the farther south he went. He couldn't trust anyone in Maryland. At least in Virginia, he felt he could trust the people. He was in Confederate territory; and he breathed a sigh of relief.

Stone thought of taking a train to New Orleans. But first he wanted to find some kind of work. A major problem remained ... his military duty. He had been thinking about it, but hesitated to resume it. Stone had decided to live like a local, at least until they caught up with him; then he would have to tell them something. What would he tell them but the truth; and he was sure they would never consider him a deserter. The Confederates would know all about him. His face was all over Maryland and he could be easily recognized. Maybe he would go back and rejoin some unit. 'Hmmm, ma'be they'd grant me a commission er a medal er somethin,' he said to Thunder.

This was one of many idyllic moments Stone reflected on. At times he would imagine himself a hero. 'Hey, not too many's gotta past like mine. I oughta git some kinda reco'nition fer the way I busted outta that prison. I sure gave the newspapers enough ta write about, huh Thunder?' His horse was becoming a part of him now and he wondered how he'd get him back to Unionville if he did go to New Orleans. Stone decided he would take one day at a time.

As the days passed, Stone found himself working as a farm hand and then in a leather shop. He even helped lay some track for a railroad company. During this time no one, journalists or other legend and fame makers could find this legendary hero.

All that they were now sure of was that Richard Harold Stone had escaped from his captors' hands into Virginia as Southern papers reported; or as Northern papers claimed, the 'mad criminal' evaded capture from the authorities in Maryland.

Stone had read some of the Northern newspapers that had found their way below the

Mason-Dixon Line as well as the Southern newspapers, which labled him a daring man of great courage and perseverance. These were the two different perceptions of Stone that each side depicted. He was temporarily famous, more as a legend and not as a real man. No one could relate to him as he was portrayed. In person no one had an even slight notion of who he really was. Around Stone, his fellow laborers would work and he would listen to their references to him as a legend.

He changed his name for jobs, because he didn't want that kind of attention or trouble to follow him. He might be expected to live up to the kind of man the newspapers and readers had made him to be. And, that would be troublesome.

Stone was no longer front page news. Time had passed, more battles were in the news and the war raged on. He held onto the same principles that he believed in before, but even more so now. He was going back to New Orleans and nobody, but nobody would take him away from there ever again.

It was December when Stone was working on a tobacco farm in Georgia. He had over three hundred fifty dollars in the bank in nearby Jasper. Christmas and New Years ended his stay in Georgia and within a week Stone was in Florida. He had worked in stables and on a cattle ranch. By February of 1864, the Confederate Army was not as strong as it once had been and Stone's absence had gone unnoticed; he was living more so the way he wanted.

On Wednesday, the tenth of February, Stone withdrew his savings of four hundred forty dollars from a bank in Lamont, Florida, a small town about twenty-five miles east of Tallahassee. The owner of the ranch liked Thunder and had paid Stone forty dollars for him, so he made his way to Tallahassee mostly by foot. Once there he hopped a freight train to Bainbridge, Georgia. He had to wait until the next day to hop another to Macon.

Stone was surprised at the loneliness of the rail yard in Bainbridge and the warm night seemed to lend an introspective mood to it all. It made the personal loneliness greater, but the unfamiliar rail yard, familiar. The moon was full and the sky was clear. He slept peacefully in a freight car that night.

Stone awoke to the crows' cawing and the sun's warm light on his face. He sat in the freight car and didn't feel like moving at all, but indulged in the moment. Slowly, he climbed out of the car. All the clothes he had were on his back except for the dark coat he was carrying in his left arm. He stepped into the lonely rail yard. Leaving his shotgun behind, he walked a small distance down some track and found himself humming the same song the poor men had played and sung on the street corners of New Orleans. It did not last long though; the blast of the whistle of an oncoming train brought him back to reality … and in a couple of hours to Macon, Georgia.

It was about noon, on a warm, sunny day that Stone arrived in Macon. He was the only 'living' passenger on board, for the rest of the train's cargo was freight. As Stone jumped from his car, he was shocked to notice that the long boxes in the next car were coffins, carrying the bodies of fallen Confederate sons.

'Man alive! I'm sure a lucky fella, aint I?' muttered Stone to himself. Thoughts of his escape from prison flooded back to him. Many times he had stopped to marvel how he had managed it. Sometimes it haunted him; and seeing those coffins made him reflect on his past as he often did.

He strolled slowly out of sight, thankful to be alive, never noticing that a large, black man was watching him. The man pulled out a pistol and was moving secretly in the direction Stone had taken. Stone, unaware of the man and his pistol, laid his coat down on the ground and started rummaging through his trouser pockets.

Quietly the black man cocked his pistol and aimed its barrel at his head. Stone thought he heard the cocking of a gun, just as the man said, "Hey white man!"

Startled Stone turned around asking, "What'd ya want?"

"Jus stand still and yo gonna live," ordered the black man.

"Hey let me tell ya. I aint got a dime."

The black man slowly moved toward Stone while his right hand kept his pistol aimed at his abdomen. "I'm not after yo money. I'm after freedom. An yo gonna help me," said the big, black man with a commanding and firm tone.

Stone swallowed hard and was at a loss for

words. He noticed how straight and smooth the black man's hair was. He looked to be about thirty, with the style and appearance of an aristocrat. Stone cleared his throat as the other man stood there with his pistol still pointed at Stone's belly.

"Mister, I'm headin fer New Orlins. Now put that thing away b'fer it goes off in ma belly." The black man stood silent, then smiled and put the gun in his belt.

"I'm Amos, jus Amos. You don't have to tell me who you are. I already know."

Stone cocked his head proudly and smiled, 'Hmm, he knows my name.' He couldn't help but be intrigued by this man.

"You see Stone, I'm one nigger who can read an write; an I'm not running an never suggested that I am. I don't run from nuthing an no one," Amos said with his hand on Stone's shoulder. "Yo name is Richard Stone an I know all about you."

With a smile Stone said, "Ya got it, an glad ta meet ya." He put his hand out for Amos to shake. Stone and Amos sensed an understanding between them and that was rare in 1864. The two men, one white and one black, seemingly to be on some kind of similar course. Both in need of freedom or in search of it and both determined enough to risk their lives for it.

The two men shook hands and proceeded

toward the railroad station. As they approached the building a sole figure was watching them. He was an old man, sitting at the ticket window trying to keep occupied on this quiet Friday afternoon.

The two men entered the station and looked at the schedule on the wall. Stone noticed that the train from Montgomery to Macon had not arrived and was twenty minutes late. He went to the ticket window.

"The train from Montgom'ry is twenty-three minutes late. What happened?" The clock on the wall showed twenty-three minutes past two o'clock.

"The track was blown up again," the man said calmly as he briefly looked at Stone and then turned away as though he wasn't there.

Stone looked at Amos and asked, "Now what do we do?"

Amos looked down at his feet, putting his left thumb in his belt so that it held back part of his coat. He looked back at Stone and replied, "Don't know. That's why I got with you. I thought you could get us anywhere."

"Hey, I don't know everythin!"

"Never said ya did." He walked away from Stone to a window and looked out over the rail yard.

Stone looked at the old man trying to catch a fly as it crawled around his hand. Then he realized he would be the one planning and making all the decisions for them.

Amos silently looked out over the rail yard unnoticeably watching Stone. "Looks like it's gonna rain."

"Would ya quit standin 'round an git yer head workin. I ain't gonna do all the thinkin fer the two of us."

Amos started to laugh, and turned to look at Stone. He easily leaned against the wall by the window and said, "Yo the one with all the experience."

"I'm serious!" Stone replied, irritated.

"Take it easy, take it ea -- sy. Don't get all undone. Now either we're going to wait here or start walkin or maybe ridin. It's that simple," Amos stated and Stone nodded.

It took them an hour to find a stable where their talents could successfully relieve the owner of two horses. It was not long until they found themselves leaving Macon and riding along the railroad tracks towards Montgomery, Alabama.

"What's taking you to New Or-leans, Stone? A woman?" asked Amos as they were riding along, side by side.

"Yea, that's one reason."

"What's her name?"

"Don't know. Aint met her yet."

"You don't know her name huh? Well where in New Or-leans will you find her?"

"Don't know fer sure, but 'tend ta find out," Stone said with a smile. Amos laughed and slapped him on the back. Stone started laughing too.

"Yo alright, white man. You are all--right!"

Chapter XIV

It did not rain as Amos had predicted. They had been riding at an easy pace for about three hours when they came upon a village. It was a very small town about five miles west of Macon. There was a general store and a saloon. That was about it for Pikesville.

It appeared to be fairly peaceful. There was no one on the main street. Even the saloon, 'Daisy's' seemed too quiet to be true. Amos and Stone secured their horses to the hitching rail in front of Pikesville's sole saloon and went inside. As they entered, they found Daisy's not so rosy. Some of the area farmers were spending a lot of their time getting drunk; and they were looking Amos and Stone up and down. The two strangers to Pikesville seemed uneasy about the saloon's clientele. A black man and a white man just don't drink together in Pikesville.

The only protection that the two men had was Amos's pistol. Not a word was spoken in the saloon; the drinking stopped and they all stared at them. This made Stone really nervous; they quickly drank their glass of beer and hurried from the saloon. They couldn't get on their horses fast enough to suit Stone.

It was about eight o'clock that evening when the two came across some unused railroad tracks. They halted their horses and looked around. Amos yawned and said, "Well, why don't we stop here? This looks like a nice place to get some sleep."

Stone didn't answer for a moment. It was as if he hadn't heard a word Amos said. "We'll be in New Orlins in a couple o days; an I think it's gonna be easy. Real ea -- sy," Stone replied with a grin.

"How do you see us in New Or-leans in a couple days?" asked the black man. Stone was surveying the tracks and Amos was confused as to what his companion was thinking.

"I figger that if we see a couple o trains go by tomorra, then the tracks have been fixed. An I figger we might ride our way in ta New Orlins that way," Stone explained. "Look ... Macon an Montgomery are two good sized towns. Ya think they're gonna leave the only rail line between 'em closed down? Certainly not. I figger we'll steal our way ta New Orlins. What d'ya think?"

Amos looked down at his saddle as the sun's faint light was dimming; it had just set minutes before. The sky was getting cloudy and Amos felt some raindrops on his head.

"I think it's gonna rain Stoney. That's what I think." Stone didn't know how to respond, so he just smiled. He couldn't quite figure out this man; but he felt he could trust him.

They headed along the railroad tracks and looked for some kind of shelter. Stone didn't think the rain would last too long or amount to very much, so he was not too worried about finding a dry place to sleep. Amos seemed more concerned about getting wet than about how they would get to New Orleans. A few drops never hurt anyone thought Stone. And that's all it was, just a few drops. Stone thought he was learning more from Amos than Amos from him. It was around ten o'clock that night when the two men decided they weren't going to find shelter; so they slept out under the stars.

Saturday arrived swiftly and the day had begun late for Stone. He had gotten up an hour and a half earlier than Amos. It was a sunny clear morning.

"Amos," wondered Stone, "why wuz ya so tir'd yesterday? Ya always go ta bed early?" he asked teasingly.

"I do when I haven't slept tha night before. An if I took the time then, I wouldn't be alive an here right now." Stone didn't say a word because he had no idea what Amos was talking about. He wasn't going to pursue it.

After a couple of minutes Amos continued, "I left a white woman behind in Florida."

"Was she married?" wondered Stone.

"She had a beau an he got after me," confessed

Amos. "I thought it best to get out of Florida as fast as I could."

"Ya don't have ta explain nothin ta me Amos." The black man smiled and they both mounted their horses and continued west.

As they rode along the railroad tracks, they heard a train whistle in the distance and a low rumbling sound on the track. It was about noon and the train was coming from the east. Stone smiled as they watched the train disappear.

At around three o'clock the whistle of another train made the two men look toward the west. "An here's the one comin from Montgomery," concluded Stone aloud. Amos didn't say anything; their eyes were fixed on the train until it disappeared.

"How do you intend to board?" asked Amos. He remembered Stone said something about 'stealing' their way to New Orleans; but he had no idea what he meant.

"We're gonna steal it an take it ta New Orlins," Stone responded calmly. Amos looked at Stone and began laughing.

Stone explained, "The impossible is *im--possible* only if ya think it is!" Amos stopped laughing and just smirked sarcastically. He was half-sold on the idea and fascinated by Stone's imagination.

"How?" asked Amos with uplifted arms.

Stone looking as though the situation was well in the palm of his hand responded, "I don't really know."

Amos's arms dropped to his side and his eyes widened as he looked at Stone in amazement. "Yo crazy, white man. Yo crazy!" Amos rubbed his temples. "I gotta headache."

"Re--lax will ya? Tomorra mornin we're gonna have us a train!"

Amos looked at Stone and said to himself, 'That white man's really serious!'

Without conversation, the two men continued along the railroad tracks toward the west. Amos could almost see Stone's mind working as they moved along glancing at each other. Amos would smile and Stone would raise his eyebrows. The black man just couldn't figure him out.

It was six o'clock and they were about twelve miles west of Macon.

"I'm gonna shoot a rabbit an make some supper."

"Why don't ya git a couple? I'm hungry too," teased Stone as Amos disappeared into the woods. He got off his horse and tied it to a nearby tree. As he sat near the side of the tracks, he realized he didn't have *his* shotgun. He ran to his horse and the saddle was empty. 'Where's my head?' Stone asked himself disgustedly.

A few minutes later a shot rang out from the woods. When Amos had gone off into the woods to find his kill, Stone had started to prepare a fire. They had moved a little ways from the track. Stone wanted to follow the rails, but at the same time stay hidden. He feared the Federals might be watching the track. They had blown it up before, and Stone didn't want to take any chances.

It wasn't long until the two men were eating rabbit for supper. Stone was angry at Amos. He had shot only *one* rabbit. "Why jest one rabbit? Why don't ya answer me? Why're we sharin one rabbit? I know! Ya ran outta bullets. **Ya ran outta bullets,** *didn't ya?"* questioned Stone with a loud voice.

"Re--lax, white man. We're not gonna kill everybody are we? You upset at me for not having bullets ... well where's yo gun? You left it somewhere huh? You've got no reason to be mad at me. Be mad at yo'self."

Amos was getting irritated with Stone who sat in silence as he ate his half of the rabbit. 'Yeah I'm mad at myself. How could I have laid my gun down somewhere an not pick it back up?' he scolded himself.

They were sitting by the fire munching on rabbit when Amos probed, "Hey Stoney, how're we gonna steal that train tomorra mornin?"

Stone looked at Amos and calmly replied, "We're gonna use yer gun. That's my plan, ta use yer gun. I left mine somewhere, so I can't get upset with you, Amos."

"All I had was one bullet anyway. So who said ya gotta use a gun ta steal a train?" Amos asked.

"Ya gotta point there," said Stone, as he began to concentrate again on how to get to New Orleans as fast as possible.

Amos and Stone laid down on the ground under a tree near their fire. The horses were tied close by munching on some lush green grass. You could hear the faint sound of rushing water from the nearby stream. 'How peaceful,' thought Stone, 'even if it's fer jest a few hours. When I git settled down I'm gonna have me a place by a stream. I wanna put that on my list Lord, if ya allow it.'

There was a full moon that night and the stars twinkled in a clear, black sky. All of a sudden ... no gun, no bullets, one rabbit ... none of it mattered. The feeling of contentment encompassed him on this tranquil night and soon sleep overtook him.

Sunday morning arrived late for Amos and Stone. As usual, Stone was up and about first. They were both on horseback by ten o'clock that morning and just riding along easily when they heard the blast of a train whistle from the east.

Amos looked anxiously over at Stone, "Have you figgured anything yet?"

"I think we'll jest hafta try an race up 'longside

an then jump on. That's 'bout all we kin do."

Amos nodded in agreement. He was a little disappointed in the new plan. *Stealing* a train was more exciting.

The two men tightened the reins on their horses as the sound of the train got closer. They looked at each other and the approaching train. It was louder now and the engine was coughing black smoke in the air. They could see it was a passenger train. Stone looked at Amos once again and yelled "**Now!**"

They smacked their horses as they began to run alongside the train. Amos swiftly placed the soles of his dusty boots on the seat of his saddle and with legs bent to his chest, he leaped successfully onto the porch of one of the cars.

Stone still on horseback, with his boots on the seat of his saddle and his legs bent, was starting to lose pace with the train. 'I gotta make ma move now er I won't git on!' he said to himself. His horse was losing pace fast, and he could see there were only a few more cars. Suddenly he threw the reigns and leaped onto the porch of the next to the last car, but not with the same success as Amos. Stone was gripping his knee as he gritted his teeth and squeezed his eyes shut in pain. Amos watched his leap and could see his landing was off.

Amos straightened his clothes and hair, then nonchalantly opened the door of the car and walked through with a smile on his face. Most of the passengers seemed to be well-to-do and appeared to be offended by a happy, self-confident black fellow walking through their railroad car. Amos was stopped at the rear door by an unattractive, older woman. She was well dressed and looked at him with a scowl on her face. He could feel her irritation at his presence. Amos nervously glanced around at the filled seats. Some of the men had suits on and the ladies wore hats and gloves. Most of them were older and some quite elderly.

He coughed and was about to say something when he heard Stone struggling with the door. Stone opened the door, entered the car and was immediately stopped in his tracks by the mean, elderly woman standing near Amos. Many of the others had seen Amos ride alongside the car and leap on. Some were laughing about it and others were talking excitedly. Then the passengers turned in their seats and saw her reaction. They quieted and became more somber, wondering what would happen next.

"Ethel, just let them be. Must you always make a scene?" said the elderly man sitting in the seat next to the now standing woman, who appeared to be his wife.

"I paid for a ticket on this train and I expected to have a decent trip to Montgomery. I did not expect a black tramp to be jumping on and upsetting everyone," the elderly woman complained angrily, and with her voice filled with arrogance yelled, "**Conductor, oh Conductor!**"

A baby started to cry in the next seat. "Now look at that poor little dear. She is frightened George," the woman blubbered. She looked at Amos, then at her husband. "What did I tell you George? **Oh Conductor!**"

"Will you shut up Ethel and sit down. You are the only one upset. Stop making a scene!" and he pulled her down into her seat.

Stone was totally confused at what he had witnessed and he pulled Amos through the door and out onto the porch. "What wuz that all 'bout?"

"Oh-h, nothing much. She saw me jump on the train. That's all." He looked at Stone and grinned. "Hey you haint walkin so good. Bad landing, Stoney? You need more practice."

Stone chuckled and said, "Yeah, I think I'll jest train jump across the country! How'd ya get so good?"

"Had my share a practice. Are we gonna stand all the way or are we gonna grab us a seat?" Amos's eyes darted back at the door. "The next three cars have plenty of empty seats an I think we'd feel better back a ways."

"Is there a mail car? I figger we'd be better off in a mail car er somethin. What 'bout the conductor? She was a callin fer 'im."

"You didn't think of them, did you."

Stone said nothing. He was slipping lately on little things ... little things that could make a big difference.

"Yo mind haint working as good as it was. What's eating at you"?

"Oh, I don know," was all Stone said. They silently walked through the next three cars and found the last one was a baggage car. The door was locked and Amos looked around for something to use to break the lock. He found a heavy wire and quickly worked the lock open.

"Ya did that fast."

Amos smiled, "Had a lot a practice."

As the train continued its way to Montgomery, the two travelers had solitude in the baggage car. It was around three in the afternoon when they finally arrived in Montgomery. They were about three hundred fifty miles east of New Orleans.

Amos and Stone left the railroad yard in Montgomery without any problems and started making their way further west. They had been walking for four days. And for four days they had been scavenging for food. They would gather together a meal from the private stocks of farmers along the way; enough to carry at a running pace. No one had much of anything to spare. The war torn South was suffering. Amos had no money and he thought Stone didn't either. But Stone had his money that he had taken out of the bank in Florida hidden in his boot. He was saving it for New Orleans.

Only two days after their departure from Montgomery, a regiment of Federal soldiers entered the city. Indeed, Amos and Stone had made their exit just in time. It would not be long until they would be in New Orleans ... the city that Stone had never stopped dreaming about; the place that had given him the motivation to keep going.

Amos was following his dreams as well. Stone didn't know much of anything about him. He didn't talk much. Women were on the minds of both men, providing them with the imaginary thrills they presently could not experience. A couple of weeks passed when the two found themselves in a small town called Hickory. There they found work at a cotton warehouse.

One afternoon, Amos staggered outside the building coughing and Stone ran after him.

"Well what ya bin doin b'sides hidin from work?" teased Stone.

"Ca ...Can't stand it ... in there. All's I do ... is cough. I can't ... work in there," gasped Amos, trying to talk and cough at the same time. The black man spat up a little mucous and doubled over slightly.

"Are ya sure ya jest got some dust in ya?" asked Stone as he helped Amos sit on the ground outside the cotton mill. Suddenly a heavy voice spun Stone around.

"Well, whatta we got here?" asked the burly man of his two workers sitting on the ground. "If yer not gonna work, ya can leave fer all I care."

"He's got some dust in his throat. He'll be alright in a minute," Stone said reassuringly.

"If you two don't wanna work, *jes say so!*" the

large man bellowed. He was a big, brawny man with more muscle than fat.

"Can't ya give the man a couple o minutes?" asked Stone

"Look, you two will get paid only if ya finish the day. If ya don't get back in there now, *git outta here!* Got it?" He picked up a piece of pipe laying in a pile of junk close by.

"Alright, we're leavin. He's too sick ta work here," said Stone as he helped Amos to his feet. They began walking west toward the small but busy town.

The large man threw the pipe down and said under his breath, "Ya squirrelly nigger lover." Then he spat toward them and went back into the makeshift warehouse.

The men went together to the town well for a drink of water. First Amos took a long drink, then Stone. A couple of men watched them taking turns drinking out of the well. They kept staring at Amos.

"Don't like what's happ'nin ta our town here. How 'bout you, Si?" said the one to the other. Both were as dusty as the street and as upstanding as the dog sleeping in the street. The other man grinned and the two of them left their place in front of a ladies' wear store and approached the two strangers. Stone noticed them, but all they could seem to see was the black man. Stone stood up straight and moved between Amos and the two men. Their eyes looked right past the white man as they got closer.

Stone was much smaller than the two town men, and was easily shoved out of their way. They grabbed Amos and started beating him until he fell to the ground. Stone and one of the men struggled, but he was knocked to the ground. He tried to get up and help Amos, but a couple of the townspeople grabbed him to keep him out of the way. The two men bound Amos' hands and feet, put a noose around his neck and tied the other end to a riderless horse. They smacked the horse, and Amos was dragged out of town.

Stone just stood there, dumb struck, not moving or saying anything, when he was suddenly knocked to the ground again by someone in the crowd of about twenty. One of the two men who started the fight yelled, "**Stay away from here, ya hear.** *Get outta our town!*"

The crowd broke up and disappeared back onto the street and into the stores as though nothing had happened. Stone was left lying in the street, shocked and sickened at what had been done so fast and easy to an innocent man. He slowly got up from the dusty street and started walking west ... alone once more.

New Orleans was ahead and Stone still intended to get there. His sole inspiration was that place and whatever he could find that would fulfill him. Friendless and alone Richard Stone once more had been spared as someone else close to him had been taken. He found himself in the country-side following the railroad tracks westward.

It was late the next morning when Stone had

noticed something peculiar, but couldn't determine what it was. He hadn't gotten much sleep during the night and thought maybe he was going crazy. But this was something strange, but friendly. He kept listening. It would fade away and then in a few minutes come back again, still unrecognizable. Stone was staying close to the railroad tracks as he continued to travel toward the southwest.

Stone was getting weary when he saw a big oak tree in a wooded area just off the side of the tracks. He sat down in the soft grass beneath it thinking he would rest a while. Soon he was asleep. He slept a couple of hours until a train passed by and woke him. He listened to the sound of the train disappear, as it went on its way east. He sat back against the tree watching a squirrel scurry around after nuts. That old squirrel wasn't paying any attention to him. He was fun to watch. He would gather some nuts and then disappear with them. He'd run chattering up and down the oak tree. 'Yer life's much better'n mine, ol squirrel. Ya don't have a care in the world.'

He was thinking of all he had been through. The North or South did not matter; it was people who did. There were good and bad on both sides. He was not going to judge anyone or any situation; he had to collect his thoughts and try to make some kind of life for himself. He looked down at his worn boots … all the places they had been together … all the running they had done.

Amos was gone and he felt very sad; so many of his friends were gone. He thought about all of them. He remembered Cynthia and O'Reilly; it really wasn't that long ago, but it seemed a lifetime had passed since then. 'Why'm I still alive?' he questioned. 'Oh, I feel like I lived a hundred years.' He took one, long last glance at the fluffy gray squirrel and said, 'Ol squirrel, yer lucky yer a squirrel.' The little creature looked up at him as if he understood what he had said, and then scurried away. Stone got up from the ground and started following the tracks again.

For the next couple of days Stone felt nothing but despair and he was beginning to wonder 'what's the use?' He felt like quitting and giving up. But deep inside, he knew he must persist.

Occasionally along the way, Stone would still hear that vague, spirited sound. He finally gave in to his curiosity, left the security of the familiar tracks, climbed up a hill and headed for the source of the sound. It was a sunny day and Stone finally reached the top of the hill. He could see a narrow, rutted, dirt road meandering between the trees and then disappearing into the woods down its twisting length. He could hear nothing. Stone slowly made his way down that winding twisting road. It seemed to be going in the same direction as the railroad tracks.

As he walked, he stuck his hands into his side pockets and strolled with a slight briskness. He felt his spirits lift and he started feeling better. Why, he didn't know. Stone hadn't eaten since yesterday; but food wasn't on his mind. 'I can't never think 'bout Hick'ry agin er I won't be able ta go on,' he said to himself. There was a cheerful gait to his walk and he could hear that sound again; it was music. It was music he had heard before. 'Am I dreamin this? Er is it real? It's like the music the men sung on the corner in New Orlins!'

'Lou'siana! Lou'siana,' Stone whispered inspiringly to himself as he kept his pace. He began looking about, determined to find the music. 'It's real. I hear it.' Smiling now, he headed toward that sound.

"Hey mon! How much ya got dere?" spoke the tall, lean, dark-tanned Cajun to another. Stone could see a group of about fifteen -- men, women and children minutes down the road. He began to walk faster. He saw one of the young men pull a bow across a fiddle and the music began again. It was that rhythm that was so movingly peculiar.

'Well, what the hell's this?' Stone asked himself aloud. He had become aware of a fear developing inside himself; he felt self-conscious about it, especially the last few weeks. Ever since Hickory, he hesitated to be around a group of people.

Stone went toward them cautiously, wondering if they would chase him off. One of the younger women noticed him and gestured to one of the men. The man looked toward Stone and slowly started toward him, but stopped. The music made the weary Rebel feel so happy, and at the same time wary of the group. The men kept their eyes on the newcomer and he on them. He stopped and stood under a tree, standing in the open while trying to hide in the shade. Stone's hesitancy was obvious to the Cajuns, so one of the young women waved to him to join them.

The Cajun musicians slowed their playing as Stone entered the group. He quietly took a seat and the music started up again. He watched the young woman come toward him. She was beautiful and he hadn't seen a woman in weeks. What a sight she was! She had long, dark hair and bright blue eyes. As she got closer, his heart started to thump and he hoped she didn't notice. Smiling at the stranger, she said, "My name's Suzanne. What's yours?"

His reply was barely audible, "Richard ... uh ... uh ... Richard Stone," almost forgetting his name. His face lit up as he looked at her. All sorts of thoughts ran through his mind.

Interrupting his thoughts, she asked him to stay for supper, adding, "I'm cookin an everyone likes my food. Would ya like to stay here with us this evenin and partake?"

Stone found refuge with the Cajuns and a hearty supper as well. He eagerly joined up with them and they all continued the following day toward Jackson, Mississippi.

The early days of March had already arrived and the temperature sometimes reached seventy degrees and higher. Stone had taken off his coat and felt comfortable as he and one of the men sat on the tailgate of the Cajuns' wagon. It was a large wagon, one like you would see in a medicine show. The others rode horses. Stone was getting anxious to get to New Orleans. Every now and then the Cajuns would stop and put on a show. They entertained in towns along the way, usually in the street for tips. Most people thought they were 'gypsies'. They were in no hurry.

Stone had been with the Cajuns for several days when he and some of the men had been talking about the Mardi Gras. It was a warm day, and Stone and a new friend, Ed were hunting for supper.

"Say mon, we gonna miss dat," said Ed as he took aim in a field not too far from the roadside where the wagon was stopped. They had decided to camp there. The Cajun had a long barreled rifle; his shot rang out in the air, but missed his prey.

"Gittin used ta me new gun. Ha! ha!" joked Ed. Stone just smiled.

"Ya think we'll miss the Mardi Gras?" asked Stone. He was anxious to get moving, but they never seemed to be in a rush for anything.

"Yea mon, we got no hurry ya know. We jus livin ev'ry day an den we got no worries like ev'ry body else," Ed explained.

Stone liked to hear them talk. They had that French accent and slow drawl that intrigued him. But he couldn't accept their slow moving approach to everything. He wished they would move a little faster. He was grateful they had let him ride along with them. He tried to hide his feelings. Stone wanted to get to New Orleans and he had no intentions of staying with them very long. He wanted to establish himself there and live life the way that suited him. They were good cooks and the girls were pretty. He was watching them get the fire started and the cooking utensils out. 'I'll tag along awhile longer,' he said to himself, 'but I aint gonna stay with em.'

Stone sat down alone watching the girls, and he began to reflect on his life again, something he had told himself he wasn't going to do. He was now going where he had intended and nothing foreseen could interfere. Richard Harold Stone had not been thinking of the Federal bounty on him; he had been too busy trying to stay alive to think of that. His eyes had acquired a shiftiness that was not obvious to him. It had come from the ever present notion that someone might be following him. He had learned to listen to the quiet and observe what he couldn't see. A tenseness had gripped him as well, an uneasiness about situations, good and bad. He was becoming fearful.

"Say mon, what ya thinkin about, huh?" Ed's voice surprised him and brought him back to reality.

It was warm by the camp fire as the rest of the group slept, for evening had come upon Stone, the Cajuns and the state of Mississippi. They would be in New Orleans in two days.

At about the same hour in the sheriff's office of New Orleans Parish, a paper was slapped on a desk by a cold, slim character by the name of Conroy Wilson Quille. He was a bounty hunter from Baton Rouge.

"How much will you give me for Richard Harold Stone's body?" asked the unemotional, calculating Quille. The dark haired man was arrogant and determined.

Suddenly, Stone started shaking, responding to a fear he could not explain.

"Ya know, ya think too much, huh?" the tall Cajun commented, noticing the man's quivering. Obviously shaken, Stone nodded and smiled weakly.

Chapter XV

It was a beautiful night. The full moon shone down on them and the stars were twinkling in the bright spring sky ... a perfect romantic night for Suzanne and Stone. He had noticed her from the time he first joined their camp. She had long, dark, flowing hair and soft, white skin; and with those deep, blue eyes her face created such a lovely picture that he couldn't take his eyes off her. This night they were sitting by a stream enjoying each other's company. She looked like a porcelain doll with her pale, blue dress and her dark curls framing her face.

This was a time for love and nothing would get in their way. This night, dreams were running high and trouble seemed far away. Stone found himself reflecting as he often did. He looked at the beautiful nineteen year old beside him and thought to himself, 'The trouble with most people is they don't know how ta live an too busy ta figger it out.' He felt content and happy lying beneath the stars with this lovely damsel. They could hear the music of the Cajun minstrels not far away. Something about that music lifted Stone above his worries and fears. He was in love once more.

By the following afternoon they crossed the Mississippi River, and that night he found love, warmth and security in Louisiana. Stone was feeling only a heartbeat away from heaven. He was so happy. Through all the trials and heartaches he had endured, had come patience; and being patient wasn't easy for him. But it was all worth it. Life's entangling and twisting ways, its cruelty, didn't seem so harsh to Stone right now. He was in Louisiana.

He was either a dreamer or a confused romantic, but life couldn't quench the spirit that sustained him. No matter how hard he tried, Stone was not as desperate at times as he was confused. He had gained strength from his ordeals and could only benefit from their lessons. Louisiana nights were warm, even in March and New Orleans was one day away.

It was Saturday morning and the sun shined brightly. Suzanne and Richard were riding in the seat up front beside Ed as he drove. Suzanne saw something deep inside him that moved her. Stone realized that he was able to handle the troubles of life, but was having a difficult time adjusting to the security the Cajuns gave him. It was a feeling that he at one moment wanted to avoid, while at another wanted to pursue. He still had something to learn. 'Nobody ever gits ta know it all. B'sides,' thought Stone, 'who'd want to?'

"Richard," Suzanne spoke softly. He looked at her wondering what she was going to say to him. "I love you ... very much." Stone was moved and at the same time surprised. He looked at her and smiled as they embraced. 'Women', he said to himself, 'ya never know what they're gonna say.'

Just northeast of New Orleans, Conroy Wilson Quille and eight civil law enforcement officers, as they called themselves, were also on horseback. They were entering New Orleans Parish on the same road the Cajuns and Stone had used. Quille was wearing a long, black coat, black hat and a fancy shirt and vest which were dusty from his journey around the Parish. He had studied all the roads Stone could possibly take to enter the Parish.

New Orleans still had that same unique look and attraction for Stone that he had found so satisfying the first time. He smiled and thought to himself, 'Here I am. I fin'lly made it!' He loved that town. It was like no other and here he would start a new life for himself, hopefully with Suzanne.

The Cajuns had just entered New Orleans at about the same time Quille had found a room. As Stone directed his friends through the streets, they caught the glances of the ladies' eyes. Suzanne noticed and held Stone's hand tightly. She wanted to show her possession. Ed smiled at them as he gazed on the new prospects. Stone looked at the ladies and smiled, then turned to Suzanne to see if she was watching. She frowned playfully and held his arm tighter.

Richard looked at her, "Hon, ya don't have a thing ta worry about. Yer the only one fer me an yer more beautiful than any girl in this city," he said reassuringly, to which she smiled and blew him a kiss.

"Hey mon, we gonna party tonight, huh?" asked Ed, his face covered with a wide, beaming grin. To this Suzanne pouted.

Stone, sitting in the middle, smacked his thighs and emitted an indecisive, "Well-l-l. I ..." Ed slapped his friend's back as Richard turned to hug Suzanne. They were all laughing then and she realized they were joking.

In his hotel room, Quille was demonstrating with his pistols to two of the men who had come with him. "Gentlemen, it will be a piece of cake," he said and smiled in a 'matter of fact' manner. He aimed one of his pistols at arm's length toward the head of one of the men. They were uneasy about the whole scheme and didn't trust Quille at all.

Saturday evening came quickly with great anticipation for the Cajun men and Stone. Their plans for the evening had excited them for hours. Quille and his men were also planning an evening, but not with the same gaiety. Carrying a noose, shotguns, pistols and wearing black hoods, they prepared to make a quick snatch of Stone and a couple of black slaves that Quille had on his list tonight; to hang them and then take their bodies to the parish authorities. The United States had opened a Federal Marshal's Office in New Orleans and they had been giving bounty hunters information on prison escapees and other criminals. They were wanted 'Dead or Alive'. Quille, like many other bounty hunters, had no loyalty for either side. It was a matter of which side paid the most.

Quille saw himself as efficient and not an egotist. He was not out for personal glory or even vengeance, but to rid the world of 'Evil Doers'. His loyalty was not to God or country, or even to himself, but to 'justice'. This was his way of justifying his actions.

In reality his form of justice was more criminal than the crime which the menace of society had committed. Conway Wilson Quille was as sick and twisted as his methods. He did it for profit; the highest bidder got his attention. He had a reputation for being successful in his line of work.

Saturday night on the twelfth of March, Ed, Suzanne and Stone were in a small place called Dolly's. It was away from the dock area where he and Ellen had had their times together.

Stone was not thinking back, for he dare not dwell on the past. He had learned that he couldn't live like that. 'Ta be fer ever sorry, is ta be fer ever sad. An ta dwell on the past causes ya ta b'come full o self-pity', he reasoned. Stone wanted to live, to find out what life, and he, were all about. He fought for life and for his own individuality. Life was a struggle and all he wanted was to be able to be himself and to go as far as he could without hurting the lives of others. Stone's mind was always working, even while he talked and played. He wondered to himself how others seemed so complacent about life ... and in these troubled times, how could that be? Stone made a conclusion about his new friends, the Cajuns and it warmed his soul; *they* were living what *they believed*.

Stone's senses were slightly dulled with drink and that was when his mind would soar. The more he drank the more philosophical he would get. He didn't like drinking too much, because that would lead him into a melancholy mood. But right now he was pondering ... life was good and he was happy in New Orleans.

He came back to the present when Ed started bellowing out his jokes. His unique 'old French' made Stone laugh. Even though he had trouble understanding Ed sometimes, the Cajuns made him feel warm and happy. Suzanne looked so quietly beautiful; and a quiet girl she was ... a truly lovely woman would be a better description. He was the first man she had known intimately and that made Richard feel very special. He had never felt so sincere about his feelings toward a woman as he did toward her. Stone had finally found something worth living for. He gazed over at her loveliness and thought to himself, 'This is the woman I'm gonna marry. I'll never let her go.'

The nightlife of New Orleans spilled into the streets again and as usual, a gaiety and a liveliness that was an intoxication. Meanwhile just a couple of miles out of town, Quille and his men had tossed a noose over a tree limb preparing to hang a black man.

"Get it good and tight, and don't be so slow!" ordered Quille. By promising them wages, he had gathered fifteen men to help him with this hanging. The young, black man tried to convince them of his innocence, but no one was listening. The poor man was now yelling and screaming. They quickly bound his arms behind his back and blindfolded his eyes, then slapped the horse. As he galloped away the black man was left hanging from the tree. It was over in quickly. He squirmed at first and then fell limp.

"John, watch that body. Don't take him down and bury him. Leave him there. **You understand?**" shouted Quille from his horse.

"**Yes, sir!** Yes sir."

"Let's get back fellas, we're going to make a heap a money come Monday morning," Quille hollered as he and the rest of his men headed back into town. Their horses left a dust trail as they rushed back in the moonlit night.

There were times when doubts about their pay would come out in the open, but Quille was quick to put an end to their worries. "I promise at least fifty dollars to each and every one of you. I can't afford to lie to any of you because you're all so important," he would reassure them.

Quille's eyes revealed his real intentions and greed. He couldn't afford them all, but he was counting on continued support from those he did pay. Some of the men had a streak of cruelty much like their leader. They didn't mind getting paid by Quille. After all they told themselves, the Federals are paying them. Why not? They too were filled with hatred and enjoyed killing. The hunter was worse than the hunted.

In the past when it came time for 'payday', his terms were weak and twisted with his long, elaborate explanations of why he couldn't pay them the amount promised. Even if an argument would follow, they would soon accept what he offered, even if they walked away grumbling. One man though had made the mistake of challenging him. He ended up dead. Quille had taken him on a search for someone who was supposedly on the run. They were alone on the trail when Quille put a bullet in his head.

After leaving Dolly's, the Cajuns and Richard made their way along the Mississippi River south toward the delta land. He had a song in his heart that no one could take away. For the first time in his life he had found true happiness.

Stone had been unaware that a couple of Quille's men had been in Dolly's and had seen him with a group of gypsies. They knew it was Stone because they were carrying in their pockets his picture on a wanted poster. They sat at the table next to him and overheard them discuss their plans of leaving town. The men reported back to their leader of what they had heard. Quille was determined to collect the five thousand dollar reward that was on the head of Richard Harold Stone. So he and his men planned to leave New Orleans the following day, also heading south.

Stone's pursuers followed him right into the bayous of Louisiana. The Cajuns were at home in the delta, but not Quille and his men. They were in unfamiliar territory and weren't welcome there. Their so called 'justice' ended in New Orleans, and once again the hunters became the hunted. Stone had found freedom at last; Quille and his men had barely escaped with their lives from the hands of the Cajuns.

It was Sunday morning when twenty Federal soldiers left New Orleans, Quille and his men not among them. The bounty hunter and some of his men had gone back to New Orleans long enough to tell the Federal officials what had happened and then left for Baton Rouge.

Later that same afternoon, somewhere in the swamplands, Colonel Dallas and his men saw a white-washed shack. They got off their horses and walked to the front porch. The Union colonel went to the door and knocked while the other two soldiers waited with the horses. Suzanne opened the door and the officer entered without an invitation, closing the door behind him. He stood there a few of moments just staring at Ed and Suzanne. Fear filled the young woman and Ed swallowed hard; no one said a word.

"I know he's here," said the quiet, middle-aged colonel suddenly, but calmly. Suzanne noticed that his hair was black and curly, as he took off his hat showing sincere respect. Stone was in the next room of the two room dwelling. Fear and guilt gripped him as he thought of all the lives lost over his quest for freedom. He was holding a pistol Ed had given him.

"We dunno who ya talkin about, mon," said Ed while Suzanne held onto his arm. She noticed the colonel's eyes showed a quiet warmth. Suddenly his eyes shot to his right ... and there was Stone sweating heavily, holding the pistol.

He had the gun aimed down at the floor and said calmly, "You can take me, but leave 'em alone. I'll go without any trouble, jest leave these people live." He looked at Suzanne and said sadly, "Hon, it's all over."

Raw emotion had tensed Stone's voice, while cold sweat ran down his neck, as he pleaded for his friends' lives.

"**No, *no, no*!** Ya can't do this. ***Don't be a fool!***" Suzanne cried. She tried to get to Stone's pistol, but he pushed her toward Ed, as he stood firm before the colonel.

Col. Dallas was different from any other military officer any of them had ever met. He seemed to understand Stone, his emotion and situation. "I've read about you Stone. I feel as though I know you. You know, I volunteered myself to your capture detail personally and I ... I understand your feelings," said the colonel honestly.

He rolled up his sleeves and Stone saw the scars of chains on his wrists, where the darkness of his skin allowed. "My mother was black and my father white," revealed the colonel softly. "I gotta career now. That's right a career ... and I'm sure proud of it!"

Col. Dallas rolled down his sleeves and replaced his hat. As he turned toward the door, Stone saluted him. The colonel nodded and said, "Best if you leave the delta land, 'cause somebody else might be looking for you." He walked out the door.

The officer looked at his men waiting outside, shaking his head and said, "Quille must've been in the sun too long. There's no one in there but a couple of old ladies and they haven't seen anybody." Col. Dallas mounted his horse, and he and his men continued down the road into the delta land.

Stone was a fighter, but he had to believe in what he fought for. He could very easily become a pacifist and right now, that's what he was. There was no more anger or fight left in him.

The Cajuns hid Richard for the next few days, but the authorities made no effort to apprehend him. He had once again evaded captivity, but Stone knew the Federals were determined to capture him. And even though Quille was gone, there would be another to take his place. He also knew that the Cajuns put themselves in danger for hiding him and they could be easily found. That bothered Richard, but he never spoke of it to Ed.

He decided he had better change his appearance. So he grew a beard and kept his hair cut short. He gained about twenty pounds, easy to do living with the Cajuns. Not only did Richard enjoy the music, but he had thrived on the food. Suzanne knew how to cook. Ed and Stone worked the bayou while she would make an irresistible supper. She would always watch for them to come home; and 'home' it was.

Ed's big plans for Mexico and his business were the talk of the table on those ever warmer evenings that always seemed to end too soon. He talked of a fishing fleet he would have someday and maybe a wife and family ... sons to help with the fishing. Richard also had his dreams.

Dawn came again and the two men found themselves back on the bayou for another day. Lately, Ed talked much of his dream for Mexico and the fleet he would have on the gulf. 'If ev'rything works out', he would always say. Stone would smile and just listen. He would let Ed have his dreams. Sometimes it seemed like it was all he'd ever have. No woman, no real job, just a wanderer. Always looking and never finding. That was Ed.

Sometimes when he and the others around the bayou got tired of 'sharecropping', the type of fishing they were doing for a large outfit in New Orleans, they would drift with their families to Florida. They had no definite route or time to get anywhere. One time they had gone to New England and worked their way down the Atlantic Coastline. Their music was well accepted by the people of the coastal towns and cities. Northerners enjoyed that special rhythm, too. The Cajuns depended on their music as well as the water for their livelihood. Since the war, they had not done any traveling north of Tennessee and Ed had been thinking they should stay in Louisiana at least for now.

Stone knew that the Federals would continue looking for him. They had lost much over the incident … loss of face and respect within the Union ranks, by those who had been responsible for his incarceration and his escape. He knew that Palmer had lost his job and the prison had closed. Stone felt sure that Palmer would do what he could to get even.

The inmates in that prison and others, saw Stone in another light. They were quietly rooting for him. After the prison closed, some were released for lack of a place to put them. Stone knew too that not many had the guts to stand up for their own beliefs. If Palmer or someone like him would shout an order, they would go right along with it. Some would follow any order given. It lessoned their guilt and reaffirmed their own sense of self-righteousness; it would make the job easier. 'Very few questioned anythin', Stone reasoned. 'That's part o the trouble today. Nobody wants ta think fer themselves. Nobody's got the guts ta stand up fer their own beliefs, except these Cajuns. I wonder if it's jest as bad ta be a criminal or ta do what a criminal orders you ta do?'

Ed was standing nearby and heard Stone muttering. "What? Yo talkin to yourself again?"

"No, jest ponderin some. Thinkin out loud, ya know ... searchin ma soul."

"Yea, yo do that a lot mon," smiled Ed.

It was the first week of May in 1864 and the summer weather had come to southern Louisiana. The bayous had come alive with trappers, hunters and fishermen. Ed said it was busier than other years probably because the war-torn South was hungry and their need for food was great. It was a long day in the mid-week when Ed and Stone had just slipped the pirogue from the bayou to land with her bow just catching the shoreline of weed and mud. A muggy seventy-eight degrees and sweet Suzanne accompanied them for supper that evening.

The sun had set behind some clouds only moments ago. Its light left a silver outline around the clouds that glowed and the horizon was bright with hues of pink to purple. Watching the evening sun go down was a time that Suzanne and Richard relished. They often sat together after the evening meal and talked of their day. This evening they were sitting under an old oak tree. Night had come and the darkness brought in a cool breeze that encircled Stone and Suzanne. Ed and some other men were talking of fishing a short distance away. They each had their own story of all that had happened that day. Richard smiled as he listened to them argue. Then his eyes glanced over at Suzanne and she responded with a long kiss that momentarily placed them both in heaven. 'This is the kind o love that lasts a lifetime.' He was so happy and content. Morning would come too soon and Ed and Richard would be off again.

Stone had been thinking quite some time now about how and where to settle down with Suzanne. He hadn't said anything to Ed yet and wondered if he would go with them. He wasn't sure what his answer would be, but he thought he would ask him when the time was right.

It was an early Saturday morning in June of that year. A man riding on horseback, wearing a black suit was a strange site here in the bayou. He was carrying a Bible and stopped to tell the Cajuns and others he passed, that he was holding a church meeting that night. He said he was going to preach on repentance.

Richard looked at Suzanne and asked, "Suzanne, will ya marry me?"

"Oh Richard! I thought you'd never ask. Of course I'll marry you," she smiled and they embraced.

"I aint got a ring fer ya, but when we git settled you'll have one!" She was smiling and a tear trickled down her check.

"**Oh Preacher**. *Preacher!*" Stone shouted after the man heading down the narrow trail to tell others.

The preacher heard a voice calling after him and he stopped. Stone was running and by the time he caught up with him, he was gasping for breath. The preacher asked, "Is something wrong boy? What can I do to help?"

"Will ya marry us … tonight … after yer meetin preacher? We wanna git married … an kin ya marry us … without a ring?" Stone was so excited he could hardly get the words out.

The preacher smiled. "What's your name boy?"

"Richard Harold Stone, sir."

The preacher looked at him for a minute and said, "I think I heard of you. You don't look like the picture though." He smiled and continued, "The church meetin will last about an hour, then I'll marry you. What's her name?"

Stone beamed and said, "Suzanne! Suzanne Lamont. We'll see ya there!"

He ran back the trail to where he had left his sweetheart waiting. He found Ed grinning, "Mon, I knowed it was gonna happen. I jus didn't know when.

Suzie, ya gots lots ta do. Yo better get busy."

Pleased beyond words, Suzanne first went through her trunk. She had saved a dress for such an occasion. It was a blue dress with puffed sleeves and a neckline of hand crocheted lace. She got her dress out and draped it over the back of the wagon to get the wrinkles out.

She decided to have a special meal, for this was a very special day for her. She prepared crawfish ... lots of them! She made a large pot of Fricassee. She wanted everyone in the camp to partake and share her big day. They would all be going to the wedding and celebrating with Suzanne and Richard.

She went for a walk along a trail in the bayou looking for wildflowers. She just had to have flowers for her wedding day. They were everywhere, so she didn't have a hard time finding them. Near the swamp, she found dark, blue irises with yellow throats. She cut the colorful wild lilies and mixed some fresh white daises in with them. Then she started looking for some green leaves to use in the bouquet. Suzanne beheld the large bunch of flowers and was pleased. She found a can and put water in it to keep the flowers fresh.

Suzanne went down to the 'Swamp Pond'. It was the place where she washed their clothes, bathed and got the water for drinking and cooking. It was a clear pool of sparkling water that came from a spring. She bathed and washed her long, dark, brown hair with jasmine. She had found morning glories and soaked them in water with some rosemary. As soon as she came out of the water, she splashed this mixture over her body. This was a day she had dreamed of for a long time and she wanted it to be perfect.

Richard and Ed had gone off to fish right after he had talked to the preacher. They wanted to get back in time to eat and clean up for the church service and the other festivities.

Oftentimes when the boats would come up the bayou to buy their fish, they used the barter system. Sometimes fish were traded for other items, such as clothing. Ed would even trade fish for gun shells. And when the Cajuns didn't need any supplies, they would sell their catch to the sharecroppers. Both Ed and Stone had some money saved. Ed always dreamed of having a real, fishing boat of his own to make a living with.

It was before noon when Ed and Stone met a boat that would take their fish. They had quite a catch this morning and the captain of the boat was happy to take them.

"Ya wouldn't have some shirts an pants, would you? I could trade fer some fish," asked Stone.

"Son, I got lots a stuff here for you to pick from. Come on board an look round. I heard ya trade now an agin, so I brought lots of stuff thinkin ya might be wantin somethin."

"Today's ma weddin day an I need a nice shirt an pants. Do ya got any shoes?"

"Let's see here. You look like this oughtta fit you. Theres some shoes over there. Jus look ta see what might fit ya."

"Hey mon, me too! I need a shirt an pants. I haint goin ta no weddin with out somethin new to wear," exclaimed Ed.

The two men proceeded to go through some of the clothing the captain had on board. Stone found a blue plaid shirt and a pair of pants. He went through the shoes and found a pair that fit. Ed, being taller, sorted through the whole pile and finally found a pair of pants long enough. He found a shirt and then decided to go through the shoes. They came away contented with their trades. The captain started to pull the anchor up when suddenly Richard remembered he didn't have a ring.

"**Cap'in,** *wait*! Would ya happen ta have a ring I could buy? I'm gettin married ... without a ring ... tonight. If you gotta ring ... I got money fer it."

The captain smiled. "I sure *do* have a ring. How big's her finger?"

"Oh, she's little. Her finger's little."

"This here's a solid, gold ring an ya ken have it for twenty dollars. It's pure gold an it'll give some. I guarantee it'll fit her," said the Captain.

Stone pulled out twenty dollars in Confederate paper money from his pocket to pay for it. The ring was carved showing a petal design for a flower.

"Do you have anythin besides this here ... Confederate money?"

"I got a ten dollar gold piece, sir."

"I'll take that," said the captain.

"One more thing, Cap'in. How hard is it to git on one o those blockade boats? I'm thinkin a gittin out o here."

"It helps to know the captain an he's gonna ask ya how you're gonna pay."

"Oh well, that shouldn't be too hard then. I don't *know* anbody, but I kin pay. Thanks fer tellin me. Guess I'll find out when I git ta New Orlins. Thanks fer yer help."

The captain nodded as he slowly moved his boat down the bayou. Stone was so excited. He looked up at Ed and slapping him on the back yelled, "*Suzanne's really gonna be surprised!*"

The two men made their way back to camp carrying their new clothes. Richard decided to surprise Suzanne at the wedding and not show her the ring beforehand.

Suzanne was busy putting the food out for everyone when they got back to camp. After the meal was over she slipped away to put her dress on. Ed and Stone had gone to the creek to clean up. When they returned she was so surprised to see Richard looking so nice and fresh.

"Where'd you get those clothes? Oh Richard you look wonderful an I'm so happy".

"Well hon, it's our weddin day an I got these clothes from the cap'in on the boat. Ed has new clothes, too. An look at you. You are beautiful Suzanne an I'm so lucky ... lucky ta be alive an lucky ta have you."

"Oh Richard, you're all I want ... the man of my dreams."

"Listen, hon, I got money saved an I'm gonna find out how ta git on one o them blockade boats. We gotta get outta here, Suzanne. I don't wanna be a hunted man the rest o my life. I want us ta live in peace ... have a family. I asked Ed ta go with us an he said he would. Wherever we go, me an Ed are goin into the fishin business. He's always wanted ta get a boat an really make money fishin. That's what we're gonna do. I'm thinkin Nasau'd be a good place fer us."

"Oh Richard, we'll figure out a way. That sounds wonderful!"

Suzanne, Richard and Ed arrived right on time. It was seven o'clock and the grassy field was standing full of bayou hunters and Cajuns. The preacher was in front and smiling.

"Well I'm surprised to see the turnout. You're gonna get a preachin sermon like you never heard. The Good Book says you must repent. Repent ... yes! *Repent!* Do you know what that means? If you're not sorry for your sinnin... you're gonna end up in hell for ever. An that's a long time."

All listened intently as the preacher described heaven and hell. The preacher led some songs with his guitar, 'Shall We Gather at the River' and 'Amazing Grace'. When the preacher was done, he said, "Now I got a weddin to perform!"

Stone quietly, but quickly ran up to the preacher with his hand held out. "Preacher, I got a ring today. Suzanne don't know she's gettin this!"

Smiling and nodding, the preacher cautiously whispered to Stone, "What are you gonna do after you're married? If I recognized you, someone else might too. You better think of gettin away from here."

"I thought o that, an I wanna get on one o them blockade ships an maybe go ta Nassau. I talked to Suzanne an she's ready ta go. Ed's goin with us, too. Do ya know anybody that can help us?"

"Yea I do. I know a captain of a ship that'll take you all to Nassau. We'll have to leave in the mornin to get to the New Or-leans' dock by tomorrow night."

Some folks hung around to see who was getting married. The Cajuns knew and they all stayed. Suzanne looked beautiful in her blue dress holding the large bouquet of colorful wildflowers. She was a ways off from everyone doing a last minute primping to her hair. She wondered what Richard was saying to the preacher. The two men soon came over to the front of the group. The Rev. Randolph looked around for Suzanne. She came forward and they stood together in front of the preacher with Ed standing next to Richard.

"Do you, Richard Stone, take this woman to be your lawful wedded wife?"

"I do."

"Do you, Suzanne Lamont, take this man to be your lawful wedded husband?"

Suzanne smiled and said, "Oh yes I do."

"Now the ring ..."

Ed pulled the ring out of his pocket and gave it to the preacher. Suzanne's eyes widened and her cheeks flushed as she caught a glimpse of the beautiful ring. The preacher blessed it and Richard put it on her finger. Tears silently ran down her checks as her husband kissed his new wife. The folks applauded, some congratulated the couple and others slowly moved on to their camp sites.

The preacher took the two aside and told them his plan of getting them to the blockade ship. The newly married couple slowly walked back to camp, hand in hand, happy to start a new life together. They could hear the music from afar. The Cajuns danced and played music long into the night. But the two of them were in a more serious mood. Thinking of tomorrow made them both anxious.

The next morning Rev. Randolph was waiting to take them to the ship.

Chapter XVI

It was early morning and the newly married couple was so anxious and nervous at the thought of actually leaving the South behind. Ed and Suzanne were frantically rummaging through their wagon sorting out what to take and what to leave when she looked up and saw the preacher standing there. Suzanne was scared, 'what would this new life bring', she wondered. She was so used to the Cajun life and its peculiarities, how would she fit in to another way of living. Having Ed come along made her feel better.

"What are you doing? You can't take much with you. Remember we gotta make our move swiftly and you can't bring all your women's things with you. It'll slow us down. I'll have you all on the ship tonight." Rev. Randolph was laughing, "Here leave this. Ya won't need that either."

"But Preacher I need these things. How am I gonna fix my hair? I need that too," Suzanne lamented as she put the items taken out of her trunk back in.

Richard was laughing but said supportively, "Hon, I think we better listen ta the preacher. A comb an hair pins won't take up much room, but some o yer clothes will jest hafta stay."

"Oh this is so hard ta do. I need everything here,

but I guess when we get to Nassau we can buy what we need. We've got some money saved."

"Suzanne, figger what ya hafta have an leave the rest. We ain't got much choice. Yer friends can use what you leave behind."

"Okay whatever ya say. I'm just happy we're together and have the chance for a new life."

"I think we're ready ta go, Preacher," said Stone.

"I got a bag, Suzanne. I can put somethin a yours in with my stuff!" Ed offered as she took clothes out and put them right back in again.

"Okay Ed. I think I'm done sortin through these things. See if you can put this in your bag an I'm done."

It was evening when they arrived at the dock. They looked at the ship Rev. Randolph directed them to, and Suzanne's mouth fell open.

"Are we gettin on that?"

"Ya sure are Missy," laughed the Preacher.

The CSS *Alliance* was a three masted blockade runner and a well-seasoned one at that, with dual boilers and very low draft. She had two funnels for her stacks from each boiler, with side paddle wheels and twin shrouded propellers. The captain would be able to bring her twin boilers to fifteen knots with the wind and they would turn red with heat as they set upon their brickwork. She would do her best at night, as fast as he could, with near explosive boiler pressures to make the eight hundred ninety nautical miles to Nassau, Bahamas.

Suzanne looked up and then to the right and left. "But it's so big an ... an lookin a bit beat up. I'm scared. I never saw anything like this in my whole life."

"It's excitin ta me," exclaimed Richard. "How about you, Ed?"

Ed loved boats, but never had he seen anything like this! He was in awe of it. "Sure is a big one all right ... but I haint scared. No mon, not a bit! Yeh this is gonna be excitin for me too."

The captain had done this many times before, even farther to Barbados and Bermuda. From New Orleans to Nassau, Bahamas was run in about three and a half days; runs from Charleston, South Carolina to Hamilton, Bermuda were done in about two days. After leaving the immediacy of the blockade, the captain could calm his ship to easier speeds. The crew would always be vigilant for the Union ships trying to chase her beyond the territorial waters of the North and South. On these runs there was no rest, but a continued fast pace to the British ports. It took a swift ship, a risk-daring captain and a tight acting crew to accomplish what few would dare to try.

Observing them all this time, the preacher was amused at their reactions as they stood wide eyed and curious. Suzanne especially, her mouth still wide open at the site, while Ed and Stone were thrilled.

"I wouldn't put ya on something I thought wouldn't make it. This captain's the best; his bark is worse than his bite too. His name's Jaspers; talks mean sometimes, but he has to. That's how he keeps the crew in line. An he carries all sorts a stuff, like supplies of cotton, guns, powder and balls for guns. I don't know what he's takin this time. The Confederacy has agents with cash waiting for these brave men on this side of the Snake, an the British have cash on their side, too. You see Missy it takes a lot of guts to run the blockade, so don't be scared of the captain."

The preacher continued in his efforts to prepare and assure the two men and the young lady about their journey. "The runs are almost always at night, best when the moon's new or the sky's overcast, with a good wind. Some of the men'll sleep a day or two so they'll be fresh and alert, ready to cut the snake, while others of the crew may wander off to Dolly's and drink their way to bravery. They have to be full of vim and vigor to race the waters, for their lives and cargo are at stake. They know the Union's out there somewhere watching and waiting to attack. Blockade running is very dangerous and there's always the chance they won't make it. But I assure ya, Jaspers' the best. I've helped others leave this land for a new life an I wanna help you all get a new start. Actually," finished the preacher," I find it all very exciting myself."

General Winfield Scott's great Anaconda Plan, referred by some in the South as 'The Snake', was to strangle the Confederates' ports into submission. This was the best of the fastest, low, draft ships that dared to challenge the Northern coercion. President Lincoln left such strategy and tactics to old General Scott (who would finally bring the Southern cause to die) to fight against Great Britain's ability to manage commerce with the South.

After thanking the preacher, Suzanne and Richard were led to a small pub near the docks. They were very hungry and it was the only safe place for Stone to go. Only captains and their crew went there. Ed remained outside talking with Rev. Randolph who would not go in. "Rev'rend, we owe ya much for yo bringin us here an we won't see ya never agin. So I want ya ta know we're beholdin to ya. I'm speakin for us all."

"Don't mention it Ed. As I said I've helped a few others get away and I sure am hopin you'll get to Nassau safe and sound. I've known Jaspers a long time. Underneath it all he's a good man. I'm going to leave you here now; I gotta be on my way. I don't stay long around these docks."

"Guess I'll go in an get them two movin."

"Yeah the quicker you all get on that boat the better," said the preacher as he disappeared out of sight.

Inside the pub, pot roast was the meal for the day and there was only a small amount left. Suzanne, Richard and Ed had the last bit. It was so delicious that they were unaware of the figure that had just slipped into the pub. The room was dimly lit with candles and kerosene lamps. The table they sat at was old and heavy, made from large boards still rough after years of use.

"Let's get this chow down an get on that boat. Bein in here makes me jumpy," mumbled Ed.

"Yeah Ed, but it tastes so good; we ain't had a meal all day. Suzanne, let's hurry an finish eatin, Ed's right."

They were getting ready to leave when suddenly a knife came straight down, right in the middle of the table! And just as suddenly, the startled trio began to choke and cough, and almost lost the food they had just eaten.

"Ah'm come ta cut de Snake!" came a raspy whisper. Then with increasing loudness, "Ar ye all ready? Huh?" "**Well, *speak up!***" now shouting into the face of Stone, while the flame of a candle flickered, almost blown out by the windy voice of one whose face was still in the shadows.

"Wh ... who are you?" Stone stuttered, trying to take all this in without showing fear, as a man emerged from the dimness.

The voice and appearance of this man shocked the threesome. They had never seen anyone like him. Suzanne shook in her shoes and was wondering if they should go through with this. Stone looked apprehensively at the stranger, but Ed was unmoved.

"Ah'm Captain Tunis Jaspers! An Ah'm gonna cut de Snake agin an ye all better be willin ta run wid de wind!" ordered the 'shadow', more visible in the light of a nearby kerosene lamp. With his torn left earlobe and his left eye in a bit of a squint, his neck showed scars as if at one time he had been hung. His beard was scraggly with rough, pale skin beneath and his right hand shook. His clothes were well worn and he carried several knives and two pistols on his belt.

"Ah'm takin ye all ta Nassau an we're leavin soon. If de wind's right we kin run with it an make it through de blockade faster an ya kin blink an eye, so we will," said Captain Jaspers in a low clear voice.

No one said a word. Suzanne was scared to death of him. The three looked at each other and moved to follow him. This was one time Richard Stone was left without words. All the prisons he had broken out of and all the colonels and sergeants he had dealt with, didn't compare to the man standing in front of him.

He was the captain of the *CSS Alliance* and he had had many close calls with the Union ships and their firepower, but so far had evaded capture. Or so he claimed. If he had been hung, he obviously survived. He surely had interesting stories to tell, if they could only ask the many questions that whirled in their heads. The main thing was to get safely and quickly to Nassau, and it would take a man like this and his crew to do it.

The CSS Alliance was about two hundred ten feet long with only about a six foot draught, very low and sleek in the now dark night. She was loaded and ready. This ship had been through the Snake many times. Looking closely, Stone could see bullet holes in the funnels and along her gunwales and hull, cracks and scrapes. Up on her flagstaff were two flags, one Confederate and below that the British. They would be hauled down before departure and only be re-flown when away from the blockade. First the British flag would be raised and then as she ported she would re-fly the Confederate.

There were known spies in New Orleans, so no one knew her departure time, except the captain, his crew and the Confederates. Union agents were showing up more often as Federal forces were making their way into the 'Crescent City'. They would finally bring more support to General Benjamin 'Beast' Butler who had been involved with bringing New Orleans under submission. He was such an unpopular commander over the citizens. His hard attitude had inspired Southern means to outwit him and the North's oppression.

While the Alliance was in port, sometimes it would even fly the American flag. For in case Union spies were nearby, she would appear to be no threat to the Union. Even loading her was done during the night for those things considered sensitive. Other cargoes that were of no relation to the war effort were loaded during the day, such as fruits and vegetables. Sometimes the day loadings were just a cover for the more important cargo that was loaded on at night.

The captain watched as the evening glided into

night. The cloud cover made sure of no stars, and her dark hull would blend into the black sea's murky surface from the night sky. This was so important for a successful run.

"Be quiet ... an move slow, make sher ye board 'long with de cargo. Act like ye are part a ma crew. Carry somethin on with ye," the captain whispered the orders firmly.

Slowly each of them, first Ed, then Suzanne and finally Richard boarded. Inside they were given rooms in the hold and told to stay put when the ship was moving fast. Jaspers ordered them to use the ropes and harnesses along the wall when the 'goin gits ruff ... an de chase is on!' That's when the ship would make sharp curves one way and then the other. Under full sail, with the paddle wheels churning at a fast clip and propellers spinning, the CSS Alliance would be extremely fast and maneuverable. All blockade runners had to maintain a difficult target.

'Hangman' McGinn, was a conniving Union opponent for those daring men willing to 'cut the Snake'. Often compared to General Grant, he was a rough sort, a drinker and a smoker of cigars. He would not return the captured crew to the proper Union authorities, but rather conduct a mock trial and then hang all those captured. He was Irish and loved to consider himself a hunter. Tonight he was on duty on board the corvette, USS Justice, and was ready for a good pursuance.

"Sir, the seas're clear at this time. Looks like a

cloudy, windy night. Quite dark out there," offered the junior officer.

"Aye, we're ta 'ave a time, fer this sea they'll try ta run. Those Secessionists shall make my huntin good sport. Ow'll run em down an haul in the damn scum an hang what's left alive!" reveled Captain McGinn.

"Aye, aye sir," quietly returned the sailor, with not quite the enthusiasm to share with his captain. To this McGinn just glared at him and roughly stole the spyglass from his junior officer's hand.

"Gi'e me the glass, Lad!" he scowled at the now humbled officer, "Ow'll enjoy this hunt ... yoo softies need ta realize that these animals need ta be stopped!"

In the port of New Orleans a small box had been removed from the Alliance and taken to awaiting men in civilian clothes, who were really Confederate officers. On the manifest it was known to Captain Jaspers that the box, containing a Faraday motor, was from Great Britain. Few knew that the British had engineers in the port with drawings of new ideas for shipbuilding. (Research was being done for batteries and electric motors for future submarines for the Southern Navy. The CSS Hunley was under consideration, but the motor did not have the power needed, so the crewmen used a crank instead. More study was going on in Britain for powering Southern ironclads to compete with the improving Union Monitor class of ships. Even batteries for torpedoes were being explored.) Some of this very equipment was awaiting pick up in Nassau for Captain Jaspers' return run to New Orleans.

The boilers were ready, getting red hot, and soon the CSS Alliance would slip from her moorings and proceed out into Lake Pontchatrain, into the delta, then the Gulf of Mexico. Soon she would make her way to a point halfway between Havana, Cuba and the Florida Keys, and then on to Nassau in the Bahamas.

The cloud cover held as the blockade runner made her way through the gulf waters. It was so dark and clear that only the most sensitive eyes would make out her silhouette on the almost imperceptible line of water and night sky. Slowly she let her speed increase causing a small noise from her wake. The wind was astern as hoped and she let out sail. Her bow was cutting the water so briskly that she would soon cross an open area between two ships of the Union Blockade, the dreaded Snake also known as Lincoln's Blockade.

With fine agility, Captain Jaspers touched and guided her rudder with his wheel, sometimes holding her steady with just two fingers. Her speed now so balanced while tilted to port, she began a curve to cross the line of fire from Union cannons waiting onboard her pursuers.

Faster and faster, at twelve knots with full sail and red hot boilers, she suddenly came out of the darkness preceded only by a rushing of wake, barely perceptible to any Union sailors' ears. She flew so fast between two of the Union boats that they completely missed the opportunity to fire.

"What! **What!** *What yoo waitin fer?"* cried Captian McGinn. **"Fire upon that damn devil!** *Stop er dead!"* he continued to yell. He rushed toward his gunners and shoved them aside. While the cannon onslaught and rifle fire was ongoing, the junior officer looked at McGinn with anger, yet obeyed.

"Go, go, be gone wi' the wind an God speed!" whispered aloud the junior officer with a sympathy bred from a superior tyranny. McGinn almost could hear and just glared at his crewman, then continued on with his verbal barrage upon his sailors to stop the Confederate snake cutter.

With cannon assault and rifled bullets raining, Captain Jaspers brought the CSS Alliance from port to starboard to port again, making his swift S course, dodging this torment of fire by such delicacy of steering and speed of his fast ship.

Meanwhile Suzanne, Richard, and Ed were in the hold while the movement of the ship went from side to side with gunfire and canons filling their ears. **"We'll never make it.** *We're all gonna die!"* cried Suzanne. *"We're gonna all drown an the sharks will eat us alive!"* She was almost out of control. They were holding on as tight as they could and Suzanne and Richard both lost their supper. Even using the harness she was thrown to the floor a couple of times.

Ed wasn't scared at all. He laughed and said, "Mon I'm glad I didn't eat like the two of you. This is excitin for me. We ain't gonna go down Suzie. Cappin's got us this far; there haint no turnin back."

Suddenly, the Alliance was out of the storm and still running fast toward her first way point between Havana and the Keys. It would soon be dawn so Captain Jaspers had her slowed to ten knots and let her ride the wind as he eased up on the boilers to slightly cool them. Now her course was straight as to make distance and time.

All was quiet and clear all the way to the horizon as the sun rose in the east. It seemed a calmer day as some of the crew and the three passengers had breakfast below deck. They were drinking coffee and it sure all tasted good. At the wheel one of Jaspers' crew was piloting the course to the southeast and straight.

"Richard do you realize this is our first breakfast together since we married. I guess this is our honeymoon. I didn't think we were gonna make it through the night."

"I love you Suzanne. Don't know if ever I said it out loud, but I do." He smiled at his wife and continued, "Yer the most beautiful woman in the world."

"Oh Richard, I never thought I'd be so happy. An my ring. Ya know I can't stop lookin at it. You surprised me so. We'll have a new life in Nassau."

"I'm excited too for a new life fer us. If it wasn't for that preacher we wouldn't be here. He sure came by at the right time. I guess there're some good people 'round. Ya know I'm still half sick from the race the cap'in made with this ship last night. He sure knows how ta cut the water. I'm lucky ta get this coffee down. I didn't wanna tell ya that. You were so scared last night an sick too."

"Now I'm so excited that I don't know what my breakfast even tasted like," Suzanne said smiling.

Ed smiled and bragged, "I didn't get sick, none at all last night. Jaspers was goin like hell hittin dem waves. I thought the ship's gonna break in two. But I didn't get sick. Stone what's the first thing we're gonna do in Nassau? I wanna see how much a fishin boat's cost us. We got money saved an now my dreams are gonna come true. Ya know I always wanted ta have my own boat."

Suzanne interjected, "Well I think I'm gonna look into running a restaurant. You two can catch the fish an I'll cook an sell the 'Catch of the Day'. Ya both keep telling me I'm a good cook. I'm tryin to think up a good name for it. I know ... I'll name it 'Chez Suzanne'!"

"Is that what ya wanna do? I thought ya wanted a family, hon." The young couple smiled at each other as he stole a kiss.

"Hmm, may be I'm gonna be an uncle, someday," said Ed thoughtfully.

The three friends spent the rest of the day planning and talking and making more plans.

The Alliance crewmen and pilot on watch felt

quite relaxed as they observed flying fish flit out of the waves to starboard and back into the sea over and over. The sun and wind felt good. The captain smiled every time he thought of the three stashed away.

"Hey Cappin it sure feels good givin them poor people a new start. An we're makin it happen," said the pilot at the wheel, as the captain passed by him making his way down to the lower deck. "Oh I know we helped others, b'fore, but these folks are somehow dif'rent."

"We haint there yet an don't go gettin lazy on me. We gotta keep our heads on what we're doin," advised Jaspers from just below deck.

Had the pilot kept his eyes near the sun to port, he would have noticed two small ships fast approaching ... Union corvettes. He had just turned to port side and quickly noticed the impending danger.

"**Cappin**! *Two devils comin from port an fast!*" he wailed down below.

Hastily Jaspers dropped his coffee cup as he barked the needed orders to begin the race to stay alive and afloat.

"Fire dem boilers ta hot as da sun, full sail an all hands tie ta da wall! Gimme sharp as sharp esses an serpentine dem varmints dizzy!" hollered the captain, as the CSS Alliance suddenly hit full steam, full sail, with side paddles spinning and wind astern.

The three had been drinking their coffee on deck when the race began. Suzanne fell to the floor of the boat with coffee all over her. "**Oh no!** *Not again.* I thought we were safe!"

Jaspers shouted at them, "**Get to da hold.** *We gotta move fast. Hold on tight or ye'll fall overboard!*"

The three sliding and tripping from side to side finally made it to the hold, the safest place to be.

The ship now tilted from port to starboard and created such a wake that the water was being cut as with a knife. Faster and faster she went her boilers at over full steam and her ducted propellers channeling waters as thrust to nearly seventeen knots (well over her stated 'fifteen knots') due to the brisk wind.

"*Shur like ta see what's goin on up there.*" shouted Ed. "I haint scared!" He started for the steps out of the hold. "I'm goin up with Jaspers. Me'be I can help."

"*You're crazy!*" wailed Suzanne.

"Now hon. It ain't that bad. We'll git through this."

"Oh Richard. I wish I was that sure."

"*Hey Cappin, I want ta help.* **What can I do?**" shouted Ed.

"*Stay ta dis gun. Iffin ye see something ... ye*

start shootin."

Now armed and ready, the two Union corvettes split and each tried to maintain a presence upon its side of the blockade runner as they raced toward her. On her port and starboard gunwales near the bow, Jaspers had three cannons of small caliber filled with powder and grapeshot. He had all of them directed at the two oncoming corvettes. His gun crews were staying below the gunwales shielded from any fire from their pursuers.

Closer and closer they all raced; two against one from out of the sun. The Alliance gunmen waited to fire at Jaspers' command who was waiting for the right moment. He wanted to avoid capture because the usual proper procedure was to stop a blockade runner and arrest the crew, seize the contraband and all the rest of the ship's manifest.

On board the corvettes, the sailors had rifles ready and each ship had a large cannon. The officers had just raised their swords to indicate to the crews to prepare to fire. At the drop of their swords the cannons and rifles would unleash the torrent of warning and destruction. Their aim was to stop the runner and not damage it so as to render it to sink, unless needed.

Suddenly the blockade runner, only yards in front of the port corvette, swerved before it and the smaller ship fired her cannon at her bow. It fired without reward into the sea. The rain from the blockade runner's grapeshot and cannon hit broadside the port corvette and her crew. Her pilot was wounded and several of the crew. The starboard corvette then had to make a large port turn to try to catch the now advancing CSS Alliance into the sun.

The remaining Union corvette now raced along the stern of the CSS Alliance, firing upon her without effect as she out-distanced the Union boat quickly. From out of the sun another larger ship appeared and was swiftly racing toward the blockade runner as she was now approaching the waters between Havana and Florida. This ship was not one to fear, for it flew the British flag and was pursuing the Union corvette also with great speed. The corvette's captain had to squint and try to acquire this new menace. As Jaspers waived his hat towards the captain of the British Man O'War, the British captain waived his hat in return. The ship's canon and rifle fire ensued and almost up on the corvette, this Man O'War raced quite dangerously.

At the last minute, the corvette turned to port and came about to the northwest, as it retreated from the cannon and rifle barrage, not only from the Alliance and the Man O'War, but unintentionally from the other corvette. The corvette sped on until it passed over the horizon, the other following in its wake. All the while, the blockade runner continued at full steam directly on toward the Bahamas and freedom.

With about two and a half days to go and without any interference from Union Naval operations, all on board began to rest and relax more as they raced eastward with Cuba on starboard and Florida's mainland on port. There were Union boats yet to be intercepted, but because of storms at sea, they would not be as effective. It was difficult to keep the blockade firm with stormy conditions, which were dangerous as well for the blockade runners; but their ability to race through so fast and straight into waves actually allowed them to be somewhat less vulnerable.

"Ed. I'm surprised at ya. Ye did good boy fer not bein a sailor. Thankin ya for da help, so I am," offered Captain Jaspers.

"Cappin, I haint had this much fun ever. Sure I'd like ta join yo crew. This sure is excitin."

"Naw I haint gonna run much longer. Dere's a couple things I need ta bring back with me an den I'm done. I'm a quittin, so I am. Hey we haint outta the fight yet. Dere's storms a facin us. I might be callin you ta help us agin."

"**I'm ready for anythin**," Ed yelled back over his shoulder as he went down to the hold to see if the newlyweds were ok.

Suzanne saw Ed coming and she wailed, "How can ya not be scared? Where are we anyway? I never dreamed it would be this bad."

"We're near Cuba an on our way ta Nassau, Suzie. I love this! Cappin says he might need me agin an I'm gonna help him as much as I can."

Night lights were sighted from two Union ships, but the CSS Alliance kept a good distance aided by ten to twelve foot waves and the wind continuing astern.

She would soon be in the Bahama Islands and then head to the southeast into Nassau Harbor.

The next day arrived with cloudy skies, some rain and a contrary wind from the northeast; so down went the sails, relying only on her engines. On she went. Now with her boilers cooling and the propellers resting, her side paddles were more useful. Her pace went to eight knots navigating the eastern Bahamas and she would port in Nassau later tomorrow if the weather remained as it was.

The CSS Alliance creaked and swayed south-southeast with the waves at three to five feet. Richard, Suzanne and Ed stood along the deck's starboard gunwale as the sun set red in the western sky. A nicer day was forecast for the morrow and hopefully for years to come, away from the tempest of not only storms at sea and war, but storms of life.

The ship had more bullet holes in her stacks; cannon balls and grapeshot had left holes in her sails, which rolled up, were more raggedy than before. Her hull had scrapes and holes and chunks missing. She sailed well, but had the scars to prove her fights and flights.

The bright evening stars were twinkling, the warm air was breezy, and the calm tropical waters were clear. On board the deck a small fire in a brickwork kept the coffee warm and gave off a soft flickering light. Richard had his arms around Suzanne as they watched the stars, and the fire warmed them as they cuddled up on the deck. The paddles continued to turn, the sails were kept away and all seemed so tranquil. Here in the Bahamas was no hint of the conflict now so far away and so aimless in its purpose.

'We aint got off the boat yet an I feel the calm. Why couldn't it be this way in the States? No fightin, jest peace. Everythin could o been so diff'rent,' thought Richard. As they left the ship, he and Suzanne looked back at her, thinking how she had saved them from storms, canon fire and war.

"Oh Suzanne I can't b'lieve my runnin is over ... over forever! Now we can settle down an we're free! I'll work with Ed ta find a boat. To really be free an no more lookin 'round ta see who's after me. I'm free ta think about our future."

"Richard I'm so happy." she said, "we're gonna have such a good life here."

They walked slowly down a street of Nassau near the docks looking for a place to stay. Captain Jaspers and his crew were staying with the ship in dock because the cargo they were to take back wasn't there yet. Jaspers was told the British ship would be bringing the batteries and motors and other secret cargo in a few days.

"We've been here only a couple of days and everybody we've met has been so friendly and helpful. Look how we were shown where to get a room ... the best place to eat. And Ed ... he might even meet someone to marry! Oh how our lives have changed so fast." Suzanne smiled at Richard and he held her tight.

In the Bahamas, as well as Barbados and Bermuda, the British without engaging in war had established a society of cooperation and prosperity. Richard was thinking about this as he would listen to the conversations in the pubs, markets and along the streets of Nassau. He knew that for each of them to find the life, liberty and the pursuit of happiness, they had to return to the British Colonies.

Captain Jaspers and his men were planning several more runs, then they were going to retire in Nassau if the South fell. They had a good ship but needed a buyer and a British steamship company was interested. The Alliance, built in Bermuda, sold to the Confederacy and now owned by Jaspers was still a great ship. It was aging from her constant speed, outrunning Union ships of a war that was winding down. The money was good for Jaspers and his crewmen, but it had come with risk, injury and at times loss of life.

In a pub the following afternoon, the captain was chatting with Richard and Ed about what kind of ship they would need. The CSS Alliance was not quite designed for a fishing boat. Ed was enthralled with the blockade runner because of her speed. Richard was more practical about such a venture and suggested to look for a more workable boat to fish with.

"Cappin, if it's up ta me, I'd buy that boat a yours. It sure does move in the water. I'm used ta her, an I like her!"

"It's some boat fer sure, but not what we need ta fish with Ed."

"O-kay, O-kay, Stone you do the buyin. I'm too attached ta this ol girl here."

Jaspers smiled at the two men, "Well I be on my way, maties! A couple more runs an I be sittin more purtty. I could spend da rest a my life right here in Nassau. Got me a buyer any time I wanna give up da blockade runnin."

"Guess I jest have a special feelin fer her too 'cause she brought us ta safety ... an a place where I can stop runnin an start a new life. But she aint gonna work fer what we want her for. It aint what we need fer our fishin business," Stone argued.

Nassau was a growing city and port with a library and government offices. It had a theater and even an art gallery and a museum. At four in the afternoon everyone on the island had tea, and Suzanne, Richard and Ed all enjoyed the quiet chat and siesta after. In the hotter climate everyone rested for the afternoon.

The Negroes and white people worked together in agriculture and trade. Socially the island was a quiet refuge and there was a sweet harmony for all. Richard, Suzanne, Ed and Captain Jaspers had left the pub and were now standing on the dock by the ship. Each one of them and the ship were worn and tired, yet full of dreams of more peaceful days ahead. It almost seemed that the CSS Alliance was listening while anchored at rest before them.

All of them, including the ship, were ending one

way of life and beginning another, in the same condition, each with their own scars, scratches, dents and holes. Whether man, woman, or ship, all had grown weary from each and every conflict including this last one shared together.

As the ship let out some soft creaking which they all could hear, Ed considered each of them and the ship. "She's talkin t'us an agrees," offered Ed, "She's tir'd an ready for the better. Cappan Jaspers, she's alive, haint she? She knows."

Captain Jaspers listened and each of them looked at the other, then turned as one to look at the ship. "Ma dear maties. She's alive an aye, she's much tarred ... an she agrees."

Then she let out a low groan and the water seemed to move around her. She slightly listed side to side and then calmed.

The friends looked at each other and the unpredictable captain just smiled, yet his eyes seemed to tear. The path they each had chosen had brought them together to a new land for a new life.

For a brief moment, they were a reflection of the same character. The wanderings of these vagabonds of war, strife and struggle had ended their quest for freedom. Now the last day of many difficult days was setting with the sun in the western sky. Tomorrow was a new day of many days to come with new lives to live.

Richard looked into Jaspers' eyes as he extended

his hand to shake the captain's. "We'll miss ya if yer headin back ta 'cut the snake'."

"Well ... I might not be goin agin."

"Hey, I thought ya said that ya might be runnin a couple more?" Richard paused, as Captain Jaspers waved him to stop.

Then staring at the CSS Alliance, the captain said, "She won't let me. She's sayin 'no'... so I'm done too, so I am. If she haint wantin ta go, den *I'm* not ta go. Without her, I wouldn't survive."

Jaspers whispered discreetly, "B'sides da British's already loaded their special machines on that other runner over yonder!"

As the sun set quietly into the twilight, the four headed back into the pub realizing that the trail of life is difficult. But with wisdom gained from their experiences, they appreciated and respected their new found freedom.